生活華語 第K2冊

Helping Tips for Teachers and Parents

妈妈　妈妈　　　　　里
媽媽ㄇㄚ˙、媽媽ㄇㄚ˙，我ㄨㄛˇ在ㄗㄞˋ哪ㄋㄚˇ裡ㄌㄧ˙？
mā ma　　mā ma　　wǒ　zài　nǎ　lǐ

宝贝　宝贝　　　　　里
寶ㄅㄠˇ貝ㄅㄟˋ、寶ㄅㄠˇ貝ㄅㄟˋ，你ㄋㄧˇ在ㄗㄞˋ我ㄨㄛˇ心ㄒㄧㄣ裡ㄌㄧ˙。
bǎo bèi　　bǎo bèi　　nǐ　zài　wǒ　sīn　lǐ
　　　　　　　　　　　　　　　　　　xīn

Mommy, Mommy! Where am I?
Baby, baby! You are in my heart.

心 ➡ 心 ➡ 心 ➡ 心

Please color it.

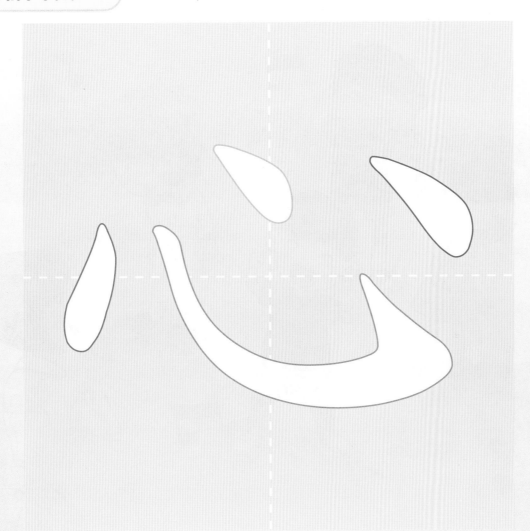

：他 在 哪 裡？
tā zài nǎ lǐ

：他 在 學 校。
tā zài syué siào
xué xiào

：你 在 哪 裡？
nǐ zài nǎ lǐ

：我 在 _____。
wǒ zài

Where is he? *He is at school.*
Where are you? *I am at ____.*

2

头
頭ㄊㄡˊ 和ㄏㄜˊ 肩ㄐㄧㄢ 膀ㄅㄤˇ ，
tóu hé jiān bǎng

脚
膝ㄒㄧ 脚ㄐㄧㄠˇ 趾ㄓˇ，
sī jiǎo jhǐh
xī zhǐ

脚
膝ㄒㄧ 、脚ㄐㄧㄠˇ 趾ㄓˇ ，
sī jiǎo jhǐh
xī zhǐ

脚
膝ㄒㄧ 、脚ㄐㄧㄠˇ 趾ㄓˇ 。
sī jiǎo jhǐh
xī zhǐ

头
頭ㄊㄡˊ 和ㄏㄜˊ 肩ㄐㄧㄢ 膀ㄅㄤˇ ，
tóu hé jiān bǎng

脚
膝ㄒㄧ 脚ㄐㄧㄠˇ 趾ㄓˇ ，眼ㄧㄢˇ 、耳ㄦˇ ，鼻ㄅㄧˊ 和ㄏㄜˊ 口ㄎㄡˇ 。
sī jiǎo jhǐh yǎn ěr bí hé kǒu
xī zhǐ

Head and shoulders, knees and toes. Knees and toes, knees and toes.
Head and shoulders, knees and toes. Eyes, ears, nose and mouth.

耳 ➡ 耳 ➡ 耳 ➡ 耳 ➡ 耳 ➡ 耳

Please color it.

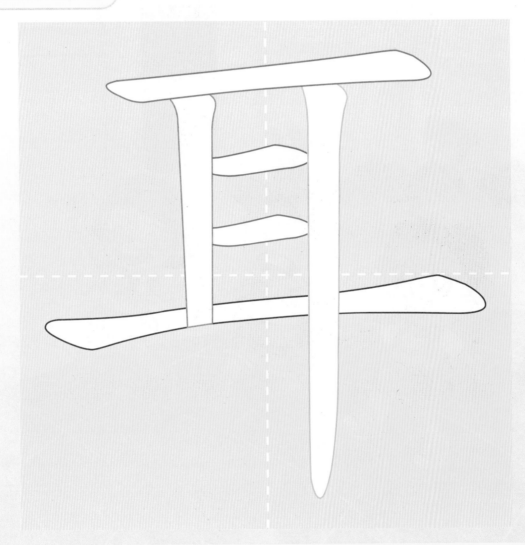

 这
這ㄓㄜˋ是ㄕˋ什ㄕㄣˊ麼ㄇㄜ？
jhè shìh shén me
zhè shì

 这
這ㄓㄜˋ是ㄕˋ耳ㄦˇ朵ㄉㄨㄛ。
jhè shìh ěr duo
zhè shì

 那ㄋㄚˋ是ㄕˋ什ㄕㄣˊ麼ㄇㄜ？
nà shìh shén me
shì

那ㄋㄚˋ是ㄕˋ嘴ㄗㄨㄟ巴ㄅㄚ。
nà shìh zhěi bā
shì zuǐ

What is this? This is an ear.
What is that? That is a mouth.

5

手 ㄕㄡˇ　shǒu　*Hand*

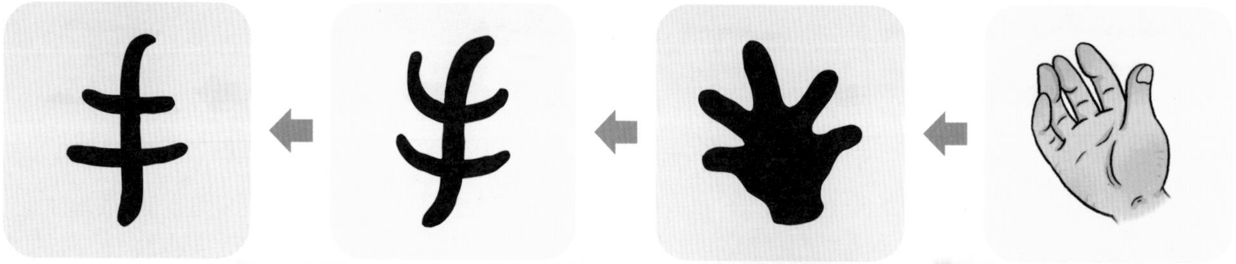

手 ← 手 ← 🖐 ← 🖐

左 ㄗㄨㄛˇ 手 ㄕㄡˇ 、右 ㄧㄡˋ 手 ㄕㄡˇ ，牽 ㄑㄧㄢ 牽 ㄑㄧㄢ 手 ㄕㄡˇ 。
zuǒ shǒu　yòu shǒu　ciān qiān shǒu
qiān

Left hand, right hand, holding hands.

左 ㄗㄨㄛˇ 腳 ㄐㄧㄠˇ 、右 ㄧㄡˋ 腳 ㄐㄧㄠˇ ，往 ㄨㄤˇ 前 ㄑㄧㄢˊ 走 ㄗㄡˇ 。
zuǒ jiǎo　yòu jiǎo　wǎng cián zǒu
qián

Left foot, right foot, walking forward.

左 ㄗㄨㄛˇ 邊 ㄅㄧㄢ 、右 ㄧㄡˋ 邊 ㄅㄧㄢ ，都 ㄉㄡ 是 ㄕˋ 朋 ㄆㄥˊ 友 ㄧㄡˇ 。
zuǒ biān　yòu biān　dōu shìh péng yǒu
shì

Left side and right side are both friends.

6

手 ▸ 手 ▸ 手 ▸ 手

Please color it.

往ㄨㄤ 左ㄗㄨㄛˇ 弯ㄨㄢ 彎。
wǎng   zuǒ   wān

往ㄨㄤ 右一ㄡˋ 弯ㄨㄢ 彎。
wǎng   yòu   wān

Turn to the left.
Turn to the right.

往ㄨㄤ 前ㄑㄧㄢˊ ＿＿＿。
wǎng   cián
      qián

往ㄨㄤ 後ㄏㄡˋ 后 ＿＿＿。
wǎng   hòu

＿＿＿ *forward.*
     backward.

聽老師唸，並貼上貼紙。Listen and place the stickers.

聽老師唸，並貼上貼紙。Listen and place the stickers.

請聽老師唸，並貼上貼紙。Listen and place the stickers.

Tones	1st tone —	2nd tone ╱	3rd tone ∨	4th tone ╲
心				
手				
耳				
口				
bí				

水 ← 氺 ← 川 ←

鱼　　　　　　　里　　　　来
魚 ㄩˊ 兒ㄦ 在ㄗㄞˋ 水ㄕㄨㄟ 裡ㄌㄧ，游ㄧㄡˊ 來ㄌㄞˊ 游ㄧㄡˊ 去ㄑㄩˋ 真ㄓㄣ 有ㄧㄡˇ 趣ㄑㄩˋ。
yú　er　zài　shuěi　lǐ　yóu　lái　yóu　cyù　jhēn　yǒu　cyù
　　　　　　shuǐ　　　　　　　qù　zhēn　　　qù

水　　　　　里　　　摇　来　摇　　　　　麗
水ㄕㄨㄟ 草ㄘㄠˇ 在ㄗㄞˋ 水ㄕㄨㄟ 裡ㄌㄧ，搖ㄧㄠˊ 來ㄌㄞˊ 搖ㄧㄠˊ 去ㄑㄩˋ 真ㄓㄣ 美ㄇㄟˇ 麗ㄌㄧˋ。
shuěi　cǎo　zài　shuěi　lǐ　yáo　lái　yáo　cyù　jhēn　měi　lì
shuǐ　　　　shuǐ　　　　　　　　qù　zhēn

Fish live in the water. It's fun to swim back and forth.
Waterweeds live in the water. They are beautiful when swaying to and fro.

水 ▶ 水 ▶ 水 ▶ 水

Please color it.

游ㄧㄡˊ 來ㄌㄞˊ 游ㄧㄡˊ 去ㄑㄩˋ。 摇ㄧㄠˊ 來ㄌㄞˊ 摇ㄧㄠˊ 去ㄑㄩˋ。 走ㄗㄡˇ 來ㄌㄞˊ 走ㄗㄡˇ 去ㄑㄩˋ。
yóu lái yóu cyù   yáo lái yáo cyù   zǒu lái zǒu cyù
         qù   qù   qù

跑ㄆㄠˇ 來ㄌㄞˊ 跑ㄆㄠˇ 去ㄑㄩˋ。 ＿＿＿ 來ㄌㄞˊ ＿＿＿ 去ㄑㄩˋ。
pǎo lái pǎo cyù   lái   cyù
         qù   qù

Swim back and forth.   Swing to and fro.   Walk back and forth.
Run back and forth. ____ back and forth.

11

火 ← 屮 ← ▽ ← 🔥

煙（烟） 火花 ， 開（开）啊開（开）， 一 朵 兩（两）朵 三 、 四 朵 ，
yān huǒ huā kāi a kāi yì duǒ liǎng duǒ sān sìh(sì) duǒ

五 朵 六 朵 七 、 八 朵 ， 趕 快 數（数） ， 開（开）了 幾（几）朵 ？
wǔ duǒ liòu(liù) duǒ cī(qī) bā duǒ gǎn kuài shǔ kāi le jǐ duǒ

Fireworks, sparkle and sparkle! One spark, two sparks, three sparks and four. Five sparks, six sparks, seven sparks and eight. Hurry up! Let's count how many sparkles?

火 ➡ 火 ➡ 火 ➡ 火

Please color it.

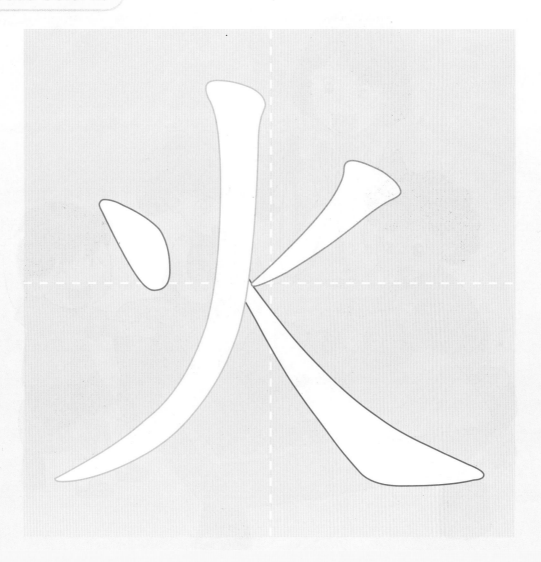

趕　　　　　　趕　　　进　来　　趕
趕ㄍㄢ快ㄎㄨㄞ跑ㄆㄠ。趕ㄍㄢ快ㄎㄨㄞ進ㄐㄧㄣ來ㄌㄞ。趕ㄍㄢ快ㄎㄨㄞ＿＿＿。
gǎn kuài pǎo　　gǎn kuài jìn lái　　gǎn kuài

Hurry up! Run! Hurry up! Come in! Hurry up! ＿＿＿＿!

土 ㄊㄨˇ tǔ *Soil*

土 ← 土 ← 工 ←

黏ㄋㄧㄢˊ 土ㄊㄨˇ 黏ㄋㄧㄢˊ 土ㄊㄨˇ 軟ㄖㄨㄢˇ 軟ㄖㄨㄢˇ 的ㄉㄜ˙，捏ㄋㄧㄝ 來ㄌㄞˊ 捏ㄋㄧㄝ 去ㄑㄩˋ 真ㄓㄣ 好ㄏㄠˇ 玩ㄨㄢˊ。
软　软　　　　　　　　　来
nián tǔ nián tǔ ruǎn ruǎn de　niē lái niē cyù jhēn hǎo wán
　　　　　　　　　　　　　　　　　　qù zhēn

圓ㄩㄢˊ 形ㄒㄧㄥˊ 方ㄈㄤ 形ㄒㄧㄥˊ 三ㄙㄢ 角ㄐㄧㄠˇ 形ㄒㄧㄥˊ，變ㄅㄧㄢˋ 來ㄌㄞˊ 變ㄅㄧㄢˋ 去ㄑㄩˋ 真ㄓㄣ 有ㄧㄡˇ 趣ㄑㄩˋ。
圆　　　　　　　　　　　　　　变　来　变
yuán síng fāng síng sān jiǎo síng　biàn lái biàn cyù jhēn yǒu cyù
　　xíng　　xíng　　　xíng　　　　　　　　qù zhēn　　qù

Clay, clay, soft clay. It's fun to mold some shapes.
A circle, a square and a triangle. It's fun to change various shapes.

Please color it.

： 什_{ㄕㄣ}麼_{ㄇㄜ}軟_{ㄖㄨㄢ}軟_{ㄖㄨㄢ}的_{ㄉㄜ}？
shén me ruǎn ruǎn de

： 黏_{ㄋㄧㄢ}土軟_{ㄖㄨㄢ}軟_{ㄖㄨㄢ}的_{ㄉㄜ}。
nián tǔ ruǎn ruǎn de

： 什_{ㄕㄣ}麼_{ㄇㄜ}圓_{ㄩㄢ}圓_{ㄩㄢ}的_{ㄉㄜ}？
shén me yuán yuán de

： ＿＿＿＿圓_{ㄩㄢ}圓_{ㄩㄢ}的_{ㄉㄜ}。
yuán yuán de

What is soft? The clay is soft.
What is round? The ___ is round.

15

石 ← 石 ← 曰 ←

剪ㄐㄧㄢ刀ㄉㄠ、石ㄕ頭ㄊㄡ、布ㄅㄨ，赢ㄧㄥ的ㄉㄜ往ㄨㄤ前ㄑㄧㄢ走ㄗㄡ，
jiǎn dāo shíh tóu bù yíng de wǎng cián zǒu
　　　　　shí　　　　　　　　　　　　　　　　　qián

输ㄕㄨ的ㄉㄜ退ㄊㄨㄟ一ㄧ步ㄅㄨ。
shū de tuèi yí bù
　　　　tuì

Scissors, stone, paper. The winner steps forward.
The loser steps backward.

石 ▶ 石 ▶ 石 ▶ 石 ▶ 石

Please color it.

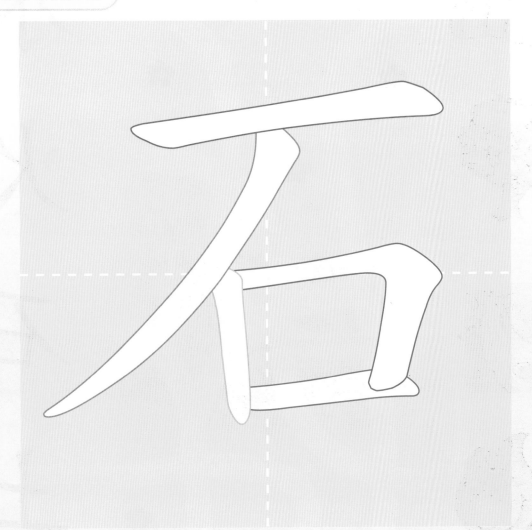

：走ㄗㄡˇ 幾ㄐㄧˇ 步ㄅㄨˋ？　：走ㄗㄡˇ 三ㄙㄢ 步ㄅㄨˋ。

走 = 几
zǒu jǐ bù　zǒu sān bù

How many steps forward?
Three steps.

：退ㄊㄨㄟˋ 幾ㄐㄧˇ 步ㄅㄨˋ？　：退ㄊㄨㄟˋ 兩ㄌㄧㄤˇ 步ㄅㄨˋ。

退 = 几　　退 = 两
tuèi jǐ bù　tuèi liǎng bù
tuì　　tuì

How many steps backward?
Two steps.

連連看 Matching game.

水

火

石

土

木

請聽老師唸，並貼上貼紙。Listen and place the stickers.

Tones	1st tone —	2nd tone ／	3rd tone ∨	4th tone ＼
石				
水				
火				
土				
木				

8

田 ㄊㄢˊ tián *Field*

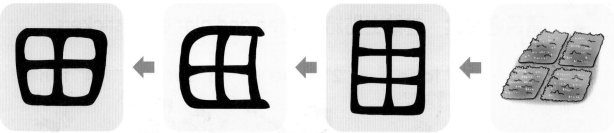

田 ㄊㄢˊ 裡 ㄌㄧˇ 有 ㄧㄡˇ 隻 ㄓ 大 ㄉㄚˋ 青 ㄑㄧㄥ 蛙 ㄨㄚ ， 愛 ㄞˋ 唱 ㄔㄤˋ 歌 ㄍㄜ ，
tián lǐ yǒu jhīh dà cīng wā ， ài chàng gē
　　　　　 zhī 　 qīng

愛 ㄞˋ 說 ㄕㄨㄛ 話 ㄏㄨㄚˋ ， 一 ㄧ 天 ㄊㄧㄢ 到 ㄉㄠˋ 晚 ㄨㄢˇ gua-gua-gua 。
ài shuō huà ， yì tiān dào wǎn gua-gua-gua 。

里　　　只　　　　　　　　愛
　　　　　　　　　　　　　　愛 说 话

20 *There is a big frog in the field. It loves singing. It loves talking.*
It says "gua-gua-gua" from day to night.

田 ▸ 田 ▸ 田 ▸ 田 ▸ 田

| Please color it. |

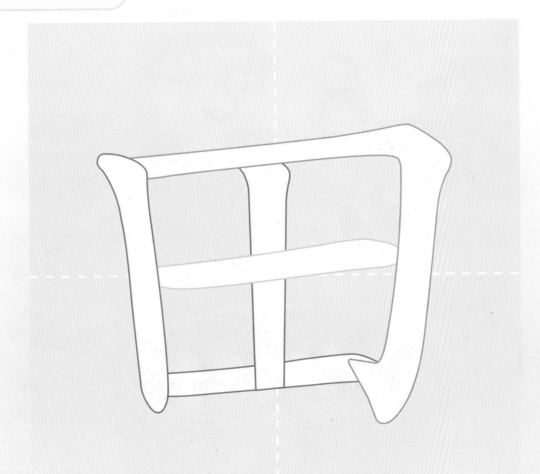

：田_{ㄊㄧㄢ}裡_{ㄌㄧ}有_{ㄧㄡ}什_{ㄕㄣ}麼_{ㄇㄜ}？
tián lǐ yǒu shén me

：田_{ㄊㄧㄢ}裡_{ㄌㄧ}有_{ㄧㄡ}一_ㄧ隻_ㄓ大_{ㄉㄚ}青_{ㄑㄧㄥ}蛙_{ㄨㄚ}。
tián lǐ yǒu yì jhīh dà cīng wā
zhī qīng

：他_{ㄊㄚ}愛_ㄞ做_{ㄗㄨㄛ}什_{ㄕㄣ}麼_{ㄇㄜ}？
tā ài zuò shén me

：他_{ㄊㄚ}愛_ㄞ唱_{ㄔㄤ}歌_{ㄍㄜ}。
tā ài chàng gē

What is in the field? There is a big frog in the field.
What does it love doing? It loves singing.

Bi-bi bo-bo Bi-bo-bo，Bi-bi bo-bo Bi-bo-bo

玉 ㄩˋ 米 ㄇㄧˇ 玉 ㄩˋ 米 ㄇㄧˇ 會 ㄏㄨㄟˋ 開 ㄎㄞ 花 ㄏㄨㄚ，

yù mǐ yù mǐ huèi kāi huā

huì

The corn, the corn is popping.

開 ㄎㄞ 出 ㄔㄨ 了 ㄌㄜ 很 ㄏㄣˇ 多 ㄉㄨㄛ 爆 ㄅㄠˋ 米 ㄇㄧˇ 花 ㄏㄨㄚ！

kāi chū le hěn duō bào mǐ huā

Look! It makes many popcorns.

米 ➡ 米 ➡ 米 ➡ 米 ➡ 米 ➡ 米

Please color it.

 ：他ㄊㄚ 會ㄏㄨㄟ (会) 做ㄗㄨㄛ 什ㄕㄣ 麼ㄇㄜ (么) ？
tā huèi zuò shén me
huì

 ：他ㄊㄚ 會ㄏㄨㄟ (会) 唱ㄔㄤ 歌ㄍㄜ 。
tā huèi chàng gē
huì

：你ㄋㄧ 會ㄏㄨㄟ (会) 做ㄗㄨㄛ 什ㄕㄣ 麼ㄇㄜ (么) ？
nǐ huèi zuò shén me
huì

：我ㄨㄛ 會ㄏㄨㄟ (会) _____ 。
wǒ huèi
huì

What can he do? He can sing.
What can you do? I can _____.

23

女 ㄋㄩˇ nyǔ / nǔ *Girl/Woman*

女 ← 虫 ←

爸ㄅㄚˋ 爸ㄅㄚ˙ 是ㄕˋ 男ㄋㄢˊ 生ㄕㄥ，媽ㄇㄚ 媽ㄇㄚ˙ 是ㄕˋ 女ㄋㄩˇ 生ㄕㄥ。
bà ba shìh nán shēng　mā ma shìh nyǔ shēng
　　shì　　　　　　　　shì　nǔ

妈 妈

Dad is a man.
Mom is a woman.

哥ㄍㄜ 哥ㄍㄜ˙ 是ㄕˋ 男ㄋㄢˊ 生ㄕㄥ，姊ㄐㄧㄝˇ 姊ㄐㄧㄝ˙ 是ㄕˋ 女ㄋㄩˇ 生ㄕㄥ。
gē ge shìh nán shēng　jiě jie shìh nyǔ shēng
　　shì　　　　　　　　shì　nǔ

Elder brother is a boy.
Elder sister is a girl.

老ㄌㄠˇ 師ㄕ 說ㄕㄨㄛ 我ㄨㄛˇ 是ㄕˋ 小ㄒㄧㄠˇ 學ㄒㄩㄝˊ 生ㄕㄥ。
lǎo shīh shuō wǒ shìh siǎo syué shēng
　shī　　　　　　shì　xiǎo xué

师 说　　　　　学

Teacher says that
I am a little student.

女 ➤ 女 ➤ 女

Please color it.

：你 ㄋㄧˇ 是 ㄕˋ 男 ㄋㄢˊ 生 ㄕㄥ 吗嗎 ㄇㄚ？
nǐ shìh nán shēng ma
shì

：是 ㄕˋ，我 ㄨㄛˇ 是 ㄕˋ 男 ㄋㄢˊ 生 ㄕㄥ。
shìh wǒ shìh nán shēng
shì shì

：不 ㄅㄨˊ 是 ㄕˋ，我 ㄨㄛˇ 不 ㄅㄨˊ 是 ㄕˋ 男 ㄋㄢˊ 生 ㄕㄥ。
bú shìh wǒ bú shìh nán shēng
shì shì

Are you a boy? Yes, I am a boy. ∕ No, I am not a boy.

25

子 ← ㅇ ←

我 ㄨㄛˇ 要 ㄧㄠˋ 做 ㄗㄨㄛˋ 個 ㄍㄜˋ 好 ㄏㄠˇ 孩 ㄏㄞˊ 子 ㄗ˙，健 ㄐㄧㄢˋ 康 ㄎㄤ、活 ㄏㄨㄛˊ 潑 ㄆㄛ、
wǒ　yào　zuò　ge　hǎo　hái　zih　　jiàn　kāng　　huó　pō
zi

有 ㄧㄡˇ 禮 ㄌㄧˇ 貌 ㄇㄠˋ，人 ㄖㄣˊ 人 ㄖㄣˊ 歡 ㄏㄨㄢ 迎 ㄧㄥˊ，人 ㄖㄣˊ 人 ㄖㄣˊ 愛 ㄞˋ。
yǒu　lǐ　mào　　rén　rén　huān　yíng　　rén　rén　ài

I want to be a good kid. I want to be healthy, active and polite.
I want to be popular and adorable.

子 → 子 → 子

Please color it.

👧：你ㄋㄧˇ要ㄧㄠˋ做ㄗㄨㄛˋ個ㄍㄜ怎ㄗㄣˇ樣ㄧㄤˋ的ㄉㄜ孩ㄏㄞˊ子ㄗˇ？ *What kind of child do you want to be?*
　　nǐ　yào　zuò　ge　zěn　yàng　de　hái　zih / zi

👦：我ㄨㄛˇ要ㄧㄠˋ做ㄗㄨㄛˋ個ㄍㄜ有ㄧㄡˇ禮ㄌㄧˇ貌ㄇㄠˋ的ㄉㄜ孩ㄏㄞˊ子ㄗˇ。 *I want to be a polite child.*
　　wǒ　yào　zuò　ge　yǒu　lǐ　mào　de　hái　zih / zi

👧：我ㄨㄛˇ要ㄧㄠˋ做ㄗㄨㄛˋ個ㄍㄜ＿＿＿＿的ㄉㄜ孩ㄏㄞˊ子ㄗˇ。 *I want to be a ＿＿＿＿ child.*
　　wǒ　yào　zuò　ge　＿＿＿　de　hái　zih / zi

圈出正確的圖。Circle the correct pictures.

1 子

2 米

3 田

4 火

5 女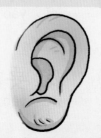

請聽老師唸，並貼上貼紙。Listen and place the stickers.

	1st tone	2nd tone	3rd tone	4th tone
Tones	ー	／	∨	＼
米				
田				
女				
子				
(好)				

小ㄒㄧㄠ 雨ㄩˇ si-li-li， 大ㄉㄚˋ 雨ㄩˇ hua-la-la
siǎo yǔ   dà yǔ
xiǎo

Si-li-li, hua-la-la. 雨ㄩˇ 傘ㄙㄢˇ 會ㄏㄨㄟˋ 開ㄎㄞ 花ㄏㄨㄚ。
        伞   会   开
yǔ sǎn huèi kāi huā
        huì

Light rain, si-li-li. Heavy rain, hua-la-la.
Si-li-li, hua-la-la. The umbrellas would blossom (turn inside out).

雨 ➡ 雨 ➡ 雨 ➡ 雨 ➡ 雨 ➡ 雨 ➡ 雨 ➡ 雨

Please color it.

：雨_{ㄩˇ}聲_{ㄕㄥ} 怎_{ㄗㄣˇ}麼_{ㄇㄜ}樣_{ㄧㄤˋ}？
　　yǔ shēng zěn me yàng

：雨_{ㄩˇ}聲_{ㄕㄥ} hua-la-la
　　yǔ shēng

：笑_{ㄒㄧㄠˋ}聲_{ㄕㄥ} 怎_{ㄗㄣˇ}麼_{ㄇㄜ}樣_{ㄧㄤˋ}？
　　siào shēng zěn me yàng
　　xiào

：笑_{ㄒㄧㄠˋ}聲_{ㄕㄥ} _____ 。
　　siào shēng
　　xiào

How does the sound of rain go? It goes hua-la-la.
How does the sound of laughter go? It goes _____ .

31

衣 ← 仌 ← 乀

爸ㄅㄚˋ爸ㄅㄚ˙ 洗ㄒㄧˇ 衣ㄧ 服ㄈㄨˊ，我ㄨㄛˇ 也ㄧㄝˇ 洗ㄒㄧˇ 衣ㄧ 服ㄈㄨˊ。
bà ba sǐ yī fú wǒ yě sǐ yī fú
　　xǐ 　　　　　xǐ

哎ㄞ 呀ㄧㄚ，小ㄒㄧㄠˇ 雨ㄩˇ 也ㄧㄝˇ 来ㄌㄞˊ 洗ㄒㄧˇ 衣ㄧ 服ㄈㄨˊ！
āi yā siǎo yǔ yě lái sǐ yī fú
　　　　xiǎo　　　　　　xǐ

Daddy is washing clothes.　I am also washing clothes.
Ai-ya, the rain is coming to wash clothes, too.

衣 ➤ 衣 ➤ 衣 ➤ 衣 ➤ 衣 ➤ 衣

Please color it.

会
我 ㄨㄛˇ 會 ㄏㄨㄟˋ 洗 ㄒㄧˇ 碗 ㄨㄢˇ ，你 ㄋㄧˇ 也 ㄧㄝˇ 會 ㄏㄨㄟˋ 洗 ㄒㄧˇ 碗 ㄨㄢˇ 嗎 ㄇㄚˊ ？
wǒ　huèi　sǐ　wǎn　　nǐ　yě　huèi　sǐ　wǎn　ma
　　huì　xǐ　　　　　　　　huì　xǐ

会
我 ㄨㄛˇ 會 ㄏㄨㄟˋ 。
wǒ　huèi
　　huì

会
我 ㄨㄛˇ 不 ㄅㄨˋ 會 ㄏㄨㄟˋ 。
wǒ　bú　huèi
　　　　huì

I can wash dishes. Can you wash dishes, too?
Yes, I can. / No, I can't.

33

刀 ㄉㄠ dāo *Knife*

刀 ← 刀 ← ㇓ ←

菜 ㄘㄞ 刀 ㄉㄠ 菜 ㄘㄞ 刀 ㄉㄠ 切 ㄑㄧㄝ 青 ㄑㄧㄥ 菜 ㄘㄞ 。
cài dāo cài dāo ciē cīng cài
　　　　　　　　qiē qīng

Kitchen knives, kitchen knives, cutting vegetables.

小 ㄒㄧㄠ 刀 ㄉㄠ 小 ㄒㄧㄠ 刀 ㄉㄠ 削 ㄒㄧㄠ 鉛 ㄑㄧㄢ 筆 ㄅㄧ 。
siǎo dāo siǎo dāo siāo ciān bǐ
xiǎo 　 xiǎo 　 xiāo qiān

Small knives, small knives, sharpening pencils.

剪 ㄐㄧㄢ 刀 ㄉㄠ 剪 ㄐㄧㄢ 刀 ㄉㄠ 剪 ㄐㄧㄢ 紙 ㄓ 張 ㄓㄤ 。
jiǎn dāo jiǎn dāo jiǎn jhǐh jhāng
　　　　　　　　 zhǐ zhāng

Scissors, scissors, cutting paper.

刀 ▶ 刀

Please color it.

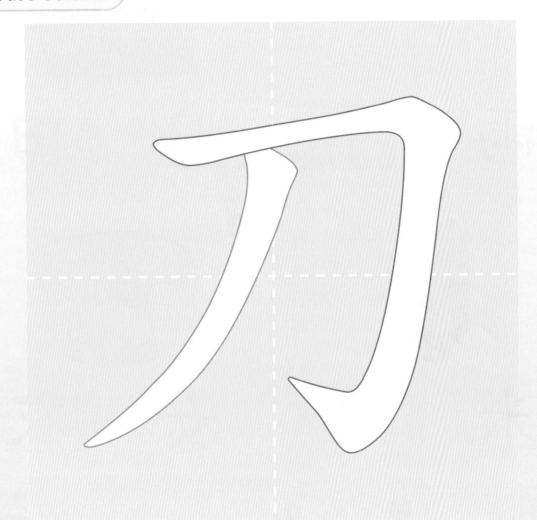

他ㄊㄚ 有ㄧㄡˇ 没ㄇㄟˊ 有ㄧㄡˇ 鉛ㄑㄧㄢ 筆ㄅㄧˇ？ : 有ㄧㄡˇ／没ㄇㄟˊ 有ㄧㄡˇ。
tā yǒu méi yǒu ciān bǐ   yǒu   méi yǒu
                         qiān

你ㄋㄧˇ 有ㄧㄡˇ 没ㄇㄟˊ 有ㄧㄡˇ 紙ㄓˇ？ : 有ㄧㄡˇ／没ㄇㄟˊ 有ㄧㄡˇ。
nǐ yǒu méi yǒu jhǐh   yǒu   méi yǒu
                    zhǐ

Does he have a pencil? Yes, he does. / No, he does not.
Do you have paper? Yes, I do. / No, I don't.

圈出正確的字。Circle the correct words.

1

雨　　耳

2

田

日　　田

3

米　　水

4

女　　衣

5

刀　　手

請聽老師唸，並貼上貼紙。Listen and place the stickers.

	1st tone	2nd tone	3rd tone	4th tone
Tones	―	／	∨	＼
衣				
雨				
刀				
田				
大				

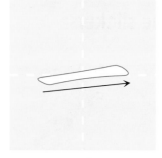

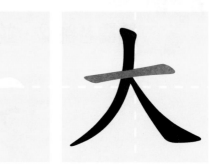

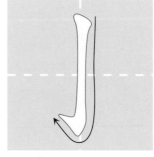

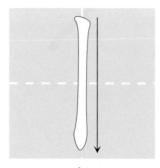

横 ㄏㄥˊ
héng

竪 ㄕㄨˋ
竪 shù

横 ㄏㄥˊ 鉤 ㄍㄡ
héng   鉤 gōu

竪 ㄕㄨˋ 鉤 ㄍㄡ
竪 shù   鉤 gōu

捺 ㄋㄚˋ
nà

水

点
點 ㄉㄧㄢˇ
diǎn

衣

撇 ㄆㄧㄝˇ
piě

手

竖
豎 ㄕㄨˋ　撇 ㄆㄧㄝˇ
shù　　piě

月

生活華語 第 K2 冊
Living Mandarin

海 外 指 導：費城頂好中文學校 Ding Hao Chinese school
　　　　　　紐西蘭華語文教學親師聯誼會
　　　　　　溫哥華台灣語言協會

輔　　　　導：教育部

策 劃 者：生活華語教材委員會

創 作 編 寫：Whitney CHUANG 莊舒雯　Betty FOO 張紀渝　YU B. C. 余伯泉

執 行 編 輯：Alice JAO 饒淑惠　Sonia CHANG 張雅容

教 學 指 引：www.skymandarin.org

美 編 印 刷：磊承印刷事業有限公司 www.lcprint.com.tw

彩 虹 筆 順：婁世美

繪　　　　圖：鍾佳吟　羅敏芬

音　　　　樂：三雅錄音有限公司

出　　　　版：台灣語言文化社

發　　　　行：藍天華語有限公司　Sky Mandarin Ltd.

發 行 部：(115)台北市南港區研究院路二段2巷28號

　　　　　　28, Lane 2, Academia Rd. Sec. 2, Taipei 115, Taiwan

　　　　　　TEL：886-2-2653-2717　886-2-2653-2718

　　　　　　FAX：886-2-2653-2719

　　　　　　e-mail：skymandarin@gmail.com

版　　　　次：2008年8月　　2009年修訂　　2010年再刷

耳　口　手　心　日　月

一　ノ　ノ　ヘ　＼　一　ノ　ノ　ヘ

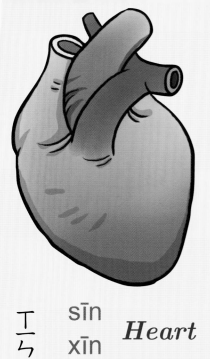

ㄒㄧㄣ sīn
xīn *Heart*

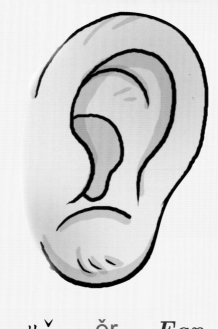

ㄦˇ ěr *Ear*

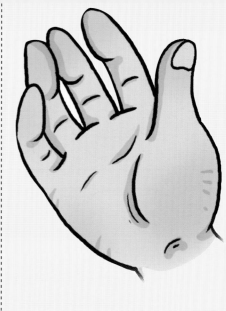

ㄕㄡˇ shǒu *Hand*

ㄊㄨˇ tǔ *Soil*

ㄏㄨㄛˇ huǒ *Fire*

ㄕㄨㄟˇ shuěi
shuǐ *Water*

ㄇㄧˇ mǐ *Rice*

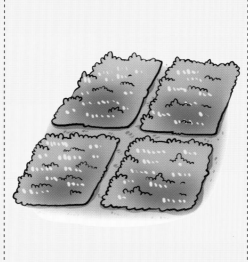

ㄊㄧㄢˊ tián *Field*

ㄕˊ shíh
shí *Stone Rock*

手	耳	心
水	火	土
石	田	米

ㄩˇ　yǔ　*Rain*

ㄗ　zih
zi　*Son*

ㄋ　nyǔ　*Girl*
ㄩˇ　nǔ　*Woman*

ㄕˊ　shíh
shí　*Ten*

ㄅㄠ　dāo　*Knife*

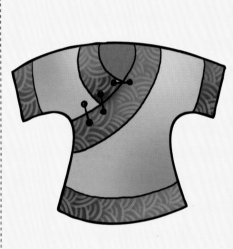

一　yī　*Clothes*

ㄋㄢˊ　nán

Man

ㄏㄠˇ　hǎo

Good

ㄊㄢ　tiān

Sky

女	子	雨
衣	刀	十
夭	好	男

SECRETS OF CHRISTIANITY

THE REAL JESUS

DETAIL FROM A WINDOW IN THE DAHLGREN CHAPEL OF THE SACRED HEART / GEORGETOWN UNIVERSITY
PHOTOGRAPH BY BRETT ZIEGLER FOR *USN&WR*

CONTENTS

A NEED TO KNOW HIM

Scientists and scholars gather fresh clues to the mystery that still obscures the man

ike massive desert sand dunes that shift and re-form, some of the most cherished beliefs about early Christianity are collapsing, and fresh ideas are replacing them. During the past six decades, crucial discoveries of ancient texts, coordinated scholarly and scientific research, and new archaeological finds have helped to reorient the thinking about a time that once appeared to be fixed in stone forever. And the most important clues have come from the Middle Eastern desert earth itself—clues that help to answer the most compelling questions of all: Did Jesus really exist, and if so, who was he?

These are, in fact, questions that have been floating about for centuries. During the Enlightenment, philosophers such as Charles François Dupuis in his *Origine de Tous les Cultes, ou la Religion Universelle*, published in 1795, began to explore the notion of Jesus as a purely mythical construct, since there seemed to be little historical record left to corroborate the few details provided in the New Testament. Following in his footsteps, David Friedrich Strauss in 1835 published *The Life of Jesus Critically Examined*, in which he treated the Gospels as "mytho-poetic" writings. Soon after, Bruno Bauer, a German theologian,

maintained in his *A Critique of the Gospels and a History of Their Origin* that Jesus never existed at all. Later, others continued the assault. In his 1927 essay *Why I Am Not a Christian*, philosopher Bertrand Russell stated that "historically it is quite doubtful whether Christ ever existed at all, and if He did we do not know anything about him." More recently, popularizers from Timothy Freke and Peter Gandy (*The Jesus Mysteries* and *Jesus and the Lost Goddess*) to Earl Doherty (*The Jesus Puzzle*) and journalist Christopher Hitchens (*God Is Not Great*) all have claimed there is no unassailable proof that the Jesus of tradition ever existed.

An ongoing quest. For many devout Christians, the idea of having to prove anything about Jesus is ridiculous: For them, the Bible is the sacred word and everything in it is infallible. Others, some of them equally devout, feel compelled to search for the historical Jesus in order to

A fragment of the Dead Sea Scrolls, first discovered in 1947 by a Bedouin shepherd

know who he really was. And so, for over 200 years, beginning with Hermann Samuel Reimarus's work on the subject and continuing through Albert Schweitzer's 1906 *The Quest of the Historical Jesus* up to the modern-day Jesus Seminar, there has been an ongoing quest to find concrete evidence of the messianic leader who lived at the time of Caesar Augustus. In recent years, this campaign to find the truth of whether Jesus existed, and what happened to him, has been launched on all fronts. To borrow a description from biblical scholar John Dominic Crossan, emeritus professor of religious studies at DePaul University in Chicago, about his own work, this effort has "established a dialectic of stone and text, an interaction of ground and gospel, an integration of archaeology and exegesis."

In the 18th century, archaeologists and scholars began to unearth and decipher important fragments of texts in a painstaking attempt to re-create the world of first-century Palestine. The picture they were able to reconstruct was very incomplete. One of the first important finds was a collection of papyrus fragments dating from the second century, discovered by Bernard Pyne Grenfell and Arthur Surridge Hunt, British archaeologists excavating at the turn of the 20th century near Oxyrhynchus, Egypt, which included a small number of the sayings of Jesus.

That discovery, however, paled in comparison with what was to come. In 1945, a major trove of manuscripts was unearthed from a cave near Nag Hammadi in Upper Egypt. Included were 52 documents in 13 papyrus books. Among the manuscripts—written in a Coptic translation of the original Greek—was the only complete copy ever found of the Gospel of Thomas, one of the so-called Gnostic Gospels (story, Page 72). This rich collection of banned religious literature included texts—and fragments of texts—that had been condemned by early champions of Christian orthodoxy such as Athanasius, Hegesippus, and Irenaeus, who wrote in the second, third, and fourth centuries. The documents in these codices, dating to the second century, were believed to have been originally part of a library at the nearby monastery of St. Pachomius.

The recovery of the complete Gospel of Thomas solved a major puzzle for scholars. It confirmed something that had been only a hypothesis. Scholars had long thought there had been a proto-gospel, a collection of sayings they dubbed the Lost Gospel Q, one of the two sources from which the Gospels of Matthew and Luke drew their material. The Gospel of Thomas proved conclusively that such sorts of codices had existed.

Between 1947 and 1956 another momentous discovery occurred. Manuscripts now known to the world as the Dead Sea Scrolls (story, Page 81) were unearthed from caves near the ruins of Khirbet Qumran, a tiny hamlet on the shores of the Dead Sea. More than 900 items were recovered, including virtually the only surviving copies of biblical documents written before A.D. 100. Most importantly, they showed that Christian sects remained essentially Jewish long after the death of Jesus. As a result, in the past 40 years there has been a new area of study concerning exactly how Jewish the early Christians—and Jesus—really were.

Other discoveries followed on their heels. One precious trove, however, was nearly lost forever. The Gospel of Judas, part of a codex discovered in the 1970s near Al Minya, Egypt, was sold to an antiquities dealer and remained beyond the reach of scholars for more than a quarter century. During that time, it deteriorated badly before it was handed over to the Maecenas Foundation in Basel, Switzerland, for restoration. Like many manuscripts that have recently resurfaced, such as those at Nag Hammadi, it is a third- or fourth-century Coptic translation of an earlier Greek text. Its particular importance to the world of biblical scholarship is in its depiction of Judas, Jesus's famous betrayer, which is markedly different—and more openly sympathetic—than that found in the canonical Gospels. In this account, Judas is Jesus's most beloved disciple and the one he specifically chose

The Qumran Caves
are where the
Dead Sea Scrolls
were found.

to hand him over to his executioners (story, Page 66).

Even as manuscripts such as this have continued to emerge from the desert, archaeologists in modern-day Israel, Palestine, and Jordan are uncovering sites that were unknown or unexcavated just a few years ago. Since the 1980s, a number of major archaeological digs have been active in Sepphoris and Tiberias, cities built or rebuilt by Herod Antipas, the governor of the Galilee at the time of Jesus. The Galilee was one of the most densely populated regions in the entire Roman empire, and Sepphoris was the market hub for a network of agricultural villages. It was rebuilt after its near-complete destruction following a Jewish uprising against the Romans in 4 B.C.

James Strange, professor of religious studies at the University of South Florida in Tampa and director of excavations at Sepphoris, has spent part of his career comparing the lifestyles in the city of Sepphoris with that of surrounding villages. As a result of this work, says Strange, "We now have a nuanced view of Jewish life in the Galilee in the Roman period from these and other sites.... Most of these were small villages dedicated mostly to agriculture, but occasionally ... to weaving, jewelry making, and bronze production. There was a thriving and complex system of trade routes between villages and towns."

The archaeologists on Strange's team make careful use of scientific methods such as stratigraphic sequencing in excavation, which involves separating out layers of occupation by color, compaction, and contents. "Everyone else thinks they pay close attention to stratigraphy too," says Strange, "but we pay as close attention to it as humanly possible, recording the stratigraphic sequences to the nearest centimeter." By using this system, archaeologists are able to date and contextualize the objects found in or near the ruins of buildings. With the help of state-of-the-art technologies such as infrared photography and scans, soil interface radar, 3-D computer mapping, GPS systems, aerial photography, and soil resistivity surveys to "see" beneath the earth, archaeologists are making significant progress in piecing together a composite picture of what life was like at a particular moment in time and in a particular place. Nazareth, a small agricultural village in Roman times, where Jesus is said to have lived as a boy, has also been located near Sepphoris and excavated.

Clues to peasant life. The ruins of two well-preserved first-century villages in the Galilee, Gamla and Yodefat, have also provided important information. All the inhabitants were dispersed by the Romans around A.D. 67 during a major Jewish revolt. Because of this, the villages can be quite accurately dated, and thus have offered up further clues concerning how simple Jewish peasants lived in the years just before the destruction of the Second Temple. In Cana, a town near Sepphoris

that survived into the second century, excavators have recently found a late first-century synagogue.

Not only does much more information exist today about the places Jesus frequented, there are many specific discoveries that seem to bear out the sparse details we have about Jesus's childhood, ministry, and horrifying death. In June 1961, for instance, Italian archaeologists uncovered a dedication to Tiberius Caesar from "Pontius Pilate, Prefect of Judea" in an ancient Roman theater near Caesarea Maritima, located halfway between Tel Aviv and Haifa. This confirmed the existence of the Roman ruler who presided over Jesus's trial the night before he died (story, Page 26). More recently, in 1990, in the middle of the Jerusalem Peace Forest, a dump truck broke through the roof of a tomb and uncovered an ossuary containing the bones of the very same high priest, Caiaphas, who handed over Jesus to Pontius Pilate (story, Page 81). In another detail that meshes with the Gospel narratives, archaeological teams brought to light remnants of the palace of Herod Antipas during excavations in 2005 at Tiberias. And the story of Jesus's crucifixion was rendered entirely plausible when, in 1968, an ossuary in a burial cave northeast of Jerusalem was opened and a victim's heel bone appeared, pierced through with a long nail. The name of the crucified man was Yehochanan. Archaeologists were able to date his remains to the first century and study the circumstances of how he died, thereby extrapolating from that the details of Jesus's crucifixion (story, Page 22).

SEVERAL SITES JESUS VISITED DURING HIS MINISTRY HAVE BEEN EXCAVATED.

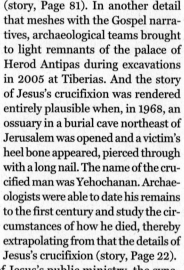

As for the years of Jesus's public ministry, the synagogue where Jesus may have prayed was found in Migdal, along the Sea of Galilee. Remains of its foundation have been discovered below the present ruins of a later Roman synagogue. The apostle Peter's house at Capernaum, on top of which an octagonal Christian sanctuary was built, has also been uncovered. Nearby, the remains of a first-century boat were pulled from a muddy lake bed in the Sea of Galilee in 1986. The relic might well be the same kind of fishing boat that Jesus used during the miraculous calming of the waters recounted in the Gospel of Mark (Mark 4:35-41). Other sites Jesus visited during his ministry, such as Caesarea Philippi, Shechem, and Bethany, have also been excavated.

Yet with all this new information and fresh insight into the world of first-century Jewish Palestine, has it changed anyone's understanding of who Jesus really was? Or does he remain maddeningly enigmatic, and does the meaning of his teachings sometimes elude certainty? And is that elusiveness a function of who Jesus was, or of what others, such as Paul and the Evangelists, have made him? As scholars such as Crossan and Jonathan L. Reed observed in their textual and archaeological work, *Excavating Jesus: Beneath the Stones, Behind*

An ancient synagogue in Capernaum, a town where Jesus was known to preach

the Texts, "Unlike earlier gospel layers, later ones tend to distance him from Judaism and 'the Jews' ... or use Jewish texts and interpretative devices to reinvent Judaism as Christianity.... And later archaeological layers commemorating Jesus's life tend to efface signs of his Jewishness in the earlier ones and replace them with features from Rome or Byzantium. On the other hand, the farther removed Jesus is from his first-century Galilean context, the more elite and regal he becomes."

An evolving history. The concept of "layers" to describe how Jesus and his circle were portrayed at various moments over time can be used just as readily to explain how subsequent church history has been reinterpreted in each age by the authors of that time. This idea has gained currency in the last half century, prompting historians such as Fernand Braudel to go back to the historical foundations, as it were, undertaking a detailed look at the many voices in everyday life at a precise moment in time through the examination of contemporary accounts and other primary documents. Using these same methods, religious scholars and researchers are taking a fresh look at many controversial areas of church history such as the Inquisition, the Crusades, the Reformation, and more recent events. Because of this renewed interest in the primary documents from certain periods of church history, an official effort has been made to open to researchers a number of collections of the Vatican Secret Archives. This is true of archives in libraries in other parts of Europe and the Middle East as well.

Because more opportunities exist now to delve into the primary documents of long ago, and to reconstruct in a more complete way the historical context and attitudes of a particular time in the past, an open and honest discussion of the history of religion becomes ever more possible—at least theoretically. In some cases, this is long overdue. The Crusades offer a good example of a subject that had largely been ignored by the general public except for references in children's storybooks or Monty Python movies. Given the Muslim-Christian tensions of the past decade, this controversial and bloody period of church history might well have merited more attention and a better understanding before now, since it has long been a rallying point for Muslim resentment toward the West. As their detractors have long alleged, the Crusaders were not always heroic champions of Christian virtues—at times decidedly outpacing the brutality of their opponents.

Yet even with all the new resources and documentation, and with better scientific knowledge and technology, many questions remain at the heart of Christianity. Certain important figures such as John the Baptist, Mary Magdalene, and Judas will remain schematic and indeterminate, despite attempts to flesh them out. The most fascinating of all these figures, of course, is Jesus himself, a brilliant, witty, intensely attractive, enigmatic, and visionary man, whose life, death, and Resurrection will continue to invite either speculation, skepticism, or fervent belief.

This gap between what has been learned about the past and what is really knowable extends even further, into other areas of inquiry. Scientific answers to questions such as how human beings were created, the nature of miracles, the existence of evil, and the ultimate fate of mankind continue to fall short of offering a fully satisfactory explanation. Not everything, it appears, can be demonstrated empirically.

And so the grand irony of Christianity remains. Even though there is much more research and far greater insight than 200 years ago, many important details elude certainty. Like the mathematical truism that a number can be divided infinitesimally without reaching zero, it seems that the world can approach, but never attain, the total truth about Jesus and the history of Christianity. ●

By Amy D. Bernstein

HIS LIFE

CHAPTER 1

DETAIL FROM A WINDOW IN THE DAHLGREN CHAPEL OF
THE SACRED HEART / GEORGETOWN UNIVERSITY

PHOTOGRAPH BY BRETT ZIEGLER FOR *USN&WR*

AND TIMES

WHO WAS JESUS?

Seeking the truth behind the man from Nazareth

hen he walked out of the Judean desert some 2,000 years ago, an unknown itinerant preacher, he proclaimed to all who would listen that the Kingdom of God was at hand. It was said that he was a healer and a gifted teacher who challenged conventional wisdom and spoke with authority and wit. In the villages and hillsides of Galilee, curious crowds would gather to witness his deeds and hear his teachings. Some followed him, believing he was God's anointed one, while others dismissed him as a pretender and a troublemaker. Less than three years after he began, he was arrested in Jerusalem and executed on a Roman cross. His death, and the testimony of his followers that he arose from the dead, would change the course of history.

Today, as in his own time, Jesus of Nazareth remains one of history's most intriguing and enigmatic figures. The religion founded on his teachings counts about a third of the world's population as members, yet his words and deeds and the meaning of his life, death, and Resurrection are subjects of intense debate and sometimes surprising interpretations. Many still ask the question of the ages: "Who is Jesus?"

For more than two centuries, biblical scholars and historians

JESUS REMAINS ONE OF HISTORY'S MOST ENIGMATIC FIGURES.

have sought to discern to what extent the Christ of faith, as perceived and experienced by Christian believers, resembles Jesus of Nazareth, the man who lived and died in Roman-occupied Palestine at the turn of the era. Using the tools of modern textual research, archaeology, and social science, they seek to reconstruct a portrait of the historical Jesus, unembellished by 2,000 years of church devotional tradition.

Judging from the number of recent books on the subject, the quest for the historical Jesus is getting a new surge of scholarly energy. In recent decades, he has been depicted variously as a magician and healer, as a religious and social revolutionary, and as a radical peasant philosopher. One author has even theorized that Jesus was the leader of the Dead Sea Scrolls community at Qumran, that he survived the Crucifixion and went on to marry twice and father three children. While such theories make for provocative reading, none has been widely accepted by biblical scholars and some have been quickly dismissed by the academic community as not much more than fanciful speculation.

Ever since the quest for the historical Jesus began in earnest during the Enlightenment, it has focused as much on the veracity of the New Testament Gospels as on the figure of Jesus himself. The late 18th-century skepticism dramatically altered the scholarly view

Jesus's reputation
as a healer
extended beyond
his followers.

of the Gospels. They came to be viewed not as pure biography or objective historical documentation, but as theological proclamation based on historical events believed to have occurred decades earlier.

In going back to those events, says Anthony Tambasco, professor of theology and associate dean in the Graduate Liberal Studies Program at Georgetown University in Washington, D.C., the Gospel writers went searching for specific kinds of stories from the oral traditions concerning the life of Jesus, stories that would illustrate what a resurrected Christ and Son of God would accomplish through the church. "They did not attempt," says Tambasco, "to reconstruct a complete account of his life and all that he spoke."

Many consider the search for the "real" Jesus in historical documents to be a quixotic task. A more reasonable objective, they say, is to learn who his contemporaries thought he was and what he thought of himself. Did he claim to be the Messiah, the divine Son of God? Did his audiences think of him in those ways?

Holy roots? In the Gospels, Jesus frequently refers to himself ambiguously as the Son of Man and to God as Father. Yet he shies away from publicly proclaiming himself Israel's Messiah. Only in the Gospel of Mark, when asked after his arrest if he is Israel's Promised One, does Jesus respond "I am." Some scholars doubt Jesus ever spoke these words. They argue instead that the declaration reflects the views of his followers as they came to understand the meaning of his life, death, and Resurrection.

Even those who take the words as authentic say it is impossible to be certain what Jesus meant by those terms or to determine when he came to recognize himself as God's promised Messiah. "The texts don't tell us,"

THE MIRACLE WORKER

ven more astounding than any of his words are the miracles of Jesus. The Gospels report 35 of them directly and allude to 12 others, from healings and exorcisms to walking on water and raising the dead. Among the most common of Jesus's recorded miracles were his healings. Yet many men have claimed such powers throughout human history, so to tell stories of Jesus making people well, says Stevan Davies, professor of religious studies at Misericordia University in Dallas, Pa., is "no more exciting than to say he was a carpenter."

Davies, who has written on the subject, says that even without believing in the supernatural, one could conclude that Jesus did heal psychosomatic illnesses—rashes, lameness, and some types of blindness, for example. Some Gospel accounts of his healings seem also to involve his use of primitive medical arts—the application of mud to the eyes of a blind man, for instance—and his appropriation of conventional religious practices, such as Jewish purification rites for those

suffering from skin diseases.

Jesus also was widely known as an exorcist. The Gospels record four instances in which he came upon people said to be possessed by demons. In one story, he casts out a "legion" of spirits, sending them into a herd of pigs that throw themselves off a cliff. "There is little doubt that Jesus performed exorcisms as they were understood in his time," said the late John J. Rousseau, an archaeolo-

THE RAISING OF LAZARUS BY CARL HEINRICH BLOCH / RESTORED TRADITIONS

says Donald Carson, research professor of New Testament at Trinity Evangelical Divinity School in Deerfield, Ill. Yet what seems clear, says Carson, is that by the time Jesus begins his public ministry he knows his special status, "and he knows he is going to be a different Messiah from what is expected."

In large measure, those seeking the historical Jesus must base their judgments of the man's authenticity on his words and deeds, much as his Galilean audiences had to do at the time. In his sermons and discourses recorded in the Gospels of Matthew, Mark, and Luke, Jesus often speaks in parables and pithy aphorisms. At the center of his teachings was the Kingdom of God—its arrival, its future fulfillment, and its implications for human conduct. He declared love the greatest of the Old Testament commandments and spoke reassuringly to the poor, the powerless, and the peacemakers. Yet he also warned of divine judgment and declared paradoxically that he had come "not to bring peace, but a sword" that would divide nations and families.

To his curious Jewish listeners, chafing under Roman rule and longing for a restoration of the glory days under Israel's great kings, historians say, the arrival of God's Kingdom would have been a tantalizing but puzzling message. In the Gospels, Jesus seldom spoke explicitly concerning the nature of God's Kingdom, but instead described it in parables with sometimes hidden meanings.

In fact, to many of his listeners, says N.T. Wright, research professor of New Testament and early Christianity at the University of St. Andrews in Scotland, it is likely that Jesus's message would have sounded subversive. He seemed to challenge the bounds of the Jewish law by declaring, for example, "the Sabbath was

The Bible gives a dramatic account of Jesus raising Lazarus from the dead.

gist and member of the Jesus Seminar, a group of liberal scholars examining the words and deeds of Christ. "It was just a natural thing to do for an itinerant charismatic healer and teacher ... and he was not the only one to do it."

Exorcisms clearly were a part of the Jewish milieu in first-century Palestine. The Judaism of Jesus's time, observed Rousseau, had been influenced by Babylonian, Persian, Egyptian, and Greek cultures. The Persian belief that demons could possess individuals and cause diseases, said Rousseau, "had gained wide acceptance, and techniques of exorcism were used for the treatment of illnesses." Often those techniques involved use of magical devices such as amulets, rings, stones, and artifacts, which have been discovered at archaeological sites.

Among the most sensational of Gospel stories, and the most problematic for historians, are those that depict Jesus performing so-called nature miracles—calming a stormy sea, walking on water, changing water into wine at a wedding feast, and feeding 5,000 people with five loaves and two fish.

Clearly the most astounding of Jesus's reported miracles are the accounts of his raising the dead. The

ONE COULD CONCLUDE THAT JESUS DID HEAL PSYCHOSOMATIC ILLNESSES.

Gospel of Luke tells of Jesus reviving a widow's son in Nain: "And he said, 'Young man, I say to you, arise!' And the dead man sat up and began to speak." And the Gospel of John records Jesus raising his friend Lazarus, who was dead for four days in Bethany, near Jerusalem. While many scholars also reject these stories as pure fiction, some have suggested that the tales may reflect honest misunderstandings. The victims may have mistakenly been thought dead and were simply revived.

Ultimately, says Paul Maier, professor of ancient history at Western Michigan University in Kalamazoo, "there is no way for historians to prove or disprove" the resuscitation stories. But he finds some historical corroboration in the subsequent history of Bethany. The town, destroyed when the Romans attacked Jerusalem in A.D. 70, was later rebuilt and was renamed by the Arabs who settled there. "The Israelis today call it Bethanya but the Arabs call it el-Azariyeh, 'the place of Lazarus,'" says Maier. "I find that fascinating. Why would they change the name of the town unless something spectacular happened there?"

Dennis MacDonald, professor of New Testament and Christian origins at Claremont School of Theology in Claremont, Calif., sees a connection between stories of Jesus's walking on water and calming the seas and Homer's *Odyssey*, in which the god Poseidon performs similar feats. Gospel writers, says MacDonald, would have been familiar with Homer's writings, which were then in common use as school texts in the ancient world. The Christian writers drew upon the familiar motif, he argues, to construct stories "in which Jesus revealed his divine identity."
–J.L.S.

made for man, not man for the Sabbath" and "not what enters into the mouth defiles the man, but what proceeds out of the mouth." He often accused the Pharisees, the leaders of the synagogues, of hypocrisy for following the letter of the law but not its spirit.

The Kingdom of God that Jesus described would include the gentiles, and many of Israel's cherished traditions would be seriously challenged by this egalitarian vision. "It would be like announcing in a Moslem country that one was fulfilling the will of Allah—while apparently vilifying Muhammad and burning a copy of the Koran," noted Wright in his book *Who Was Jesus?* "It's no wonder Jesus needed to use parables to say all this." While some of Jesus's listeners were prepared to follow him, forsaking all, says Edwin Yamauchi, professor emeritus of history at Miami University in Oxford, Ohio, "many more were either skeptical or aghast at his apparent disregard of Moses's teachings and his claim of a special relation with God the Father."

Feats of wonder. Of course, much of the renown of Jesus was due to the miracles associated with him, from healings and exorcisms to walking on water and raising the dead. Implied in the modern debate over whether or not Jesus performed such feats is the ultimate question of his identity: Was he the divine Son of God, as the church would come to believe, or was he

The Sermon on the Mount includes some of Jesus's best-known teachings.

just a uniquely gifted teacher and perhaps a prophet?

The significance of the issue was recognized early on by leaders of the church. The Christian apologist Justin Martyr, writing in about A.D. 160, referred to the healing miracles of Jesus as the fulfillment of Messianic prophecies in the Book of Isaiah, written about 700 years before Jesus's lifetime:

... the eyes of the blind will be
opened and the ears of the deaf
unstopped; then the lame shall
leap like a deer, and the tongue
of the speechless sing for joy.

Jesus performed healing miracles, Justin Martyr wrote, to elicit recognition that he was indeed the prophesied Messiah. But many who witnessed Jesus's miraculous feats, he noted, drew the opposite conclusion: "They said it was a display of magic art for they even dared to say he was a magician and deceiver of the people." To label someone a magician and a deceiver in antiquity, wrote the late New Testament scholar Graham N. Stanton, "was an attempt to marginalize a person who was perceived to be a threat to the dominant social order."

Jesus's criticisms of the legalistic excesses of Judaic law could easily have been perceived as a challenge to the religious customs and traditions of his time, Stanton contended in his book *Jesus of Nazareth in New Testament Preaching*, and would certainly have set the Temple priests and the leaders of the synagogues against him.

Today, there is broad consensus among even the most skeptical of scholars that Jesus probably did perform feats that would have been perceived as miracles at the time (box, Page 14). They find considerable evidence, for example, that Jesus's reputation as a healer and miracle worker extended beyond his own circle of followers. The Jewish historian Josephus, writing near the end of the first century, wrote that Jesus was known as "a doer of startling deeds" and a teacher who "gained a following both among many Jews and many men of Greek origin." The Jewish Talmud relates that "on the eve of Passover, Yeshu was hanged ... because he has practiced sorcery and led Israel astray."

Some biblical experts argue that his performance of "startling deeds" does not make him entirely unique in his place and time. Among the most common of Jesus's recorded miracles were his healings. Yet theologians point out that every culture—before, during, and after Jesus's time—has produced similar tales tied to others. Nonetheless, the fact that Jesus was widely known as a healer makes it likely that he did indeed engage in such activity, noted the late Robert Funk, director of the Westar Institute in Salem, Ore., and cofounder of the Jesus Seminar, a group of liberal scholars who examine Jesus's words and deeds. Still, to say that Jesus was known for engaging in these types of events, Funk said, "is far different than saying he healed this particular man in this particular way, as recorded in the Gospels."

Many scholars do believe that Jesus probably did perform some miracles. While it may not be possible to determine which ones were authentic, says Georgetown's Tambasco, "we can, however, be reasonably sure that all of the healings taken together witness to the fact of miracles in the life of Jesus."

Dangerous game. Though it is not depicted as a miracle, Jesus's chasing of the money-changers from the Temple in Jerusalem is clearly one of the most dramatic and significant of his reported deeds. Beyond the religious symbolism of the act—purifying what the Gospels said had become "a den of thieves"—it was a definitive event leading to his arrest and Crucifixion. But the account in the Gospels of Matthew, Mark, and Luke of Jesus doing this after his final entry into Jerusalem, just days before his arrest, conflicts with John's Gospel, which seems to have him performing the deed at the very beginning of his ministry. Is either of the accounts accurate?

Again, there is wide disagreement on the historicity of the specific details. The story, says Paula Fredriksen, a professor of religion at Boston University, "is excellent theology. It's just terrible history." Selling of sacrificial animals in the Temple court, she notes, was a long-standing practice that enabled pilgrims to meet their religious obligations. And portraying Jesus as chasing the money-changers from the Temple, noted Funk of the Westar Institute, "is not a realistic picture. There must have been hundreds of them, especially on a festival day."

Nonetheless, there is broad consensus that underlying the Gospel anecdote is some Temple incident that is somewhat akin to the accounts of Jesus's bold and decisive act. Some have suggested that he protested the Temple tax or the use of coins with pagan images. Others theorize he was angered that the selling of animals had taken over the only area in the Temple where gentiles were permitted to pray. Whatever the exact nature of Jesus's deed, says Bruce Chilton, Bernard Iddings

SOME BIBLICAL EXPERTS NOTE THAT JESUS'S PERFORMANCE OF "STARTLING DEEDS" DOES NOT MAKE HIM ENTIRELY UNIQUE IN HIS PLACE AND TIME.

Bell professor of religion at Bard College in New York, "an act against the Temple would have been perceived by the Romans as an attack on the status quo." And that would have made him a prime candidate for arrest in the eyes of the authorities.

Regardless of the controversy it generates and the lack of consensus over what it may produce, the quest for the historical Jesus is certain to continue. If some clearer, purer vision of Jesus of Nazareth is to be found, it may very well come not from some obscure text or ancient scroll buried in the Judean desert. Perhaps it will be as the scholar and humanitarian Albert Schweitzer wrote early in the 20th century, after he concluded his own search of the evidence and found the historical Jesus as elusive and mysterious as ever. "He comes to us as One unknown, without a name," Schweitzer concluded, "as of old, by the lakeside, He came to those men who knew Him not. He speaks to us the same word: 'Follow thou me!' and sets us to the tasks which He has to fulfill for our time." ●

By Jeffery L. Sheler

THE FIRST CHRISTMAS

New evidence helps experts separate fact from folklore

Behold, I bring you good tidings of great joy, which shall be to all people. For unto you is born this day in the city of David a Saviour, which is Christ the Lord.

—The Gospel according to Luke

o Christians through the ages, the Christmas story proclaims the advent of a Savior, the imponderable miracle of God's invasion of human history through a stable in Bethlehem 2,000 years ago. Yet as familiar and enchanting as it is, the Christmas story—like much of the Bible itself—has come under intense scrutiny in recent years. While recent archaeological discoveries and ancient nonbiblical writings have shed some new light on the historical context of the events, the New Testament remains virtually the only source of details concerning the birth of Jesus of Nazareth. Even there, birth accounts appear in only two of the four Gospels—Matthew's, believed written about A.D. 90, and Luke's, written a few years before. The Gospels of Mark and John begin with the baptism of an adult Jesus.

Many scholars conclude that the Nativity stories were not part of the earliest Christian traditions. While the Resurrection of Jesus was celebrated from the very start, observance of the Nativity did not gain a wide following until the fifth century A.D. The first Christian preaching, as recorded in the Book of Acts and in the epistles of Paul, also focused on the Resurrection as evidence that Jesus was the Christ, but made no mention of a miraculous birth accompanied by the acclaim of angels and visiting Magi. Had New Testament writers "seen anything worthy of note in the events connected with Jesus's conception and birth, it seems they would have made thousands of references to it," according to the late Rolland Wolfe, who for many years taught biblical literature at Tufts University.

Where, then, did the stories come from? Most scholars agree that they took shape as a result of the growing curiosity of Christians who, believing Jesus to be both human and divine, sought to understand how and when he came to be. While the texts do not spell out their sources, some scholars have suggested that Luke's version is based on Mary's recollections, while Joseph is the source of Matthew's narrative. The writer of Luke explains in his opening lines that he "investigated everything carefully" in order to write "the exact truth" about events he had not personally witnessed. Many scholars find no reason to doubt that Luke may have spoken to Mary or at least obtained her story from others.

Some experts, however, argue that sharp disagreements on some details make it unlikely that family members could have been the source of the infancy material. Matthew, for example, has Joseph and Mary taking the newborn baby to Egypt to avoid a plot on his life. Luke has them staying in Bethlehem and Jerusalem for at least a month and then going home to Nazareth. Some scholars seek to harmonize such differences by explaining that the writers selected different anecdotes in order to address different questions. Others see the discrepancies as more problematic. "The two narratives are not only different," wrote the late New Testament scholar Raymond E. Brown, "they are contrary to each other in a number of details." Brown, in his widely cited book, *The Birth of the Messiah*, concluded it is "unlikely that either account is completely historical."

Few scholars are terribly concerned by the discrepancies. Most agree that writing an objective history was not at all what the Gospel writers had in mind. "The main question for the people at the time was 'What does this birth mean for our faith?'" says Brennan Hill, professor emeritus of theology at Xavier University in Cincinnati. The Nativity story, adds Donald Hagner, a New Testament scholar with the Fuller Theological Seminary in Pasadena, Calif., "was not told for the sake of facts alone, but in order to illustrate a deeper meaning—the theological significance of Jesus as the fulfillment of Old Testament prophecy." On that score, wrote Brown, whatever doubts may be cast on the Nativity accounts as history, as theological truth they remain intact.

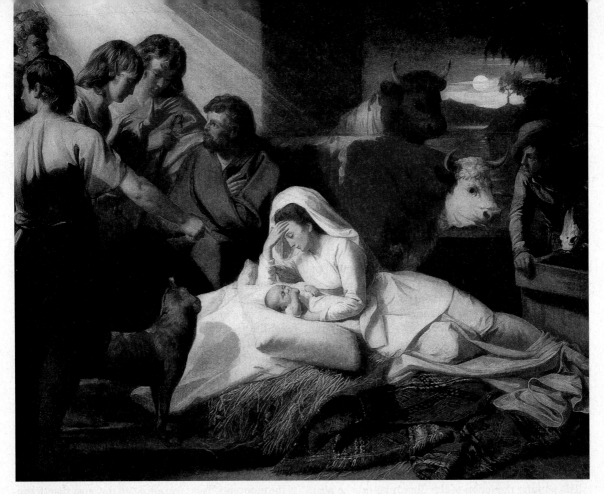

THE NATIVITY BY JOHN SINGLETON COPLEY / RESTORED TRADITIONS

THE BIRTH

And Joseph also went up from Galilee ... unto the city of David, which is called Bethlehem ... to be taxed with Mary his espoused wife.... And so it was, that, while they were there ... she brought forth her firstborn son, and wrapped him in swaddling clothes, and laid him in a manger.

—The Gospel according to Luke

Though differing in other details, Matthew and Luke agree Jesus was born in Bethlehem.

hatever their differences on other details of the Nativity, the two Gospels agree that Jesus was born in Bethlehem near the end of the reign of Herod the Great, perhaps between 6 B.C. and 4 B.C., to a virgin named Mary whose husband, Joseph, was a descendant of King David's. All of this, according to the Gospel writers, was to fulfill Old Testament prophecies that "a virgin shall conceive and bear a son, and shall call his name Immanuel," and that out of Bethlehem "one will go forth ... to be ruler in Israel."

While the virginal conception of Jesus seems not to have been a part of the earliest Christian preaching and is mentioned only in Matthew's and Luke's Gospels, most scholars are convinced it has some basis in early Christian tradition. Yet whether it is strictly historical or merely a vehicle for theological teaching, it remains, as it has been for centuries, a subject of considerable dispute. In A.D. 178, the pagan writer Celsus wrote a fanciful parody of Matthew's Gospel, portraying Jesus as the illegitimate son of a Roman soldier. In a more modern attack on the doctrine, retired Episcopal Bishop John Spong, in his book *Born of a Woman*, describes the virginal conception as a myth and asserts that Jesus may have been born to a sexu-

ally violated girl. In the final analysis, says John P. Meier, a professor of New Testament at the University of Notre Dame, judging the historicity of the virgin birth must depend on "one's philosophical views about the miraculous and the weight one gives to later church teachings."

The setting of Jesus's birth in the Christmas story is nearly as important as its nature. The fact that, during his ministry, Jesus was known to have come from Nazareth rather than from Bethlehem "constituted a problem" for the writers of Matthew and Luke, says Hagner of Fuller Theological Seminary. Listeners familiar with Old Testament prophecies no doubt would have questioned how a native son of Nazareth could be the Messiah. That complication, says Hagner, may explain why both Matthew and Luke emphasize Bethlehem as Jesus's birthplace and why they tell intricate and seemingly differing stories to get him back to Nazareth.

In Luke's Gospel, Joseph and Mary go to Bethlehem from their home in Nazareth to be counted in a census "of all the inhabited earth" ordered by Caesar Augustus. The census, Luke says, "was the first taken while Quirinius was governor of Syria," and it required all to go to their native cities to be counted. Some scholars who see this part of the story more as myth than history ask why a very pregnant Mary would make such an arduous 80-to-90-mile trip when Joseph could easily have responded to the census by returning to his native city alone (as only men were counted).

But Paul Maier, professor of ancient history at Western Michigan University in Kalamazoo, in his book *In the*

Fullness of Time, suggests that Mary "had every reason to make the trip." She probably knew of the Old Testament prophecies that the Messiah was to be born in Bethlehem, says Maier, and no doubt was puzzled about why God had chosen a girl from Nazareth. The Roman emperor's census decree, says Maier, put "the last piece of the divine-human puzzle into place."

But many historians have found Luke's reference to an empire-wide census puzzling. Outside of the Bible, there is no historical record of a universal census ordered by Caesar Augustus, nor, as New Testament scholar Brown observed, of a "census requirement that people be registered in their ancestral cities." While records do exist of censuses ordered by Augustus in 28 B.C., 8 B.C., and A.D. 14, they all apparently involved only Roman citizens.

There also are records of many smaller censuses of non-Romans in the provinces, mainly for taxing purposes. Some scholars suggest it may have been one of those that Luke recalled. However, the only known census involving Quirinius as governor of Syria occurred in A.D. 6. That was nearly a decade after the death of Herod the Great, a key figure in Matthew's Nativity story. More important than the details, noted Brown, may be Luke's purpose in reporting the census as the reason for the trip: "To show that the Roman emperor, the mightiest figure in the world, is serving God's plan ... by providing the setting for the birth of the Savior."

The popular depiction of the Christmas creche also has been subjected to revisionism. In the traditional interpretation of Luke, Joseph and Mary arrive late in Bethlehem and, finding no room at the inn, spend the night in a stable or cave where the baby is born. But Kenneth E. Bailey, a New Testament scholar at the Tantur Ecumenical Institute in Jerusalem, describes that as a creative expansion of Luke's Gospel, which says simply that after Mary gave birth to Jesus she "laid him in a manger; because there was no room for them in the inn."

Bailey thinks Jesus was born not in a stable but on the ground floor of a typical two-level Bethlehem house, in a room where animals were led in at night. He argues that the Greek word for "inn" also can be translated "house" or "guest house." Mary and Joseph, says Bailey, probably were invited into the ground-floor room because the guest room was full. Instead of being rejected by a "mean old innkeeper" and sent to a "cold drafty stable," says Bailey, "Joseph finds shelter for his family in a simple peasant home."

Matthew's Gospel seems to give a much different picture of events surrounding the birth. There are no depictions of the Nativity scene itself, nor of Joseph and Mary traveling from Nazareth. In fact, there is no mention of their ever living there together before the birth of their son. The narrator simply states that "when Jesus was born in Bethlehem," Magi from the East came to visit. When they arrive, the Magi enter "into the house." While some scholars believe that Matthew simply chose to omit the details of Mary and Joseph's travels, others conclude from the Gospel that the couple lived in Bethlehem all along. For Matthew, the more fascinating

chapter of the Christmas story entails the holy family's move from Bethlehem to Nazareth following the birth. It is a dramatic story of a wicked king and a terrifying plot against Jesus's life that Luke does not tell.

THE VISITORS

There came wise men ... to Jerusalem, Saying, Where is he that is born King of the Jews? for we have seen his star in the east, and are come to worship him.

—The Gospel according to Matthew

he holy family did not celebrate the Nativity alone. In Luke's Gospel, an angel announces the royal birth to local shepherds, who find their way to the baby's side. In Matthew's account, Magi, or "wise men" in some translations, arrive bearing precious gifts to pay homage to the newborn king. But the Magi's courtesy call, as Matthew tells it, was just the beginning of a harrowing chapter in the Christmas story. When the Magi stopped in Jerusalem to ask directions, their inquiries about a newborn king immediately stirred up trouble. A jealous King Herod, hearing of the Magi's quest, secretly plotted to find and kill the child. The plot sent Joseph, Mary, and their newborn into Egypt as refugees and resulted in the slaughter of all of Bethlehem's male infants.

While these are easily the most dramatic of the Nativity episodes, Matthew's visit of the Magi and "slaughter of the innocents" have also attracted the most skepticism through the years. Many scholars have simply dismissed the stories as nonhistorical, citing a lack of corroboration from other sources either for the atrocity in Bethlehem or for an astral phenomenon over the Middle Eastern skies that might have been the Magi's guiding star. They view the tales as midrash, theological elaborations of other biblical motifs, or as allegories intended to evoke the story of Moses, who also escaped an infant slaughter and "came out of Egypt." Some see the Magi mainly as an allegorical symbol for gentiles of Matthew's time who responded as believers to the Christian message when many Jews did not.

A number of scholars, however, are now convinced that the stories have been dismissed too easily. They contend that there is reason to believe that the Magi, the star, and the atrocity at Bethlehem are rooted in history, although getting to those factual roots requires peeling away layers of embellishment from the intervening centuries. The Magi, for example, are often depicted today as "three kings from the Orient," even though Matthew does not describe them as royalty or say how many there were. Those traditions, New Testament scholar Brown noted, grew up in the church between the second and fifth centuries. The number three was probably affixed based on the three gifts of gold, frankincense, and myrrh that Matthew describes. By the sixth century, the tradition had been elaborated to the point of assigning the Magi names—Gaspar, Melchior, and Balthasar—as well as ages and skin color. Little weight is given to those traditions today.

What seems more likely to some biblical scholars is

that the Magi of Matthew were astrologers from Persia or Mesopotamia who were drawn to Bethlehem by a significant alignment of stars and planets indicating to them that a ruler had been born. According to Maier of Western Michigan University, just such a configuration occurred in 6 B.C., when Jupiter, Saturn, and Mars drew close in the constellation of Pisces, an event that occurs every 805 years. In ancient astrology, says Maier, Jupiter was considered the "king's planet" and Saturn the shield of Palestine, while Pisces represented epochal events. So to astrologers of the time, he says, the conjunction "would have meant that a cosmic ruler or king was to appear in Palestine at the culmination of history."

To many scholars, this is more plausible than the sudden appearance of a spectacular star in the night sky, as depicted by tradition. It also would explain why Herod and his court seemed unaware of the star and why no other historical sources mention it. But it does not explain what Matthew seems to describe as a star moving and standing over the house "where the young child was." While a few have suggested the Bethlehem star might have been a comet or a nova, those scenarios have drawn fewer supporters. Some biblical commentators argue simply that the Bethlehem star must be chalked up as a unique supernatural event that cannot be explained naturally.

Some speculate the Magi may have been astrologers from Persia or Mesopotamia.

Well-worn arguments against the historicity of the Bethlehem slaughter are also getting new scrutiny today. The presumption in most academic circles has long been that an atrocity of the magnitude that Matthew describes—the killing of all boys up to 2 years old in the town and vicinity—certainly would have been noted by the first-century historian Josephus, who documented the final years of Herod's reign. Some church estimates have set the death toll as high as 64,000. But some scholars now argue that the incident must have been much smaller in scope. Hagner of Fuller Theological Seminary estimates that the population of Bethlehem in those days was probably no more than 1,000, and that there could have been as few as 20 infants under 2. As despicable as it was, says Hagner, the massacre of 10 or 12 babies in a small town may well have escaped Josephus's attention, especially when compared with other grisly deeds of Herod's that the historian did record. Herod had a number of Torah scholars burned alive for removing Rome's golden eagle from the Temple gate, for example. He also had his wife and some of his sons murdered because he considered them a threat to his throne. To assure there would be universal mourning associated with his death, he ordered thousands of men locked inside the hippodrome in Jericho to be massacred when he died—an order never carried out.

Provided Josephus had even heard of the Bethlehem murders, Maier asks: Which events would he have been likely to include in his history as he was "trying to wind up Herod's rotting life?" While scholars who make such arguments concede there is no direct evidence corroborating Matthew's account of the Bethlehem slaughter, they say the story is far from implausible. The manic Herod who appears in the Gospel, says Hagner, is "entirely consistent" with Josephus's portrait and "reflects the way Herod would have responded to the Magi." Even the Roman Caesar Augustus is quoted as saying of his Judean pawn: "I'd rather be Herod's pig than his son."

Ultimately more important in Matthew's story is that Joseph, alerted to the peril by an angel, escaped with his wife and child to Egypt unharmed. Exactly where they lived and how long they stayed in Egypt, Matthew does not say, although a number of legends have survived. In Old Cairo's Coptic quarter, a crypt under the church of St. Sergius is venerated as the place where the holy family stayed for three months. At another site outside Cairo, near the Heliopolis, Christians since the fifth century have honored the "Tree of Mary," a sycamore under which Mary is said to have sought shade.

Apocryphal writings from the second century purport to provide some additional details about the family's life in exile. The Arabic Gospel of the Infancy, for example, describes the holy family's being waylaid by robbers on a road in Sinai. When the highwaymen found nothing worth stealing, they took pity on the family and sent them on their way with fresh provisions. According to the tale, one of the robbers turned up 30 years later as one of the two thieves crucified with Jesus—the repentant one to whom Jesus said, "This day you'll be with me in paradise."

The sojourn in Egypt ended, according to Matthew's Gospel, when Herod died and an angel gave Joseph the all-clear to return with his family to Israel. But when Joseph and Mary learned that the new ruler, Herod's son Archelaus, had begun his reign by slaughtering 3,000 Jews in Jerusalem, they decided to look north toward the more pastoral region of Galilee. They settled in the dusty little town of Nazareth. ●

By Jeffery L. Sheler

WHY JESUS HAD TO DIE

His acts of defiance would launch a major religion

nd there was one named Barabbas, which lay bound with them that had made insurrection with him, who had committed murder in the insurrection. And the multitude crying aloud began to desire him to do as he had ever done to them. But Pilate answered them, saying, Will you that I release to you the King of the Jews? For he knew that the chief priests had delivered him for envy. But the chief priests moved the people, that he should rather release Barabbas to them. And Pilate answered and said again to them, What will you then that I shall do to him whom you call the King of the Jews? And they cried out again, Crucify him. Then Pilate said to them, Why, what evil has he done? And they cried out the more exceedingly, Crucify him. And so Pilate, willing to content the people, released Barabbas to them, and delivered Jesus, when he had scourged him, to be crucified.

It is called the Passion—the dramatic Gospel accounts of the suffering and death of Jesus Christ in Jerusalem nearly 2,000 years ago. To the apostle Paul, the Crucifixion of Jesus was the very heart of the Gospel, "the power of God unto salvation." Early church martyrs faced persecution and death emboldened by the familiar stories of Jesus's suffering at the hands of his enemies. And in every generation since, Christians have found spiritual sustenance in the story of Christ's sacrificial death recounted in the celebration of the Eucharist and in annual observances of Holy Week. When Christians around the world celebrate the liturgy and pageantry of Easter, they retrace once again the familiar Bible narrative, grieving the betrayal of an innocent Savior, mourning his lonely death on a common cross, and rejoicing in his

"CRUCIFIXION WAS A ROMAN FORM OF PUBLIC-SERVICE ANNOUNCEMENT."

vindication in the miracle of the Resurrection.

But while the Gospel story has inspired piety and devotion through the centuries, it also has spawned darker emotions: From the rise of the Holy Roman Empire to the fall of the Third Reich and even today, purveyors of anti-Semitism have sought to justify their prejudices by appealing to the Gospels' depiction of Jews as jealous villains who plotted against Christianity's founder. Such hatefulness permeates Western culture. For centuries, even the Good Friday liturgy of the Roman Catholic Church included prayers "for the perfidious Jews." Only at the Second Vatican Council in the mid-1960s did the church officially renounce the concept of "deicide"—a term historically associated with Jews as "Christ killers." And in 2000, Pope John Paul II apologized for Christianity's sins against Jews. Pope Benedict XVI's analysis of the trial of Jesus has been widely praised by Jewish leaders for its repudiation of collective guilt. (Page 26).

Some doubt whether, despite the sincerest remorse, Christianity can ever fully repent its anti-Semitic excesses, since the New Testament is permeated with passages that seem to cast "the Jews" as enemies of Jesus and of the church. But biblical scholars contend that such passages contain more polemics than real history, reflecting conflicts that arose between Christians and Jews late in the first century A.D.—when the Gospels were being written and Christianity was evolving from a messianic Jewish sect into a predominantly gentile religion. "As long as Christians were the marginalized and disenfranchised ones," wrote New Testament scholar John Dominic Crossan in his 1995 book *Who Killed Jesus?*, "such Passion fiction about Jewish responsibility and Roman innocence did nobody much harm. But, once the Roman

WEEPING OF CHRIST FOR THE FAMILY OF HOLZSCHUHER BY ALBRECHT DÜRER / RESTORED TRADITIONS

A tableau of mourning the fallen Jesus.

Empire became Christian, that fiction turned lethal."

Still, other scholars maintain that while later Jewish-Christian conflicts may have colored some of the rhetoric, the New Testament stories preserve the "historical core" of the events surrounding the Passion. The Gospel writers, says Scot McKnight, a professor in religious studies at North Park University in Chicago, "were not attempting to give a careful piece of history as to why Jesus died." They were telling "the story of Jesus—a story that has within it conflicts with Jewish leaders and with Roman leaders." While the precise nature of those antagonisms may not be fully explained, he says, "the Gospel writers give us enough evidence to see that a complex set of factors" led to Jesus's death.

Indeed, from a historian's point of view, the events preceding the Crucifixion present a tantalizing puzzle. First of all, Jesus's arrest and execution came during a week that began with public adulation as he entered Jerusalem to shouts of "Hosanna!" and ended with angry crowds shouting, "Crucify him!" According to the Gospels, Jesus was arrested by order of the Jerusalem high priest, Caiaphas, who accused him of blasphemy; he was tried before the Sanhedrin, a council of Jewish officials;

OPPOSITION TO JESUS AMONG JEWISH LEADERS WAS BY NO MEANS UNANIMOUS.

was delivered to Pontius Pilate, the Roman governor and chief judicial officer of Judea; and was condemned to crucifixion for claiming to be king of the Jews, an act of sedition in the view of Roman officials. But the seeming simplicity of the story line belies some bewildering complexities involving the charges and evidence against Jesus, the motives of his accusers, and the swiftness and ruthlessness of his execution.

Scholars begin their search for answers with a historical reconstruction of Jesus himself. Who was he and what might he have said and done during his brief ministry to inspire the authorities to turn so viciously against him? A broad scholarly consensus today affirms first the indisputable Jewishness of Jesus and of the early Christian movement. The Judaism of Jesus's day, most scholars now agree, was not incidental or peripheral to his life and ministry. Raised a Jew in Galilee, he read and revered the Torah, was an ardent defender of Jewish law, and carefully observed the Jewish festivals at the Temple.

To attempt to detach Jesus from that religious and cultural context is to obscure a proper understanding of the man and his message. Jesus was "fundamentally a Jew-

ish prophet," observes Darrell Bock, research professor of New Testament studies at Dallas Theological Seminary. "He went to the Jewish people, calling for renewal of the Jewish religion." The Jewish leaders, he says, naturally would have been "concerned by his calls for reform, which threatened the status quo and their own positions."

Yet this portrait of Jesus as a Jewish reformer does little to explain why he was put to death in the manner that he was. "The single most solid fact [known] about Jesus's life is his death," wrote Boston University scholar Paula Fredriksen in her book, *Jesus of Nazareth, King of the Jews*. "He was executed by the Roman prefect Pilate, on or around Passover, in the manner Rome reserved particularly for political insurrectionists, namely, crucifixion."

Spokesman for God. And what might Jesus have done to make the authorities perceive him as a threat? While it may be customary in Christian tradition to think of Jesus as meek and mild, the Gospels sometimes depict him in a different light. In his 1994 standard work, *The Death of the Messiah*, the late biblical scholar Raymond E. Brown noted that a careful reading of the Gospels reveals "a Jesus capable of generating intense dislike." He easily could have offended religious leaders, wrote Brown, "if he told people that God wants something different from what they know and have long striven to do, and if he challenged established sacred teaching on his own authority as self-designated spokesman for God."

Yet the extent to which Jewish authorities contributed to the death of Jesus is a complicated issue. The Gospels suggest that opposition to Jesus among Jewish leaders was by no means unanimous. Indeed, at least two members of the Jewish high council—Joseph of Arimathea and Nicodemus—are portrayed as sympathizers. But he certainly had plenty of enemies among Jewish leaders in Jerusalem. According to the Gospels, he had accused the Pharisees of hypocrisy, challenged the Sadducees' theology, and espoused unconventional interpretations of the Torah. But perhaps most important, what had been perceived by some as his threat to "destroy the Temple" was an affront that neither the priests nor the Romans could tolerate.

But what had Jesus said to provoke this accusation? The Gospel authors merely attribute to him a prediction that the Temple would be destroyed—"Do you see these great buildings? Not one stone will be left here upon another; all will be thrown down"—and claim that his enemies falsely accused him of threatening the Temple. And, in fact, some scholars argue that Jesus probably never said anything like the words ascribed to him in Mark. His prediction so closely presages what the Romans actually did in A.D. 70, they argue, that it almost certainly reflects an attempt by the authors, writing after the destruction of Jerusalem, to enhance Jesus's reputation as a prophet. (Others disagree. As New Testament scholar E.P. Sanders argued in *The Historical Figure of Jesus*, the prediction was not precisely fulfilled. When the Romans destroyed the city some 40 years later, they

had hailed Jesus as "the son of David," a messianic title, are the real audience whom Pilate addresses by sending Jesus to the cross.

It was the crowds assembled for Passover in Jerusalem, not Jesus's close associates, that first proclaimed him Messiah, Fredriksen wrote, "in all the excitement, panoply, and ritual re-enactment of the holiday that commemorated the liberation and redemption of their people." Their enthusiasm for Jesus and his message, she contended, led directly to his death.

Squelching an uprising. Whether Pilate thought Jesus was the Messiah, or even if Jesus thought of himself in that way, was not important, noted Fredriksen. But the fact that only Jesus was killed, and none of his disciples were, suggests that Pilate did not consider Jesus a real threat. What Pilate did find threatening was a city crowded with messianic pilgrims who believed God was about to intervene on behalf of his people, defeat the Roman occupation, and restore the throne of David in Jerusalem. When the crowds began hailing Jesus as a messiah, Pilate moved swiftly and ruthlessly to squelch a potential uprising.

The disciples who had accompanied Jesus to Jerusalem at Passover, Fredriksen observed, were expecting an astounding spiritual event, the arrival of God's kingdom. "What they got instead," she wrote, "was the Crucifixion." But then the truly unexpected happened: "God, they became convinced, had raised Jesus from the dead." Energized by that belief, they began preaching the arrival of God's kingdom, which they now believed would be fully inaugurated with the Second Coming of the resurrected Christ.

Four years after that fateful Passover in Jerusalem, both Pilate and Caiaphas—the two men at least officially responsible for Jesus's death—were deposed by the Roman legate in Syria for failing to keep order within Jerusalem. The unpopular "reforms" that Caiaphas had imposed on the Temple, and which apparently had prompted Jesus's violent protest, were reversed. And the small core of Jesus's followers, who had scattered frightened and confused at his Crucifixion, were by then a rapidly growing sect whose astounding message of a risen Messiah was spreading through the synagogues of the region.

The Roman destruction of Jerusalem in A.D. 70 would deprive Christianity of its Judaic "mother church" and hasten its transmutation from a Jewish sect to a distinctly gentile religion. Yet after 2,000 years, buffeted by the sometimes brutal tides of history, it remains as it was in the beginning—a faith rooted in the life and teachings of an enigmatic Jewish rabbi whose vision of God's kingdom and whose death on a Roman cross would change the world. ●

By Jeffery L. Sheler

left much of the Temple's retaining wall intact. Bogus prophecies created after the fact are almost always exact, he pointed out.)

Still, not only Jesus's words, but also his actions drew attention. There was his violent demonstration on the Temple Mount, an incident described in all four Gospels as his "cleansing of the Temple." Most scholars today see the incident as the key event that led to his arrest. As the Gospels describe it, shortly after arriving in Jerusalem for the Passover feast, Jesus and his disciples stormed into the Temple, and he began overturning the tables of money-changers and chasing animal vendors out of the court. The high priest had moved the animal stalls to the Temple from a nearby hill, making it easier for pilgrims to buy beasts for sacrifice and for the authorities to profit from those sales. Jesus, says Bruce Chilton, a professor of religion at Bard College, would have objected to such crass commercialism being attached to the sacred offerings. The Temple takeover, as Chilton describes it, may have involved as many as 200 zealous followers, and it may have succeeded at least temporarily in disrupting commerce. That, he says, would have provided ample motivation for both religious and civil authorities to move against Jesus.

Yet if the Jewish authorities had wanted him out of the way, and Pilate consented to do the job, asked Fredriksen, "why not a simple, private murder?" The answer, she wrote, is that "crucifixion was a Roman form of public-service announcement" intended to get the attention of those watching. The crowds in Jerusalem who earlier

The astounding message of a risen Messiah would quickly spread beyond Jerusalem.

THE TRIAL OF THE MESSIAH

The pope looks at the forces behind a historic prosecution

fter three years of publicly proclaiming the advent of the Kingdom of God, Jesus of Nazareth's ministry reached its climactic moment around the spring of A.D. 30 as he rode into the Jewish capital of Jerusalem. Jubilant crowds of pilgrims greeted him with messianic fervor. Jesus, however, would turn the crowd's expectations upside down. For he cleansed the Temple not of the Romans, but rather of Israel itself, calling for the Temple to be a house of prayer for all nations and claiming that it had been turned into a den of thieves.

In Jesus's day, the Jewish religious leadership had great influence over political affairs and was marked by two vital groups: the Pharisees, whose name in Aramaic means "separated ones," and who pushed for Jewish purity and religious zeal; and the Sadducees, who consisted of the ruling priestly families and were led at this time by the high priest Caiaphas. The Pharisees refused to share Jesus's inclusive view of the Temple as a house for all nations, and the chief priests and Sadducees felt *themselves to be the target of Jesus's condemnation for turning the Temple into a den of thieves. Both groups also felt threatened by Jesus's claim that the religious and political spheres should be separated from each other.*

By depicting Jesus as a political threat to Rome, these two groups could reap the benefit of ridding themselves of him without having to take responsibility for his death. Thus, they were more than willing to conspire to turn him over to Pontius Pilate, the Roman procurator, or governor, of Judea. In this excerpt from his book, Jesus of Nazareth: Holy Week: From the Entrance into Jerusalem to the Resurrection, *Pope Benedict XVI draws on the Gospels and the work of leading historians to probe the historical forces behind the events of Jesus's last week and the trial of one of history's most compelling figures. His analysis has been widely praised by religious leaders for repudiating the idea that the Jewish people as a whole bore collective guilt for the death of Jesus.*

Introduction by Tim Gray,
professor of Scripture at the Augustine Institute in Denver

---

n the early stages of Jesus's ministry, the Temple authorities had evidently shown little interest in the figure of Jesus or in the movement that formed around him; it all seemed a rather provincial affair—one of those movements that arose in Galilee from time to time and did not warrant much attention. The situation changed on "Palm Sunday." The Messianic homage paid to Jesus on his entrance into Jerusalem; the cleansing of the Temple with the interpretation he gave to it, which seemed to indicate the end of the Temple altogether and a radical change in the cult, contrary to the ordinances established by Moses; Jesus's teaching in the Temple, from which there emerged a claim to authority that seemed to channel Messianic hopes in a new di-

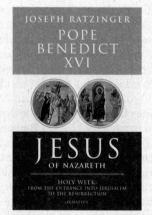

rection, threatening Israel's monotheism; the miracles that Jesus worked publicly; and the growing multitude that gathered around him—all this added up to a situation that could no longer be ignored.

In the days surrounding the Passover feast, when the city was overflowing with pilgrims and Messianic hopes could easily turn into political dynamite, the Temple authorities had to respond. John tells us that the chief priests and the Pharisees were gathered together. These were the two leading groups within Judaism at the time of Jesus, and on many points they were opposed to one another. But their common fear was this: "The Romans will come and destroy both our holy place [that is, the Temple, the holy place for divine worship] and our nation." One is tempted

to say that the motive for acting against Jesus was a political concern shared by the priestly aristocracy and the Pharisees. Yet through the message that he proclaimed, Jesus had actually achieved a separation of the religious from the political, thereby changing the world.

Jesus fights, on the one hand, against self-serving abuse of the sacred space, but his prophetic gesture and the interpretation he gave to it go much deeper: The old cult of the stone Temple has come to an end. The Temple of stone must be destroyed, so that the new one, the New Covenant with its new style of worship, can come. Yet this means that Jesus himself must endure crucifixion, so that, after his Resurrection, he may become the new Temple. This means, though, that the Cross corresponded to a divine "necessity" and that the high priest Caiaphas, in making the decision he did, was ultimately carrying out God's will, even if his motivation was impure and reflected, not God's will, but blind self-seeking. John expressed this striking combination with great clarity. While the Council members were perplexed as to what should be done in view of the danger posed by the movement surrounding Jesus, Caiaphas made the decisive intervention: "You do not understand that it is expedient for you that one man should die for the people,

Pope Benedict XVI drew on decades of research to produce his bestselling work on Jesus.

and that the whole nation should not perish."

The immediate consequence of Caiaphas's statement was this: Until that moment, the assembled Council had held back in fear from a death sentence, looking for other ways out of the crisis, admittedly without finding a solution. Only a theologically motivated declaration from the high priest, spoken with the authority of his office, could dispel their doubts and prepare them in principle for such a momentous decision. This fundamental decision to take action against Jesus, reached during that meeting of the Sanhedrin, was put into effect on the night leading from Thursday to Friday with his arrest on the Mount of Olives. Jesus was led, still by night, to the high priest's palace, where the Sanhedrin with its three constituent groups—chief priests, elders, scribes—was evidently already assembled. It now seems reasonable to assume that what then took place was not a proper trial, but more of a cross-examination that led to the decision to hand him over to the Roman governor for sentencing.

Two charges. After the cleansing of the Temple, two charges against Jesus were in circulation. The first had to do with his interpretation of the prophetic gesture of driving cattle and traders out of the Temple, which seemed like an attack on the Holy Place itself and, hence,

The prisoner was
brought before
Pontius Pilate.

on the Torah, on which Israel's life was built. I consider it important that it was not the cleansing of the Temple as such for which Jesus was called to account, but only the interpretation he gave to his action. We may conclude that the symbolic gesture itself remained within acceptable limits and did not give rise to public unrest. The danger lay in the interpretation, in the seeming attack on the Temple, and in the authority that Jesus was claiming to possess.

In Jesus's trial, witnesses came forward who wanted to report what Jesus had said. But there was no consistent version: His actual words could not be unequivocally established. The fact that this particular charge was then dropped reveals a concern to observe juridically correct procedure.

On the basis of Jesus's teaching in the Temple, a second charge was in circulation: that Jesus had made a Messianic claim, through which he somehow put himself on a par with God and thus seemed to contradict the very basis of Israel's faith—the firm belief that there is only one God. We should note that both charges are of a purely theological nature. Yet the charges do also have a political dimension. As the place of Israel's sacrifices, to which the whole people comes on pilgrimage for great feasts, the Temple is the basis of Israel's inner unity. The Messianic claim is a claim to kingship over Israel. Hence the placing of the charge "King of the Jews" above the Cross, to indicate the reason for Jesus's execution.

There were certain circles within the Sanhedrin that would have favored the liberation of Israel through political and military means. But the way in which Jesus presented his claim seemed to them clearly unsuited to the effective advancement of their cause. So the status quo was preferable, since Rome at least respected the religious foundations of Israel, with the result that the survival of Temple and nation could be considered more or less secure. After the vain attempt to establish a clear and well-founded charge against Jesus on the basis of his statement about the destruction and renewal of the Temple, we come to the dramatic encounter between the serving high priest of Israel, Caiaphas, the highest authority of the chosen people, and Jesus himself, in whom Christians recognize the "high priest of the good things to come" (Hebrews, 9:11).

According to Mark, the high priest's question is: "Are you the Christ, the Son of the Blessed?" And Jesus answers: "I am; and you will see the Son of Man sitting at the right hand of Power, and coming with the clouds of heaven." From all this we may conclude that Jesus accepted the title Messiah, with all the meanings accruing to it from the tradition, but at the same time he qualified it in a way that could only lead to a guilty verdict, which he could have avoided either by rejecting it or by proposing a milder form of Messianism. In any

event, as far as the high priest and the members of the assembly were concerned, the evidence for blasphemy was supplied by Jesus's answer, at which Caiaphas "tore his robes, and said: 'He has uttered blasphemy.'" There now erupts over Jesus, who had prophesied his coming in glory, the brutal mockery of those who know they are in a position of strength: They make him feel their power, their utter contempt. Jesus was found guilty of blasphemy, for which the penalty was death.

Jesus before Pilate. Since only the Romans could carry out the death sentence, the case now had to be brought before the Roman Governor Pontius Pilate and the political dimension of the guilty verdict had to be emphasized. With cockcrow, daybreak had arrived. Jesus is now led by his accusers to the praetorium and is presented to Pilate as a criminal who deserves to die.

In all essentials, the four Gospels harmonize with one another in their accounts of the progress of the trial. Only John reports the conversation between Jesus and Pilate. Charles K. Barrett in *The Gospel According to St. John* wrote: "John's additions and alterations do not inspire confidence in his historical reliability." Yet Barrett also noted "that John has with keen insight picked out the key of the Passion narrative in the kingship of Jesus, and has made its meaning clearer, perhaps, than any other New Testament writer." We may assume that John was able to explain with great precision the core question at issue and that he presents us with a true account of the trial.

Now we must ask: Who exactly were Jesus's accusers? According to John it was simply "the Jews." But John's use of this expression does not in any way indicate—as the modern reader might suppose—the people of Israel in general, even less is it "racist" in character. After all, John himself was ethnically a Jew, as were Jesus and all his followers. In John's Gospel this word has a precise and clearly defined meaning: He is referring to the Temple aristocracy. In Mark's Gospel, the circle of accusers is broadened in the context of the Passover amnesty: The "ochlos" enters the scene and opts for the release of Barabbas, another condemned man, over Jesus. "Ochlos" in the first instance simply means a crowd of people, the "masses." The people, as so often with such amnesties, have a right to put forward a proposal, expressed by way of "acclamation." Effectively this "crowd" is made up of the followers of Barabbas who have been mobilized to secure the amnesty for him. As a rebel against Roman power he could naturally count on a good number of supporters. So the Barabbas party, the "crowd," was conspicuous, while the followers of Jesus remained hidden out of fear.

Let us move now to the judge: the Roman Governor Pontius Pilate. While Flavius Josephus and especially

SOME SOURCES PORTRAY PILATE AS DECISIVE, PRAGMATIC, AND REALISTIC.

Philo of Alexandria paint a rather negative picture of Pilate, other sources portray him as decisive, pragmatic, and realistic. The image of Pilate in the Gospels presents the Roman prefect as a man who could be brutal when he judged this to be in the interests of public order. Yet he also knew that Rome owed its world dominance not least to its tolerance of foreign divinities and to the capacity of Roman law to build peace. This is how he comes across to us during Jesus's trial.

You are a king? The charge that Jesus claimed to be king of the Jews was a serious one. Rome had no difficulty in recognizing regional kings like Herod, but they had to be legitimated by Rome, and they had to receive from Rome the definition and limitation of their sovereignty. A king without such legitimization was a rebel who threatened the Pax Romana and therefore had to be put to death. Pilate knew, however, that no rebel uprising had been instigated by Jesus. Everything he had heard must have made Jesus seem to him like a religious fanatic, who may have offended against some Jewish legal and religious rulings, but that was of no concern to him. Yet during the interrogation we suddenly arrive at a dramatic moment. To Pilate's question: "So you are a king?" he answers: "You say that I am a king. For this I was born, and for this I have come into the world, to bear witness to the truth. Everyone who is of the truth hears my voice."

This "confession" of Jesus places Pilate in an extraordinary situation: The accused claims kingship and a kingdom. Yet he underlines the complete otherness of his kingship. If power, indeed military power, is characteristic of kingship and kingdoms, there is no sign of it in Jesus's case. And neither is there any threat to Roman order. This kingdom is powerless. It has "no legions." After the interrogation, Pilate knew for certain what in principle he had already known beforehand: This Jesus was no political rebel; his message and his activity posed no threat for the Roman rulers. Whether Jesus had offended against the Torah was of no concern to him as a Roman. Yet Pilate seems also to have experienced a certain superstitious wariness concerning this remarkable figure. John tells us that "the Jews" accused Jesus of making himself the Son of God, and then he adds: "When Pilate heard these words, he was even more afraid."

Jesus's accusers obviously realize this, and so they now play off one fear against another. Against the superstitious fear of a possible divine presence, they appeal to the entirely practical fear of forfeiting the emperor's favor, being removed from office, and thus plunging into a downward spiral. The declaration: "If you release this man, you are not Caesar's friend" is a threat.

In the end, concern for career proves stronger than fear

THE SOLDIERS ARE PLAYING CRUEL GAMES WITH JESUS; NOW IT PLEASES THEM TO HUMILIATE HIM.

of divine powers. Before the final verdict, though, there is a further dramatic and painful interlude in three acts. The first act sees Pilate presenting Jesus as a candidate for the Passover amnesty and seeking in this way to release him. In doing so, he puts himself in a fatal situation. If the crowd has the right of acclamation, then according to their response, the one they do not choose is to be regarded as condemned. In this sense, the proposed release on the basis of the amnesty already tacitly implies condemnation. According to our translations, John refers to Barabbas simply as a robber. In the political context of the time, though, the Greek word that John uses had also acquired the meaning of terrorist or freedom fighter. It is clear from Mark's account that this is the intended meaning: "And among the rebels in prison, who had committed murder in the insurrection, there was a man called Barabbas."

Jesus's followers are absent from the place of judgment, absent through fear. But they are also absent in the sense that they fail to step forward en masse. The second act is succinctly summarized by John as follows: "Then Pilate took Jesus and scourged him." In Roman criminal law, scourging was the punishment that accompanied the death sentence. In John's Gospel, however, it is presented as an act during the interrogation, a measure that the prefect was empowered to take on the basis of his responsibility for law enforcement. It was an extremely barbaric punishment, noted Josef Blinzler in *Der Prozess Jesu*, his classic study of the trial of Jesus. The victim was "struck by several torturers for as long as it took for them to grow tired, and for the flesh of the criminal to hang down in bleeding shreds."

The third act is the crowning with thorns. The soldiers are playing cruel games with Jesus. Now he is in their hands; now it pleases them to humiliate him. They pay homage to him: "Hail, King of the Jews"; their homage consists of blows to his head, through which they once more express their utter contempt for him. Thus caricatured, Jesus is led to Pilate, who takes his place on the judgment seat. Once again he says: "Here is your King!" Then he pronounces the death sentence. In this case peace counted for more than justice in Pilate's eyes. Perhaps this was how he eased his conscience. For the time being, Jerusalem remained calm. Later, though, it would become clear that peace, in the final analysis, cannot be established at the expense of truth. ●

From *Jesus of Nazareth: Holy Week: From the Entrance into Jerusalem to the Resurrection* by Joseph Ratzinger, Pope Benedict XVI, Ignatius Press, San Francisco. Copyright©2011 by Libreria Editrice Vaticana by arrangement with Ignatius.

THE WORLD

CHAPTER 2

Some 3,000 years after
King David's day, believers
of three great faiths call
God's City home
34

A modern photographic
tour of the path Jesus is
thought to have traveled,
from the site of his birth to
that of the Holy Sepulchre
40

A WINDOW IN THE DAHLGREN CHAPEL OF
THE SACRED HEART / GEORGETOWN UNIVERSITY

PHOTOGRAPH BY BRETT ZIEGLER FOR *USN&WR*

HE LIVED IN

GOD'S OWN CITY

A guide to 3,000 years of Jerusalem history

*"Of the 10 measures of beauty that came down
to the world, Jerusalem took nine."* —The Talmud

"No people blessed so as thine, no city like Jerusalem."
—Christian hymn

"One prayer in Jerusalem is worth 40,000 elsewhere."
—Islamic saying

t was a procession of joy, a pageant of history and faith gladful enough to have pleased the Shepherd King himself. In 1995, marching through the hills of Judea almost to within the shadow of the hand-carved stone walls of the ancient Holy City, 80,000 dancers, musicians, and performers from Israel and around the world celebrated the 3,000th anniversary of King David's establishment of Jerusalem.

Though central to the Jewish soul as Israel's "eternal capital," Jerusalem is vitally holy to all three of the world's great monotheistic faiths: Judaism, Christianity, and Islam. And it is all the more celebrated during the Hanukkah and Christmas seasons. The city is hailed as a gathering spot of civilizations, saints, and prophets and is seen as a sacred place for pilgrims and their prayers. To believers, it is God's own city, a place infused with signs and symbols of the holy. And that in no small measure explains why its history is one of nearly ceaseless strife. Each event that takes place, each piece of ground that is disturbed, each artifact that is dug up can stir ancient hopes and resentments. With Israelis and Palestinians still unable to reach a final peace, some critics deemed Israel's yearlong celebration of the trimillennium a provocation as much as a statement of history.

Still, it is through the Holy City that one "can learn almost everything even remotely connected to the ancient Near East," argues biblical archaeologist Hershel Shanks in his stunning book, *Jerusalem*. Across its hilltops have marched Canaanites, Israelites, Egyptians, Assyrians, Babylonians, Persians, Seleucids, Romans, Arabs, Seljuks, crusaders, Saracens, Mamelukes, Ottomans, Britons, Palestinians, Jordanians, and Israelis. In its history, blood-drenched stones and archaeological treasures are keys to understanding the essence of the human spirit.

THE CITY OF DAVID

*"David took the strong hold of Zion: the same is
the city of David."* —2 Samuel 5:7

Jerusalem's Chalcolithic roots predate David by almost 2,500 years. First mentioned in Egyptian hieroglyphics as the Canaanite *Urushamem* and *Urusalim*, the city was visited by Abraham, says Genesis. But it was David who established its historic and holy standing. The son of Jesse ruled Israelites from the southern city of Hebron when he first set his sights on the Jebusite fortress of Zion in about 1004 B.C. A political and military genius, the young king wanted a strategically located capital to unite fully the loosely linked tribes of Israel. And Jerusalem's citadel loomed over the Jordan Valley, standing about halfway between the northern and southern halves of the Holy Land.

Moving swiftly, recounts the second book of Samuel, David took Zion in a bloodless raid, renaming it *Ir David*, the City of David. A later account in 1 Chronicles implies that Joab, David's nephew and general, surprised the Jebusites by entering the town through a water shaft. One such shaft was discovered by Sir Charles Warren, a

Islam's Dome of
the Rock in the
Old City

British surveyor who explored Jerusalem in 1867, and it was cleared in 1979 with the help of South African mining engineers by archaeologist Yigal Shiloh. Though archaeologists now doubt that Warren's shaft was actually used as a passageway by Joab during the Israelite assault, the 40-foot-long tunnel connects underground to the gurgling Gihon Spring, for centuries Jerusalem's only steady source of water.

The triangular 12-acre city David built lay some 350 feet to the south of the walled Jerusalem of today, on and beyond the eastern ridge called the Ophel. Archaeologists, who have uncovered 21 strata there ranging from the fourth millennium B.C. to the 15th century, estimate that the Davidic city's population never exceeded 4,000—largely members of the court. Until fairly recently, the biblical references to David and the city's structures were not corroborated archaeologically. But in the early 1990s, a team digging in northern Israel uncovered a ninth-century B.C. stone tablet bearing a clear reference to the "House of David" and "King of Israel," says former Jerusalem District Archaeologist Dan Bahat, now a professor of biblical archaeology at the University of St. Michael's College in Toronto.

Archaeologists now believe that a 13th-century B.C. stepped stone tower first uncovered in the 1920s and later explored by Britain's Kathleen Kenyon may be part of the mysterious "Millo" around which the Bible says David built his city. Further evidence of the Davidic dynasty was found in 1986 by archaeologist Eilat Mazar. Digging on the southeast Ophel slope, she discovered an eighth-century B.C. gate that may well have led to the First Temple area. Beyond it: an area that appears to have been a royal administrative center.

Eventually David's kingdom stretched from Egypt to the Euphrates River. With great flourish, relates the Bible, the poet king had the Ark of the Covenant moved to Jerusalem. The city had become Israel's political, military, and religious center. It would fall to David's son and heir, Solomon, to build the Temple atop the windswept Moriah plateau that David purchased as a threshing field. And the Hebrew name became *Yerushalayim*, or City of Peace.

IN THE STEPS OF JESUS

*"And ye shall be witnesses unto me both in Jerusalem ...
and unto the uttermost part of the earth."*　　　—Acts 1:8

By the time Jesus first passed through the Golden Gate, Jerusalem had been the holy center of the Jews for more than 10 centuries. The Bible chronicles its glories and the steady beat of its conquest by outsiders: the destruction of Solomon's Temple by Nebuchadnezzar, the painful exile of the Jews to Babylonia. The Holy City then stretched well beyond David's hilltop fortress. Yet even by the standards of Roman times, the city was small, its population less than 80,000.

The Temple was still incomplete when Jesus came to pray and preach there. Before then, Herod the Great, eager to outdo the great Solomon, had begun to expand the modest Second Temple built after Jews re-

turned from Babylonia around 539 B.C. The surface of Mount Moriah was enlarged by Herod, who built vast platforms—remnants of which were uncovered during the second half of the 20th century. As many as 18,000 workers hauled material to the site: mammoth stone blocks for the walls, cedar limbs for the roof, and great columns of marble for structural support.

Beyond the teeming, rectangular Court of the Gentiles lay a series of 13 gates through which only Jews could pass on their way to the Temple proper. Each was deemed more beautiful than the last. The most famous, the bronze Nicanor Gate, was so heavy that it needed 20 men to open it, an event that signaled each new day. This area is also close to where Jesus is believed to have overturned the tables of the money-changers and today is part of the open court of Islam's Dome of the Rock.

In A.D. 70, about 40 years after the accepted date of the Crucifixion on Golgotha, Rome destroyed Jerusalem as punishment for a revolt by Jewish freedom fighters. Temple treasures were carted off, Jews enslaved and exiled, Jerusalem's land salted to keep it fallow. All that remained of the Temple compound were its four outer retaining walls. One of them—the Western Wall—would come to be known as the "Wailing Wall" and be sanctified by centuries of Jewish tears and prayers for the redemption of Zion and a return to Jerusalem. It remains an irony of history, notes Shanks, that "Judaism's holiest shrine was built, not by Solomon ... but [largely] by Herod, who was one of the most hated kings ever to rule the Jews." A descendant of converts, Herod observed Judaism's rituals in public but eschewed its morality in his rule. "I'd rather be Herod's pig than his son," Emperor Caesar Augustus reportedly quipped. The reason: Herod murdered three of his sons but refrained from eating pork.

Many of the holy places where Jesus is said to have walked are pinpointed more by tradition than by archaeology. Archaeologists now theorize that Gethsemane was not a garden but a nearby cave where olive oil was pressed—the meaning of *gat shemanim*. Archaeologists like Bahat are convinced that much more of the Jerusalem of Jesus's time lies buried around the Temple Mount. Digging a tunnel along the northern end of the Western Wall, Bahat has found a Herodian gate leading to the Temple area. To the south, in the site explored by Benjamin Mazar (Eilat's grandfather) in 1967, workers uncovered a set of massive steps and a stone with an inscription that mentions the *zakenim*—the elders. Wonders Bahat: "Are these the Temple steps where the New Testament says a 12-year-old Jesus stood when he taught the rabbis?"

THE MIDDLE AGES

*"Come forward to the defense of Christ.... Wrest
[Jerusalem] from the evil race, and keep it for yourself."*
　　　　　　　　　　　　　　　　　　—Pope Urban II, 1095

Roman Emperor Constantine's conversion to Christianity in the early fourth century ensured the future of the new church and gave it Jerusa-

lem. But some 300 years later, the followers of the powerful new faith of Prophet Muhammad seized the city, building great Islamic shrines and centers of study of their own.

For almost 400 years, church leaders seethed as Christianity's holiest sites remained "in the hands of heretics." Finally, in 1095, Pope Urban II called for the "deliverance" of Jerusalem through Holy Crusade. Tens of thousands of Europeans—soldiers, peasants, and mobs of the unemployed—marched and sailed to the Holy Land.

Their assault was the most fearsome Jerusalem had ever witnessed. And on July 15, 1099, after 41 days of deadly siege, the armies of the Holy Crusade raised the banner of Christ atop the Temple Mount. Two days later, when the crusader princes came to pray at the Church of the Holy Sepulchre, the traditional site of Christ's tomb, they marched through a deserted city. Jerusalem's Christians had fled before the battle. Its Muslims and Jews had all been sold as slaves or slaughtered by the rampaging victors. Mutilated corpses were piled knee high. Blood still literally ran in the streets, down to the Valley of Kidron. It was a sight, wrote the crusaders' historian William of Tyre, "that roused horror in all who looked upon [it]."

The crusaders' Jerusalem kingdom would last 87 years—transforming Jerusalem into a capital city for the first time since Jews ruled there. The knights wasted no time re-creating a European feudal society. Dividing Jerusalem's stone houses among themselves, they banned Jews, limited the number of Muslims, and imported Christian settlers from Syria and Jordan. With the enthusiastic blessing of Rome, they feverishly built new churches and monasteries. Some have survived, like the elegant Church of St. Anne, built over the possible site of the Virgin Mary's birth. The Byzantine Holy Sepulchre, consecrated anew, was greatly expanded and took the Romanesque crosslike shape it still bears. In the early 1990s, Bahat says, a renovation at the Old City police station revealed the foundations of the crusader royal palace.

The crusaders also took their turn reshaping the Temple Mount. Romans had replaced Herod's Temple with a pagan shrine. The Byzantine Christians destroyed that in 629, then heaped the mount with trash and dung to show disdain for Judaism. Arab conquerors cleansed the site in 638 and built two great shrines: the golden Dome of the Rock and the great Al-Aqsa Mosque. Now it was the crusaders' turn. They made Al-Aqsa headquarters for the Knights Templar and transformed the Dome, one of the world's most beautiful examples of Islamic art, into a church. The knights also erroneously dubbed an underground labyrinth of vaulted storage chambers "Solomon's Stables" and used it accordingly.

Such sacrilege by "infidels" stuck in the throats of Islamic believers. Though never mentioned by name in the Koran, Jerusalem was revered by Muslims as a city whose holiness was outshone only by Mecca and Medina. The Temple Mount, called *Haram esh-Sharif*—the Noble Sanctuary—was treasured as the place from which Muhammad made a mystic flight to heaven, and Muslims later came to revere it as the rock where Abraham was commanded to sacrifice his son Ishmael (Isaac to Christians and Jews).

In 1187, the Saracen warrior Saladin defeated the crusader forces near the Sea of Galilee and then marched south to wrest Jerusalem from the Christians. The crusaders surrendered without battle. Christian pilgrims could still visit Jerusalem's holy places, but only upon payment of tribute and with eyes blindfolded as they passed through Muslim areas. It was not until Britain took Jerusalem during World War I that the city of Jesus would truly see another Christian ruler.

GLORY AND DESOLATION

"We toiled up one more hill, and every pilgrim and every sinner swung his hat on high! Jerusalem! ... [Yet] Jerusalem is mournful and dreary and lifeless."
—*The Innocents Abroad*, Mark Twain, 1869

Between 1538 and 1541, slaves of Ottoman Sultan Suleiman the Magnificent built the graceful limestone walls that still surround the Holy City. Since retaking the city, Islam would rule supreme in Jerusalem for more than 700 years. But by the mid-19th century, American and European churches began staking out their own claims, opening missions to convert the Jews and building hostels for the thousands of pilgrims who made the arduous, dangerous sea and land trek to the site of Christ's Passion.

Devotion ran deep. When the 6-ton bell for a new czarist-built cathedral arrived at the port of Jaffa in 1885, a small army of Russian Orthodox pilgrims, mostly women, helped haul it up the mountains to Jerusalem's Mount of Olives.

The 19th century also saw Jerusalem's first archaeological explorers. Some were adventurers and not a few used science as a cover for military espionage. The best made major discoveries. France's Louis Felicien de Saulcy found great tombs just north of the Old City. In 1870, Britain's Charles Warren, who explored the city's water shaft, completed the first—and until now the last—scientific survey of the Temple Mount itself.

But under increasingly corrupt Ottoman rule, 19th-century Jerusalem itself was reduced to the status of what the Turks called a *sanjak*, a provincial backwater whose streets were filled with sewage and whose tight quarters bred disease. Its religious communities, said the late Israeli author and journalist Amos Elon, were "islands unto themselves." But they were not immune to communal warfare. Muslims pelted Christians with garbage during Easter. Both barred Jews from each other's shrines and took great pleasure in driving cattle through

the crowds swaying in prayer at the Western Wall. Nowhere was the religious battle fiercer than in the Holy Sepulchre, where monks from myriad Christian sects fought pitched battles over which order had the right to clean its sacrosanct floor.

For the Jews, Jerusalem was their capital of memory. Like Christian pilgrims, they were inexorably drawn by religious fervor. By 1870, Jerusalem's population had grown to 25,000 and Jews had become the majority. Most Old City Jews devoted their days to study, prayer, and rebuilding the spirit of the city stone by stone. Many lived off *chalukah*—charity collected in the ghettos of Eastern Europe and among the thriving Sephardic communities of the East.

Life for most within the walls was squalid. But with bandits holding sway over the hills, few ventured beyond the Old City gates after dark. All that changed after 1860 when Sir Moses Montefiore, the Jewish philanthropist and sheriff of London, built a row of workshops cum homes on a hill facing the western ramparts. Other Jews began to construct neighborhoods beyond the walls. Christians and Muslims moved to the north and south, and Jerusalem was soon surrounded by growing suburbs.

As the century turned, Jerusalem received a new influx of Jewish immigrants who called themselves "Lovers of Zion"—Zionists. They were determined not just to pray for salvation but to rebuild a desolate land.

1948: DIVIDED CITY

"It is our Holy City ... [but] we will strangle Jerusalem!"
—Abdul Khader Husseini, Palestinian commander

"Without Jerusalem, the land of Israel is as a body without a soul." —David Ben-Gurion, the first prime minister of Israel

Jerusalem thrived under the British Mandate of Palestine that began when Lord Allenby captured the Holy City from the Turks during World War I. Building boomed. The Hebrew University, with its own archaeological institute, opened atop Mount Scopus, followed by the Rockefeller Museum near Herod's Gate. Both promoted new excavations. But the crosswinds of Arab and Jewish nationalism would soon overwhelm all other pursuits. A 1947 United Nations Partition Plan dividing Palestine between Jews and Arabs internationalized Jerusalem. The Jews, eager for a state at all costs, accepted the plan. The Arabs, convinced they could win all of Palestine by force, vehemently rejected it.

Even before Britain withdrew, Jerusalem fell under siege. The city's Arabs received supplies and armed reinforcement from neighboring Arab states. By the beginning of 1948, the highway to Jerusalem was all but impassable. The city's Jews, cut off from the coastal plain, were reduced to eating weeds. Hours after David Ben-Gurion proclaimed Israel's independence on May 14, six Arab armies invaded. "Our 'heavy' artillery consisted of two 2-pounder cannons," recalled Teddy Kollek, who would serve as mayor of Jerusalem from 1965 to 1993. Later the arsenal was rounded out by three homemade 6-inch mortars affectionately dubbed "Davidkas." The Arabs fled from the city's southern suburbs but held the

walled Old City and the eastern hills. The Jews stood firm in the western New City. The Old City's Jewish Quarter, with its mostly elderly population of 2,000, was the weakest link. The 80 Jewish commandos who managed to sneak into the quarter were no match for the Arab armies that advanced house to house in the narrow stone-walled alleys and in their path destroyed 27 of the Old City's historic synagogues.

On May 28, two weeks after Israel's birth, the Old City's Jews surrendered. As the last survivors left through the Zion Gate, an aged rabbi among them thrust a package into the hands of a Christian Arab for "safekeeping." It was a 700-year-old Torah scroll. Moments later the Zion Gate closed. For the first time in its multimillennial history, Jerusalem was truly divided.

THE GOLDEN CITY NOW

The ugly barricades bisecting Jerusalem were torn down when Israeli forces captured the Old City during the 1967 Six-Day War. Unlike conquerors past, Israel left the Temple Mount in the hands of its latest occupants: Muslims. But the dingy alley before the Western Wall was broadened to a great plaza to accommodate the hundreds of thousands of Jews now free to worship there. And Kollek, who would serve as the tireless Israeli mayor of "united Jerusalem" for nearly three decades, launched an ambitious restoration of Old City glories.

Israel's determination that Jerusalem remain open to all faiths brought the nation almost universal praise. But

Sights along the Via Dolorosa, thought to be the path Jesus walked while carrying the cross

its encirclement of the city with new Jewish neighborhoods and the decision to declare all of it Israel's "eternal capital" sparked angry protests in the Arab world, especially among Palestinians. The Holy City's final political disposition remains one of the sorest points of Mideast peace negotiations. But debate also rages over how best to preserve its position as a uniquely historic place, a sacred monument, and a modern city. One key: the continued ban on facing new buildings with anything but the classic local stone. "The history of Jerusalem is writ in stone," says architect and former Jerusalem town planner David Kroyanker.

Its stones also remain the key to revealing its still-hidden secrets. Yet the quest is not without controversy. An attempt in 1995 to reconstruct part of a seventh-century Umayyad palace adjoining the Temple Mount sparked protests from Jews and Muslims alike. Orthodox rabbis argued that the palace was built with Temple stones tossed from the mount when the Romans destroyed it and that their use to rebuild was a double sacrilege. Muslim leaders said the excavations disturbed ancient graves and expressed fears they were the precursor to an archaeological invasion of the Temple Mount. Despite the objections, the project was eventually completed and is now part of an archaeological park. But the debate it brought about has become known irreverently as the "war of the stones and bones." And it is one more reason, as David the Psalmist once urged, to pray for the peace of Jerusalem. ●

By Richard Z. Chesnoff

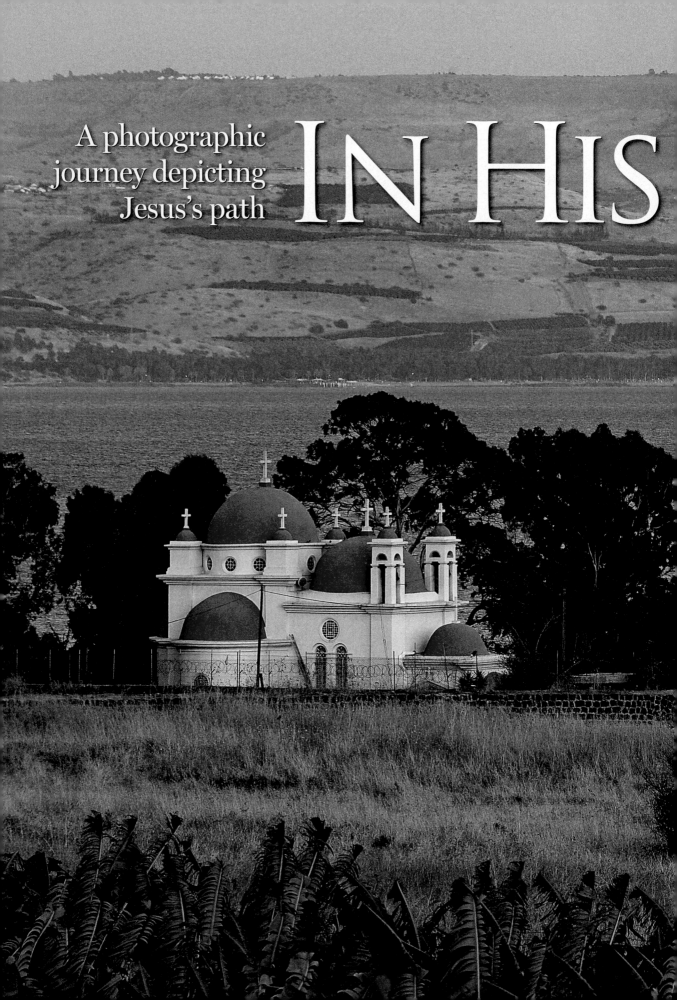

A photographic
journey depicting
Jesus's path

IN HIS

FOOTSTEPS

he Gospels say that Jesus Christ was born in the town of Bethlehem and grew up in Nazareth. Around the age of 30, he was baptized in the Jordan River by his cousin, John the Baptist. From then on, answering his calling, Jesus traveled and preached to his people, the Jews of Palestine. During his years of ministry, Jesus walked hundreds, perhaps thousands, of miles, crisscrossing the countryside from Capernaum on the Sea of Galilee to the Mount of Olives in Jerusalem carrying his message of salvation. Here, in a series of panoramic shots and close-up views of the magnificent land that has long been sacred to people of three faiths, modern pilgrims can step back in time and retrace the route that led from Jesus's birth to his Crucifixion.

GREEK ORTHODOX CHURCH, CAPERNAUM (PREVIOUS PAGE)

Located on the northern shore of the Sea of Galilee, Capernaum was in Jesus's day a bustling fishing village and trading center. Jesus often used the town as his base, and it's known as a place where he taught at a synagogue and healed several sick people. The modern church is built on the ancient village ruins.

THE CHURCH OF THE NATIVITY, BETHLEHEM

Built over the grotto (at left) where Jesus is said to have been born, the Church of the Nativity lies in the Palestinian territory of the West Bank. The basilica was completed under the Emperor Constantine in A.D. 333 and then was rebuilt after burning to the ground around 565. It is one of the oldest Christian churches in the world and is venerated today as a major holy site.

Photography by Ahikam Seri for *USN&WR*

JORDAN RIVER, NEAR JERICHO

In these waters, near the town of Qasr el Yahud, Jesus was baptized, at about the age of 30, by his cousin John the Baptist some 2,000 years ago. According to the Gospels, the Holy Spirit came upon Jesus and he heard God speak to him. After his baptism, Jesus began to travel and teach in earnest.

BETHLEHEM, WEST BANK

The city revered as Christ's birthplace (above) is considered sacred to Jews as King David's home and to Muslims as well as Christians. In 1995, control of Bethlehem reverted from Israel to the Palestinian National Authority.

"NAZARETH VILLAGE"

A historic re-creation (at left) captures life in first-century Nazareth where, the Gospels say, Jesus spent his childhood. Developers drew on the New Testament and archaeological findings to create the site where people acting the part till soil, herd sheep, bake bread, and carry water, and a carpenter's workshop features tools Joseph might have used.

THE SYNAGOGUE OF CAPERNAUM

During his ministry, Jesus often prayed at a synagogue in Capernaum. In excavations over the past century (at left), archaeologists have turned up evidence of a first-century synagogue lying beneath the foundation of a newer structure. Thus far, analysis suggests the older building dates back to Jesus's time.

THE NINTH STATION, VIA DOLOROSA, JERUSALEM

On the "Way of Sorrows" (at right), a street in Jerusalem's Old City believed to be the path that Jesus walked while carrying the cross, a woman passes by the spot where he is said to have fallen a third time on the way to his Crucifixion. The location is the ninth of the 14 Stations of the Cross; the 14th is at the site of Jesus's burial in the Church of the Holy Sepulchre.

THE GARDEN OF GETHSEMANE

According to the Gospels, Jesus went with his disciples to pray in the garden at the foot of the Mount of Olives (above) the night before the Crucifixion. The Basilica of the Agony (left) sits at the site today.

CHURCH OF THE HOLY SEPULCHRE

The holy site where Christ is believed to have been crucified and buried is today the shared responsibility of the Roman Catholic, Eastern Orthodox, Armenian Apostolic, and Ethiopian, Coptic, and Syrian Orthodox Churches. At left, people sit by the Ethiopian section.

THE STONE OF ANOINTING

Inside the Church of the Holy Sepulchre lies the stone where Jesus's body is believed to have been laid after the Crucifixion and then smeared with oil in preparation for burial. Today, visitors from around the world come to honor the Messiah by touching or kissing the slab.

FAMILY AND

DETAIL OF A WINDOW IN THE DAHLGREN CHAPEL OF
THE SACRED HEART / GEORGETOWN UNIVERSITY

PHOTOGRAPH BY BRETT ZIEGLER FOR *USN&WR*

FOLLOWERS

A MOTHER'S TALE

The Bible offers surprisingly little on Mary's life

Inside Paris's Notre Dame cathedral, dedicated to the Virgin Mary, a soprano's voice floats plangently upward in Bach's spectacular "Magnificat," the sound hovering in the soaring space before the chorus rises joyously to join it. "Behold, from henceforth, all generations shall call me blessed," Mary proclaims in her paean to God, accepting that she will be the mother of Christ.

Inspiration for some of history's most sublime musical, architectural, and artistic creations, the peasant girl from Nazareth also embodies Christianity's thorniest paradoxes. She is a virgin, yet also a mother. She is God's obedient handmaid, yet she is also a strong woman in her own right, a woman of valor, the patroness of victory. She rejoices in the birth of her son, but her salvation comes only through his death.

To the Roman Catholic and Orthodox faithful, Mary remained a virgin throughout her life, and she was herself immaculately conceived—that is, untainted by the original sin of sexual conception. She rose "body and soul" to heaven, the church teaches in a highly polarizing dogma that caused an uproar when Pope Pius XII declared it in 1950. As the Mother of God, she sits in heaven with the Trinity; she is above all saints, yet she is human. And that—her humanity—is the key.

Over the centuries, true believers and skeptics alike have spoken to Mary as a protector, a guide, even a friend in a way they cannot with God and Christ. "Closer to the human plane, she is more approachable by those who have reason to fear, or who cannot comprehend, the ineffable mystery of God or the stern authority of Christ," Steven Botterill, chair and associate professor of Italian studies at the University of California–Berkeley, has written. Even Protestants, who broke from the Catholic Church in part because of what Martin Luther abhorred as the "abominable idolatry" of Mary, are giving her a more prominent place in their hearts.

In the West, the Virgin Mother is ubiquitous. Mary has been the favorite baptismal name for girls for centuries; the Ave Maria is repeated millions of times daily.

MARTIN LUTHER ABHORRED THE "ABOMINABLE IDOLATRY" OF MARY.

Almost certainly, she has been portrayed in art and music more than any other woman in history. Even in Asia, Mary is a growing presence. Churches as far-flung as South Korea and East Timor honor her name with elaborate shrines.

Revered as a symbol that bridges disparate cultures, Mary appears prominently in the Koran, where she is compared to Hagar, the mother of Ishmael, whose descendants became the Arab peoples. In Mexico, where she appeared to an oppressed Aztec Indian in the 16th century, she is Nuestra Señora de Guadalupe, focus of a cult of near-fanatic devotion. Ten million pil-

Mary is
venerated around
the world.

grims a year flock to a shrine honoring the dark-skinned Madonna, a political as much as a religious symbol for the poor and downtrodden, "the mother of Mexico," in the words of the Mexican poet Octavio Paz.

Apparitions. Mystical Marian visions have been reported thousands of times, beginning with the "woman clothed with the sun" of Revelation and cresting in the 20th century with more than 200 apparitions cited since 1930. Such is Mary's power that Pope John Paul II credited her with saving his life when he was gravely wounded in an assassination attempt on May 13, 1981—the same day and hour Mary reportedly appeared to three children at Fátima in Portugal 64 years earlier. It's a lucky thing Mary inspires, because sketching a picture of her from the meager biblical references requires not a mere leap but an Olympian broad jump of the imagination. In all the Gospels, she appears fewer than 15 times, in accounts that take up a total of less than four pages.

Named for Moses's sister, Mary (*Miriam* in Hebrew or *Maryam* in Aramaic, the language she spoke) grew up in Nazareth, a hill town of olive groves, vineyards, and hard-scrabble farms 70 miles north of Jerusalem. Nazareth means "small fort," probably its original function, given the site's commanding view overlooking the Jezreel Valley. On an extension of the Silk Road far below, camel and mule caravans bearing silk and saffron made their stately progression from the Jordan River to the eastern Mediterranean port of Caesarea.

Nothing is known of Mary's family, although legends later held that she was the daughter of an elderly couple, Anna and the priest Joachim. In *Mary: A Flesh-and-Blood Biography of the Virgin Mother*, writer and Middle East historian Lesley Hazleton speculated that Mary may have been a shepherd, herding sheep and goats on the craggy hillsides and learning about healing and herbal cures from village women, techniques she passed along to her son.

Witness to injustice. In Hazleton's account, Mary considered herself an Israeli Jew from the province of Galilee, a region that had been occupied for more than a millennium by foreign rulers, from Babylonians to Persians, Greeks, Seleucids, Parthians, and Romans. Although she could neither read nor write, she most likely absorbed oral histories of David, Solomon, Elijah, and Ruth from the elders.

Mary almost certainly witnessed peasant farmers ruined by onerous taxes and saw them beaten and imprisoned by soldiers, a recurrent shame that may have deepened her indignation at injustice and nurtured sympathy for the poor and oppressed people all around her. The Galileans groaned under the brutal rule of

Herod the Great, a shockingly rapacious client king of the Roman Empire who built innumerable palaces while his subjects were literally taxed to death. Debt-ridden and living on the edge of starvation, Mary's neighbors no doubt served as the inspiration for Jesus's demands in the Lord's Prayer: "Give us this day our daily bread. And forgive us our debts."

It is against this tumultuous background that the angel Gabriel, in the Gospel of Luke, appears to Mary in what has come to be known as the Annunciation—a startling vision mingling alarm, illumination, and willing submission. The earliest representations of the event appeared in the Roman catacombs, and the scene was later interpreted by Matthias Grünewald, Simone Martini, Raphael, and hundreds of artists over the centuries.

When Gabriel appears, Mary is a mere teenager, betrothed to Joseph, a figure who remains even more mysterious than Mary throughout the Gospels. He is a descendant of King David, Luke says, a crucial element for fulfilling Hebrew prophecy that the Messiah would be a descendant of the royal house of Israel. Trembling in spite of the angel's entreaty not to be afraid, Mary is incredulous when she receives the news that she is to bear the Son of God.

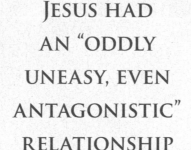

JESUS HAD AN "ODDLY UNEASY, EVEN ANTAGONISTIC" RELATIONSHIP WITH HIS PARENTS.

"How shall this be, seeing I know not a man?" she asks. "The Holy Ghost shall come upon thee, and the power of the Highest shall overshadow thee," replies Gabriel. With unnerving self-possession, the peasant girl gives her assent. "Behold the handmaid of the Lord; be it unto me according to thy word," she says. In a stroke, Mary's obedience to the will of God absolves the disobedience of Eve, maintained second-century theologian Irenaeus. It is significant that Mary, like Eve, acts without compulsion, a sign of God's grace and a promise that human beings would exercise freedom in their destinies.

Some religious historians, like the late Raymond E. Brown, author of *The Birth of the Messiah*, argue that early Christians viewed Jesus as becoming the son of God not at birth but at the Resurrection. The idea of the virgin birth arose later, they theorize, with the Gospels of Matthew and Luke, written after A.D. 60. Others, like Jane Schaberg, emeritus professor of religious studies and women's/gender studies at the University of Detroit Mercy, have even raised the explosive possibility that Mary was raped. Schaberg takes a piece of second-century, anti-Christian propaganda, the story that a Roman soldier called Panthera was Jesus's father, and turns it on its head. If Mary were raped, she says, the Holy Spirit transforms an illegitimate child into God's anointed son and Mary's potential disgrace becomes an exalted

The celebrated *Pietà* by Michelangelo at St. Peter's Basilica in Vatican City

grace of redemption. Although some feminist theologians side with Schaberg, conservative Catholics furiously dismiss her proposition as borderline heresy.

Still other historians, like Hazleton, suggest that there was a sort of dual paternity, with Joseph the human father and the Holy Spirit the divine one, a scenario similar to birth legends about Helen of Troy or Alexander the Great, both sired by the god Zeus and human fathers. Certainly, in cults across the Middle East, goddesses like Isis, Ishtar, and Diana who were both virgin and fertile exemplified a commonly accepted paradox. In any event, when Joseph learns his betrothed is pregnant, he considers leaving her until "an angel of the Lord" reveals to him in a dream that she has conceived the child through the Holy Spirit.

Whatever the literal or metaphysical truth surround-

ing the virgin birth, the mystery rests intact. The very fact that the concept goes "against nature and against proofs" invests the faith with its power, according to the 17th-century French thinker Blaise Pascal.

Soon after the Annunciation, Mary visits her pregnant elderly cousin Elizabeth. Her husband, Zechariah, has also had a vision of Gabriel foretelling the birth of a son, later known as John the Baptist. When Mary greets her cousin, Elizabeth feels the child leap in her belly in joyful recognition of the holy infant growing in Mary. "My soul doth magnify the Lord," rejoices Mary, in the words that open the ancient "Magnificat." Repeating themes and language used by Hannah in the Old Testament to give thanks for the birth of her son Samuel after years of infertility, Mary prophesies the revolutionary kingdom to come. In the future, the Lord will act as he has in the past when he "put down the mighty from [their] seats, and exalted them of low degree. He hath filled the hungry with good things; and the rich he hath sent empty away." In this 27-line poem, Mary prefigures "virtually every theme in Jesus's teaching and ministry," says Scot McKnight, a religious scholar at North Park University in Chicago.

After staying with Elizabeth for three months, Mary next appears at the Nativity, a miracle of humility enacted in countless Christmas pageants and an amalgam of accounts from Luke and Matthew (story, Page 18). Some scholars have suggested that Mary and Joseph were summoned to Judean Bethlehem for a census. Whatever the reason, they are unable to obtain a room at an inn, and Mary gives birth in a manger. Shepherds flock to see the newborn child along with three wise men bearing gold, frankincense, and myrrh.

A perilous flight. In Matthew, the story is told of King Herod's ordering the massacre of infants in Bethlehem after hearing of the birth of the future ruler of Israel. Mary and Joseph flee with their son to Egypt. Mary next appears in Luke during the purification ritual for her baby. A seer named Simeon blesses Jesus and direly predicts to his mother that "a sword shall pierce through thy own soul also," an ambiguous foreshadowing of Mary's suffering at the Crucifixion as she watches a Roman soldier thrust a sword into her son's side.

Madonna of the Pear by Giovanni Bellini, the influential Italian Renaissance painter

Twelve years later, Mary and Joseph lose young Jesus in Jerusalem. After searching for him for three days, they find him at the temple and gently upbraid him for causing them anxiety. The boy calmly replies: "How is it that you sought me? knew you not that I must be about my Father's business?"

Mystified, Mary keeps this answer in her heart, along with the puzzling adoration of the shepherds and wise men at his birth, perhaps fearing the ultimate purpose God intends for her and her son. From then on, Jesus maintains an "oddly uneasy, even antagonistic" relationship with his parents, Hazleton has written, addressing Mary not as "mother," but as "woman." At a wedding in Cana, Mary tells Jesus there is no more wine. "Woman, what have I to do with thee?" he replies testily. "Mine hour is not yet come." Patient as always, Mary instructs the servants to follow Jesus's orders, which were to fill some jars with water. Her son then performs a minor miracle by turning the water into wine.

Mary is also an essential presence at the Crucifixion, where she agonizes for hours as her son dies, comforted by her sister (or sister-in-law), also named Mary, and Mary Magdalene (as well as Salome, says Mark). As Mary stands next to John, the youngest disciple, Jesus tells her: "Woman, behold thy son!" These are his last words to Mary. Turning to John, he says: "Behold thy mother!" binding them together. After he dies, Jesus is lowered into his mother's arms in a scene depicted in Michelangelo's transcendent *Pietà*.

In Mark and Luke, Mary arrives at the tomb two days later with Mary Magdalene to anoint Jesus with perfumes but is greeted by an angel or angels who bid them to tell the disciples that Christ is risen. She does not actually see Jesus herself. Mary's final appearance in the Bible is anticlimactic. In the book of Acts, she is given a brief mention when she joins the apostles to pray at Pentecost (50 days after Jesus's Resurrection at Easter) in the "upper room," where the Last Supper was held.

From then on, Mary's story is taken up by various Apocryphal and Gnostic texts. Although they recount diverse opinions about where she goes, some placing her with John in Jerusalem, Nazareth, Mount Zion, or Ephesus in present-day Turkey (according to the Eastern Orthodox tradition), most sources also place her at the center of a group of female disciples continuing Jesus's message of forgiveness. The Gnostic *Pistis Sophia*, which means "faith wisdom" in Greek, shows Mary as one of 17 disciples, the others being the 12 male apostles plus Mary Magdalene, Salome, Martha, and Martha's sister Mary of Bethany.

According to the 20th Discourse of the Apocryphal New Testament, Mary, dying of old age, gathers the community of women around her, instructing them to follow Mary Magdalene when she's gone. "Behold your mother from this time onwards," she says. On her death, says the text, Christ descends from heaven. "Her soul leaped into the bosom of her own son, and he wrapped it in a garment of light." At Jesus's instructions, the apostles remove her body to the Vale of Jehoshaphat in Jerusalem, the current site of Mary's Tomb. Three days later, Christ returns to raise her into heaven with him, accompanied by a choir of angels as Peter, John, and the other apostles lose sight of them. ●

By Richard Covington

A LONG MISCAST OUTCAST

Mary Magdalene is finally getting her due

he woman kneels at Jesus's feet, wiping them with her abundant tresses. In Giovanni Domenico Tiepolo's drawing, taken from several passages in Luke, the dinner guests are up in arms, waving in protest that this sinner from the city has the gall to seek forgiveness. Jesus does forgive her and tells the protesting guests, "Her sins, which are many, are forgiven; for she loved much." The 18th-century Italian artist mistakenly identifies her as Mary Magdalene, but he can be forgiven, too.

Few characters in the New Testament have been so sorely miscast as Mary Magdalene, whose reputation as a fallen woman originated not in the Bible but in a sixth-century sermon by Pope Gregory the Great. Not only is she not the repentant prostitute of legend, medi-

CONVERSION OF MARY MAGDALENE BY PAOLO VERONESE / WIKIPAINTINGS

Jesus is said to have cured Mary of seven demons.

tating and levitating in a cave, but she was not necessarily even a notable sinner: Being possessed by "seven demons" that were exorcised by Jesus, she was arguably more victim than sinner. And the idea, popularized by *The Da Vinci Code*, that Mary was Jesus's wife and bore his child, while not totally disprovable, is the longest of long shots.

But arguments over whether Mary Magdalene was Jesus's wife, a reformed harlot, or the adulterous woman Jesus saved from stoning pale in comparison with the most rancorously disputed aspect of her legacy—what exactly she witnessed at Jesus's Resurrection. In his

Many artists have portrayed Mary as a saint in ecstasy; others, as a reformed temptress.

book *Mary Magdalene: A Biography*, Bard College theologian Bruce Chilton contends that Mary witnessed not the resurrection of a flesh-and-blood Jesus but a spiritual visitation. This is one of the principal reasons that she has been sidelined in the New Testament, he says. Like the apostle Paul, who claims that only a "fool" could believe in the physical resuscitation of the body, and Jesus himself, who maintains men will be reborn "like angels," Mary perceives the risen Christ as a "sequence of visions," shared by the disciples, Chilton argues. (Luke, of course, insists that Jesus is bodily resurrected. "A spirit has not flesh and bones as you see that I have," Jesus tells the disciples in Luke, then eats broiled fish to drive his point home.)

Mary Magdalene's nonphysical interpretation of resurrection was ultimately suppressed, Chilton says, because it came uncomfortably close to the view of the Gnostics, a heretical sect of Christianity that flourished in the second and third centuries. But it came to light in 1896 when the early third-century Gospel of Mary was acquired by a German scholar. In this fragmentary eight-page papyrus text in Coptic, Mary has a vision in which Jesus tells her she witnessed his reborn image with her "mind." This is followed by a section of likely elaboration that may have been purposely ripped from the manuscript to discredit her, says Chilton. She then urges the apostles to follow Jesus's instructions to spread his teachings to nonbelievers. When Peter angrily scoffs at the idea that Jesus would entrust such an important vision to a woman, another disciple, Levi, rebukes him as "hot-tempered."

But now, after centuries of neglect, outlandish distortions, and outright male fantasies, Mary Magdalene is beginning to regain her place as what Chilton terms "one of the prime catalysts and shaping forces of Christianity." Catholic groups around the country celebrate July 22, the anniversary of her death, as Mary Magdalene's feast day, using the occasion as a way to counter myths surrounding her and promote the ordination of women. "We're trying to right a 2,000-year-old wrong," Christine Schenk, executive director of FutureChurch, a Cleveland-area organization behind the movement, told *U.S. Catholic* magazine in 2000.

A devoted follower. Mary first appears in the Bible around A.D. 25 in Capernaum, a fishing town on the Sea of Galilee, where Jesus is rapidly gaining a reputation as a healer. Afflicted with "seven demons," this single woman is probably 25 or 26. A few years older than Jesus and Jewish as well, she has made her way from Magdala (the origin of her name Magdalene), a cramped, smelly fish-processing town seething with angry, dispossessed farmers seven miles to the southwest. It's not hard to picture Mary fleeing this hellhole in desperation, full of gratitude for finding someone who might save her from her demons. After an arduous, year-long treatment, writes Chilton, she is finally cured by Jesus, who exorcises all the unnamed psychological torments.

Although Luke speaks of Mary as one of the women who provide for Jesus "out of their means," the Gospel does not say she is rich, like Joanna, another follower, who is married to King Herod's steward. And it's not easy to imagine anyone wealthy coming from a place like Magdala. Still, Renaissance painters like Caravaggio

and others portrayed the wealthy, fallen Mary as a red-haired siren draped in ermine, silk, and pearls. In these fantasies, the idly rich woman turned to prostitution not for money but for vanity, making her repentance and forgiveness that much sweeter.

After Jesus cures her, Mary becomes the most influential woman in his movement, the oral source for the accounts of other exorcisms in the New Testament. According to Chilton, she teaches Jesus to use his own saliva for healing a deaf-mute and a blind man, an account that appears in Mark, the oldest Gospel, but is dropped from subsequent Gospels as women's magic.

Mary also figures prominently in rituals of healing and anointing, practices intended to invoke the Holy Spirit.

FOR HER PIVOTAL ROLE IN THE RESURRECTION, SHE BECAME KNOWN AS THE "APOSTLE TO THE APOSTLES."

In one episode in Mark, where she seems to foreshadow Jesus's burial, she incurs the wrath of some of the disciples for pouring expensive spikenard ointment over Jesus's head. We could have sold the ointment and used the money to help the poor, they complain. Sternly upbraiding them, Jesus praises Mary for her beautiful gesture. "For you always have the poor with you," he says, "but you will not always have me. She has anointed my body beforehand for burying."

Mary Magdalene is unquestionably one of Jesus's most faithful followers, witnessing the Crucifixion with his mother, Mary, while the male apostles flee to avoid arrest. In all four New Testament Gospels, Mary Magdalene is the first (either alone or with a group of women) to arrive at Jesus's tomb, where she encounters an angel (or a pair of angels) who instructs her to go tell the disciples that Jesus has risen.

In John, she later encounters the resurrected Christ, who warns her not to touch him, perhaps because he is an intangible spirit, not flesh and blood. In works by Giotto, Fra Angelico, and other Italian artists, a joyous but frustrated Mary reaches to Christ with intense longing, so near yet so far. Nine verses further on in the text, Jesus orders doubting Thomas to place his hand in Jesus's side. A possible explanation of this seeming inconsistency is that the first episode stems from Mary herself and the episode with Thomas arises from another witness.

It is not by chance that Mary Magdalene is among the first to learn of Jesus's rebirth. Surely, the divine prophet who foresaw his own crucifixion also foresaw the witnesses of his resurrection; in a sense, Jesus chose Mary Magdalene as the herald of his return. For her pivotal role in the Resurrection, she became known as "the apostle to the apostles," a figure powerful enough to chide the apostles to follow Jesus's command to preach to nonbelievers, despite the risks.

In Eastern Orthodox tradition, Mary Magdalene travels to Rome, where she preaches to Tiberius, then settles in Ephesus, in west Turkey, with Mary, the mother of Jesus, and the apostle John. Other accounts place her in southern France or even in India with the apostle Thomas. According to Chilton, she returns to Magdala, where she continues preaching, healing, and anointing. In A.D. 67, she becomes one of thousands of victims massacred by the Romans in reprisal for an armed rebellion.

Politicizing Mary's role. Soon after, the early leaders of the emergent church, including the authors of the New Testament Gospels, written around A.D. 70–95, con-tinued a process of erasing Mary Magdalene and other female followers that had begun with Peter and the other male disciples. In one text, the heretical Gnostic Gospel of Thomas, Jesus himself makes the astonishing statement that Mary, and indeed all women, cannot enter the kingdom of heaven unless they become male. In order to offer a moral alternative to the decadent Roman religion, the emergent church trumpeted male-dominated traditional family values. "This allowed Christianity to make great strides in the Greco-Roman world, but at the enormous price of forgetting about the movement's influential women," says Chilton.

MIRACLES OF THE BONES

After Jesus's death, Christians believed Mary Magdalene to be so important, wrote Victor Saxer in his 1959 book *Le Culte de Marie Madeleine en Occident*, that between the 8th and 16th centuries hundreds of different sites in Western Europe claimed to have her relics. In the Middle Ages, notes Bruce Chilton, a professor of religion at Bard College, relics were determined to be authentic based solely on their capacity to produce miracles. In Mary Magdalene's case, this phenomenon took flight.

A cult sprung up around her starting in the 6th century that was inspired by stories about her from the New Testament and later combined with the tales of other women, like Mary of Bethany and the secular Mary of Egypt. By the time of the Crusades, Mary Magdalene's heroic persona barely resembled the New Testament figure, but it was a perfect fit for the times because of the redemptive nature of her personality and her supposed stand against false idols. Many religious sites, during this period, found it important politically and monetarily to be recognized as a valid pilgrimage destination for the faithful. So as the cult of Mary Magdalene grew, so too did the assertions by different authorities that

In the sixth century, Pope Gregory the Great brought Mary firmly back into the picture—not the way she was but as the church wanted her to be. With breathtaking oversimplification, Gregory conflated Mary Magdalene of the seven demons with the unnamed "sinner" who washed Jesus's feet with her hair in Luke (a close reading of Luke 7 and 8 shows that they are not the same woman) and also Mary of Bethany, who anoints Jesus with nard in John.

Gregory reasoned that if a woman like Mary, who had fallen so low, could be forgiven through faith and the church, her carnality transformed into spirituality, the worst sinners could hope for salvation. Mary Magdalene wiped away Eve's original sin. "In paradise, a woman was the cause of death for a man; coming from the sepulcher, a woman proclaimed life to men," Gregory declared in his famous sermon in 591. The Eastern Orthodox Church, however, never accepted Gregory's melding of the three women. In short order, Mary Magdalene soon became identified with the adulterous woman Jesus saved from stoning in John and with another woman who is not even mentioned in the New Testament—Mary of Egypt, a fourth-century prostitute who converted to Christianity and lived in a cave for the rest of her life. Feminist biblical scholar Jane Schaberg coined the term

A bone at Vézelay reputed to be Mary Magdalene's

they alone possessed her "true" relics.

While many sites would claim to have skulls, fingers, or other parts of Mary, only two—both in France—rose to prominence. The first to gain notoriety was Vézelay, located in Burgundy. Local legend describes how, in A.D. 749, a monk named Badilus managed to steal Mary's skeleton from an area in the region of Provence. Over time the "stolen" relics displayed at Vézelay began to be credited with miracles allegedly experienced by people brought into contact with them. As Michael Haag relates in his book, *The Templars: The History and the Myth*, Mary's bones were "associated with the liberation of prisoners, assistance with fertility and childbirth, spectacular cures and even the raising of the dead."

After the fall of the Mesopotamian city of Edessa in 1142, the Catholic church felt a new crusade was needed to save the Holy Land. When St. Bernard of Clairvaux preached about this second Crusade from Vézelay in 1146, it only added to the mystique surrounding Mary's bones there.

A prince's vision. However, the town's claim to have Mary's true relics would be challenged a century later by Saint-Maximin-la-Sainte-Baume in Provence. Charles, Prince of Salerno, had a vision in 1279 telling him that a sarcophagus containing Mary's bones was buried in the vicinity of Saint-Maximin. He famously took part in the excavation, and popular legend maintains that when the bones were found, a patch of skin incredibly still remained on her forehead where Jesus had touched her, and a green plant was seen to be growing out of the skull. Because of Charles's prominence within the church, the growing reputation of the relics for producing powerful miracles, and the fact that even the bones claimed by Vézelay had come from the same area, Saint-Maximin gradually became the preferred destination for pilgrims. Over time, the friars of Saint-Maximin would chronicle the wondrous events associated with the relics in a work entitled *Book of Miracles of Saint Mary Magdalene*.

Whether either of these French towns holds the true remains of Mary Magdalene may never be resolved, as the bones have never been carbon dated or otherwise tested. As David B. George, professor of classics and archaeology at St. Anselm College in Manchester, N.H., and director of the Institute for Mediterranean Archaeology, says, "Is it possible that those bones are Mary Magdalene? I guess it's possible," but "I have a suspicion, given what happened when the church turned over the Shroud of Turin for analysis (story, Page 81), and it was shown to be a medieval forgery, that that would be the last relic that they turned over for scientific analysis."

In the end, author Meera Lester, who has written three books on Mary, says people visiting these sites may not need to have proof the bones were actually hers. Gazing upon the relics that stand for her, Lester says, allows each person to reflect on the "sacred truth to be found within one's own heart." For this reason alone, the faithful will no doubt continue to make their pilgrimages to Saint-Maximin and Vézelay. –*Rett Fisher*

"harlotization" to describe Mary's negative makeover, a process that disempowered a powerful leader of the faith.

Tales about the hermit Mary clawing her breasts and tearing out her hair in penance for her sins abounded, inspiring the creation of orders of flagellant monks. Painters like the 13th-century Italian Master of the Magdalen, Hans Holbein, and William Blake focused on her role in the Resurrection, while artists like Titian portrayed the saint in ecstasy, barely covering her naked body with long reddish-blond hair. Victorian photographers posed seminude adolescent girls, many living in charity schools named after her, as "Magdalenes," a prurient mixed message perpetuating the saint's image as the vixenish Lady Godiva of Christianity.

Finally, in 1969, 1,378 years after Gregory fused three

When Mary encounters the resurrected Christ, he warns her not to touch him.

New Testament women into Mary Magdalene—and more than 450 years since religious scholars rejected this fusion confusion—the church officially corrected the mistake. Even so, the legend of the repentant prostitute still exercises a tenacious hold on the public imagination. Filmmakers like Martin Scorsese in 1988's *The Last Temptation of Christ* and Mel Gibson in *The Passion of the Christ* in 2004 keep the fiction alive.

The sexy, reformed Mary Magdalene is a symbol that's proven difficult to abandon. But the visionary Mary, full of faith at the foot of the cross and messenger of the Resurrection, a founding disciple entrusted by Jesus with a special mission to spread God's word, carries the greater ring of truth. ●

By Richard Covington

NOLI ME TANGERE BY TITIAN / RESTORED TRADITIONS

MODELS OF DEVOTION

Scholars still debate the roles of Mary and Martha

In his earliest known painting, *Christ in the House of Martha and Mary*, Jan Vermeer recasts the biblical sisters of Lazarus as two sturdy young Dutch women. Good Martha, all bustle and industry, is just setting down a woven basket containing a perfect round loaf of golden bread in front of Jesus.

Sitting at Jesus's feet, sister Mary is a picture of repose, one hand propping up her head in a traditional thinker's pose, taking in Jesus's teachings. Above her, Martha and Jesus are locked in a gaze. One can imagine that Martha, hot from the kitchen and exhausted from cooking and cleaning—what must it take to host the Son of God?—has just finished delivering perhaps the most famous sibling whine of all time. "Lord, don't you care that my sister has left me to do the work by myself? Tell her to help me!"

Jesus responds, maybe a bit sharply, "Martha, Martha, you are worried and upset about many things, but only one thing is needed." And here comes the zinger: "Mary has chosen what is better, and it will not be taken away from her."

Painted sometime in the 1650s, Vermeer's version of events reflects what New Testament scholars believed about Mary and Martha for centuries: two sisters in a deep rivalry—one self-righteously busy with women's work and the other in calm discipleship with the Lord. The tale has often been interpreted as a model for two kinds of Christian devotion—a quiet solitary life of contemplation, in the tradition of monkhood, or a life of active secular engagement, as a member

THOUGH DEPICTED AS BICKERING SISTERS, MARY AND MARTHA MAY HAVE BEEN MISSIONARY LEADERS.

of the clergy. As two of the few named women in the New Testament, Mary and Martha have also been beloved by women readers. Even if Jesus might appear to denigrate Martha's domestic work, he also praises Mary for her discipleship—affirming the importance of women taking active personal roles in devotion.

A fresh look. However, new scholarship points toward entirely different layers of meaning hidden within the tired bickering of Mary and Martha. Scholars are questioning just who these sisters were, why Jesus came to their home and not the house next door, whether they were sisters at all, and why, for two millenniums, Martha has been forever stuck in the kitchen, while Mary sits at Jesus's feet.

"The story has often been read in a very domesticated way," says Warren Carter, professor of New Testament at Brite Divinity School in Fort Worth, Texas. "People have often thought that Martha is serving dinner. She's distracted by her many tasks, but these are not the tasks of what vegetables to cook." In fact, Martha's "tasks," translated from the Greek *diakonia*, related to the verb *diakonein*, are used throughout the New Testament to refer to both domestic service and Christian ministry. The word deacon is derived from the same noun. Patriarchal association of women with the domestic meant that scholars routinely missed this important detail. This double meaning opens up a new vantage point from which readers can view Mary and Martha.

"It seems likely to me these were two women who were famous among early Christians, perhaps as missionaries, but certainly as leaders," says Mary Rose D'Angelo, an

Vermeer's *Christ with Mary and Martha*

associate professor of theology at the University of Notre Dame. In Luke 10:38, Jesus and his disciples "came to a village where a woman named Martha opened her home to him." The language suggests that Martha owned the house—not unlikely, as women did own property in ancient times. D'Angelo takes the interpretation a step further: "Early Christians didn't have churches; most seem to have gathered in private houses, and perhaps Martha was the host of a house church."

That Mary and Martha were actually a pair of missionary leaders and not merely bickering sisters is a theory that gained support with the advent of the women's movement, as the role of women in church leadership and the question of ordination were increasingly debated. "The church has a very bad history in terms of treatment of women, and I imagine this story has continued to be very significant in our own time because it's a rediscovery of a part of the heritage," says Carter.

In fact, the New Testament points to the early Christian movement as having extensive female leadership. For instance, in the last chapter of Romans, Paul commends 27 people for their missionary tasks—one third of these are women, including the pair Tryphena and Tryphosa. Missionaries tended to be named in pairs, and male-female pairs are assumed to be married couples. This assumption has led to some speculation on the nature of Mary and Martha's relationship. In translation, they are called sisters, but in the original Greek, the language is less exact—sisters could mean sisters in Christ, siblings, or possibly even a same-sex relationship. The idea of a romantic relationship has been bandied about in recent scholarship, but the text lacks support.

A bold proclamation. Whatever the exact nature of their relationship, the story of Mary and Martha does not end in the book of Luke. The sisters reappear once more in the Gospel of John. Here, they have a brother that the writer of Luke doesn't mention—the famous Lazarus. When Jesus comes to the town of Bethany, Lazarus has already been dead for four days, and Mary and Martha are in deep mourning. Mary stays home, and Martha, again the more active sister, greets Jesus in town and makes the astonishing statement in John 11:27: "I believe that you are the Christ, the Son of God, who was to come into the world."

Margaret Guenther, associate rector at St. Columba's Episcopal Church in Washington, D.C., and a former seminary professor, says that Martha's profession of faith is an underappreciated moment in the Bible. "It's

a bold proclamation, and she made it before many of the men did," says Guenther. "We have a special day in January where we celebrate Peter's recognition of Jesus as the Messiah, but Martha doesn't quite make it into the book."

In contrast to their apparent rivalry in the Gospel of Luke, the Mary and Martha of the Gospel of John work in concert. After Lazarus is raised from the dead, Jesus again comes to their house for dinner. Here, Mary commits an act of great devotion and significance: She washes Jesus's feet with "a pint of pure nard, an expensive perfume" that Judas says is worth a year of wages. With this poetic act wherein "the house was filled with the fragrance of the perfume," Mary powerfully presages Jesus's death—the oil was saved for the day of his burial. She also provides a model of Christian service and devotion. Christ later echoes her act when he washes the feet of his disciples.

The appearance of Lazarus only in the Gospel of John might raise doubt that the Mary and Martha of Luke are the same as the pair in John. Scholars point out that there seemed to be relatively few personal names in biblical times, and the authors of the Gospels may have recycled the same names for different stories. If so, did these women exist at all? "That there were a significant pair of leaders called Mary and Martha who were well known, I don't see any reason to doubt," says Carter. And to a lay reader, Mary and Martha have always been the same sisters.

> MARY COMMITS AN ACT OF GREAT DEVOTION AND SIGNIFICANCE: SHE WASHES JESUS'S FEET WITH AN EXPENSIVE PERFUME.

What becomes of these women? Popular folklore traces Martha's path from her house in Bethany to the South of France, where she supposedly traveled as an evangelist. Some even say that she tamed a dragon along the way. And to this day, several churches in France claim to be the site of Martha's tomb. "It's folk piety," says Guenther. "People want to know more about these women, so somebody makes up these terrific stories, and they grow and grow."

Mary and Martha need not tame dragons to engage the modern reader. Whether one imagines the sisters in a dusty biblical town, in Vermeer's 17th-century Holland, or even as contemporary women, they have much to offer beyond their imagined rivalry. In Vermeer's painting, Jesus points toward Mary, not as a rebuke to Martha but as a gentle reminder that leadership demands both the ability to listen and the ability to act. Finally, Mary and Martha are not at odds but form two parts of a whole. ●

By Caroline Hsu

JUDAS AGONISTES

A recovered text says Jesus told his apostle to betray him

 priceless archaeological treasure was unearthed from a cave near Al Minya, Egypt, in the 1970s but remained in private hands until it was made public by the National Geographic Society in 2006. Known as the Judas Gospel, it has been published in translation by Karen L. King, Hollis professor of divinity at Harvard Divinity School. Here, in an excerpt from their book Reading Judas, King and co-author Elaine Pagels, Harrington Spear Paine Foundation professor of religion at Princeton University, relate why the Judas Gospel enhances our understanding of how early Christians viewed Jesus's death and Resurrection.

For thousands of years, Christians have pictured Judas as the incarnation of evil. Motivated by greed and inspired by Satan, he is the betrayer whom Dante placed in the lowest circle of hell. But the Gospel of Judas shows Judas instead as Jesus's closest and most trusted confidant—the one to whom Jesus reveals his deepest mysteries and whom he trusts to initiate the Passion. Startling as this sounds, the familiar New Testament Gospels have long offered hints of this. All the New Testament Gospel writers agree that Jesus anticipated, even embraced, his own death. The Gospel of Mark says that right before Jesus led his followers toward Jerusalem, where he would suffer and die, he secretly told them that it was necessary for all these things to happen (Mark 8:31). The Gospel of John suggests that Jesus himself was complicit in the betrayal, that moments before Judas went out, Jesus had told him, "Do quickly what you are going to do" (John

13:27). The Gospel of Judas follows these hints to their logical conclusion. And yet it, too, does not resolve the issue finally but only succeeds in raising again—and more forcefully than ever—the question of why Jesus was betrayed and what his death means.

The New Testament Gospels show that after Jesus's shocking arrest, torture, and slow, horrifying public execution, various groups of his followers told and retold these events as they struggled to understand how things could have gone so wrong. If Jesus had been God's chosen one, how could his enemies have gained power to kill him? Who actually engineered the plot that succeeded? What role did Judas really play? Despite all that the New Testament Gospels say, the various anecdotes about Judas left many questions open—questions that have baffled and intrigued people ever since. Now, however, the Gospel of Judas, along with many other ancient Christian texts discovered recently, from the Gospel of Mary of Magdala to the Apocalypse of Peter, lets us see that the New Testament writers were not the only ones troubled by these questions. Various Christians among the earliest generations asked—and struggled to answer—fundamental questions that look past Judas to Jesus. Who was—or is—Jesus?

That Jesus was crucified is acknowledged not only by every one of the four New Testament Gospels and the letters of Paul but also by many gospels outside the New Testament, including the Gospel of Truth, the Gospel of Philip, the Secret Book of James, the Apocalypse of Peter, and the Letter of Peter to Philip, to mention only a few. But when these followers try to say what Jesus's execution could mean, agreement ends. For

> IF JESUS HAD BEEN GOD'S CHOSEN ONE, HOW COULD HIS ENEMIES HAVE GAINED POWER TO KILL HIM?

those who left the movement it seemed that the Crucifixion proved that Jesus was not God's chosen one, or at least that God had abandoned him. Paul admits that when he preached among Jews, the terrible fact that Jesus had been crucified presented a nearly insurmountable obstacle to any who heard him; among gentiles, his claims about an executed criminal sounded ridiculous (1 Corinthians 1:17-24). Outsiders confirm this: The philosopher Celsus says that many people despised Christians because, in his words, "they worship a crucified sophist." Yet for Paul, the meaning was clear: "Christ died for our sins in accordance with the scriptures" (1 Corinthians 15:3).

The Gospels differ, to some extent, on how much Jesus planned his own betrayal.

Others devoted to Jesus, like the author of the Gospel of Mark, expressed concerns about what Jesus's Crucifixion might mean. But unlike Paul, the Gospel of Mark addressed the problem by constructing a detailed story about Jesus's arrest and execution. What could it mean to proclaim that Jesus not only *was* but still *is* God's anointed king when the Gospel admits that he fell, helpless, into Roman hands to be tortured and killed, abandoned by everyone, and even, as Jesus himself cried out as he died, abandoned by God (Mark 15:34)? How could the story the author tells possibly be what his opening words

The NEW YORK TIMES Bestseller
ELAINE PAGELS
and
KAREN L. KING

READING JUDAS

THE GOSPEL OF JUDAS AND THE SHAPING OF CHRISTIANITY

led the hearer to expect—"the *good news* of Jesus Christ, the Son of God" (Mark 1:1)?

This earliest Gospel proved enormously influential, since the authors of the Gospels of Matthew and Luke, writing about 10 to 30 years after the Gospel of Mark was written, both copied much of what its author wrote, sometimes nearly word for word, into their own, longer, Gospel narratives. Each of them based his own Gospel on the Gospel of Mark's story line and amplified what he found in the Gospel of Mark by adding more material, in the process giving his own emphasis and interpretation of the story.

When they wrote about Jesus's arrest, for example, each one, including the author of the Gospel of Mark, had to explain how Jesus's enemies succeeded in capturing him. What, then, do they say about Judas? The evidence suggests that Jesus's followers knew that someone had betrayed him, a person the Gospel of Mark names as Judas Iscariot. The author of Mark's Gospel, who wrote the earliest version we have of the story, apparently includes Judas among the disciples who it says heard Peter blurt out to Jesus, "You are the Messiah" (Mark 8:29). But the Gospel of Mark says that immediately afterward, Jesus confided to them that he expected to suffer terribly and be killed by his enemies. When Peter, shocked and

THE GOSPEL OF JUDAS SAYS THAT JESUS TOLD JUDAS TO HAND HIM OVER, SO THAT WHAT HAD TO HAPPEN COULD HAPPEN.

troubled, expressed horror, Jesus's response was unexpectedly harsh: "Get behind me, Satan!" indicating that he could not—would not—evade what he insisted must happen, a necessary course of events, divinely ordained.

Then, before Jesus shared the Passover meal with his disciples, right after he repeated his prediction that he would die, the author of the Gospel of Mark says that

At the Last Supper, Jesus tells the assembled disciples that one of them will betray him.

"Judas Iscariot, who was one of the 12, went to the chief priests in order to betray him to them" (Mark 14:10). Intriguingly, the author refrains from suggesting a motive. Yet he does speculate that the chief priests gladly seized on the opportunity Judas offered them, hoping to find Jesus and his followers alone at night, apart from the crowds that often surrounded him, in order to kill him. The author of the Gospel of Mark says that they offered to pay Judas, apparently to add incentive (Mark 14:11). The most striking change Matthew made was to suggest a motive. He says Judas was the one who initiated negotiations with the chief priests by demanding money. Of all the New Testament Gospels, the famous account of Judas's remorse, despair, and suicide is found only in the Gospel of Matthew's version. Thus each of the Gospel writers boldly confronts what Paul calls the "scandal" of Jesus's shameful death by insisting not only that Jesus had to die, as the Gospel of Mark put it (Mark 9:31), but that he did so knowing and accepting that his death was essential to God's plan of salvation. We can see, too, that each version pictures Jesus increasingly in control of what happens. The vulnerable Jesus becomes more powerful from Gospel to Gospel, from earlier accounts to the later ones.

When we look at the Gospel of Judas, then, we can see that all this author does is to take one step further this tendency to show Jesus in control. Just as the Gospel of Mark says that Jesus instructed specific disciples to set up the Passover meal and his entry into Jerusalem, and just as the Gospel of John says that Jesus himself told Judas to go out and "do what you have to do," so too the Gospel of Judas says that Jesus told Judas to hand him over, so that what had to happen could happen. But the Gospel of Judas ends the story there. There is no story of arrest, no torture, no Crucifixion, no Resurrection. As a result, the Gospel of Judas succeeds in shifting the focus from Jesus's death to what he reveals to Judas before he dies—the mysteries of the kingdom.

But where in all this is the history? What really happened? Today, New Testament scholars differ in judgment about what and how much in the Gospel stories is based on actual history. By comparing the accounts we can see that the Gospel writers elaborated on stories of

LAST SUPPER BY GIOTTO DI BONDONE / RESTORED TRADITIONS

Jesus's death in order to express the theological points they wanted to emphasize—and to address the basic problem that God's Messiah had been put to a horrible death as a criminal at the hands of the occupying Roman government. How much did they invent? Is it possible that those events, which are so clearly inspired by the prophetic writings, were actually written from them, with no historical basis at all? The New Testament scholar John Dominic Crossan puts the question this way: Are the details of the Crucifixion accounts "history prophesied" or are they "prophecy historicized"?

Scholars who see this story as "prophecy historicized" have argued that the Gospel writers selected passages like these and pieced them together to come up with the story of Judas. Some conclude, then, that the account of Judas's betrayal has no historical basis whatsoever. While this is not impossible, it leaves the question of why Jesus's followers would have made it up. For to admit that one of Jesus's closest followers actually had turned on him

> **Matthew says Judas was paid 30 pieces of silver to turn on Jesus, then repented and hanged himself.**

and betrayed him was an enormous disgrace. If it was not true, would Jesus's followers have risked bringing such shame upon the movement? And if someone outside the group had invented a character like this, wouldn't Jesus's followers have been likely to denounce it as a slanderous lie? Since the story was widely known and not challenged, it is likely that someone in the movement did betray Jesus. For as we have seen, instead of denying this embarrassing fact, the New Testament Gospel writers all attempted only to mitigate its impact—first, by claiming that Jesus knew and accepted what would happen; second, by placing this event, too, in the context of prophecies, to show that nothing, however horrible, happens apart from God's divine plan. ●

JUDAS RECEIVING PAYMENT FOR HIS BETRAYAL BY GIOTTO DI BONDONE / RESTORED TRADITIONS

RELICS AND

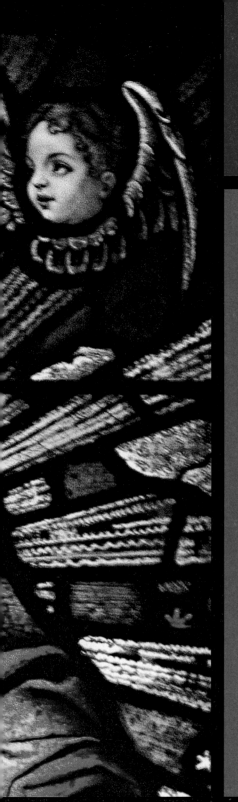

Ancient Gnostic writings
challenge orthodox views
of Christianity
72

Truth or tall tale?
Elaborate forgeries were
common in biblical times
76

What recently discovered
artifacts, real and fake, say
about Jesus and his times
81

DETAIL FROM A WINDOW AT
THE FRANCISCAN MONASTERY OF THE HOLY LAND IN AMERICA

PHOTOGRAPH BY BRETT ZIEGLER FOR *USN&WR*

RIDDLES

THE GOSPEL TRUTH

Gnostic writings challenge orthodox Christianity

hat does the bestselling novel *The Da Vinci Code* have to do with a letter written by the Archbishop of Alexandria in the year 367? As it turns out, quite a lot. Call it part of the Gnostic connection, a long, fine thread of influence connecting contemporary cultural debates with an important struggle in the early Christian movement to define the meaning of Jesus's life and teaching. In that struggle—arguably the most important waged by self-styled correct believers against so-called heretics—orthodox Christians battled Gnostic Christians over their respective interpretations of divinity, human nature, sin, salvation, and other crucial theological and philosophical points. The soldiers of orthodoxy, as we now know, ultimately prevailed, confirming their claim to be the true Christians. But Gnostic principles lived on in isolated communities and, occasionally, sparked Gnostic-like revivals.

Indeed, in recent decades, thanks to the recovery and scholarly interpretations of a trove of Gnostic documents,

Pages from a Gnostic text, the Secret Book of John

the ideas of that ancient movement have come to play a surprisingly prominent role in our current culture wars. Luke Timothy Johnson, a biblical scholar and professor at Emory University in Atlanta, may be right in saying that a new Gnosticism once again "threatens the shape of Christian faith." But the return of Gnostic ideas has also contributed to a larger debate between progressives and traditionalists that goes beyond the strict concerns of one religious tradition.

If all of that seems a bit of a stretch, consider the far-reaching historical consequences of Archbishop Athanasius's letter from 367: In addition to providing the first-known list of the 27 books that would eventually constitute the official canon of the Christian New Testament, the letter ordered all Christians to repudiate an assortment of "illegitimate and secret" Gnostic texts that Athanasius deemed heretical. In that one Easter epistle, Athanasius enunciated two bedrock principles of orthodoxy and traditionalism: the importance of scriptural canon, and apostolic authority to determine what is, and is not, acceptable Christian thought.

To be sure, Athanasius was not the first church father to consider Gnostic writings beyond the Christian pale. Written mostly in the second century A.D., these works had circulated widely in Christian communities around the Mediterranean basin, often translated from the original Greek into other languages. Bearing names like the Gospel of Truth, the Secret Book of John, the Gospel of Judas (story, Page 66), and the Gospel of Thomas, they offered a strikingly different slant on the teachings of Jesus, one that emphasized esoteric knowledge (*gnosis* in Greek), and particularly self-knowledge, as the path to salvation. More troubling to those who claimed to be orthodox Christians, Gnostic writers tended to view the virgin birth, the Resurrection, and other elements of the Jesus story not as literal, historical events but as symbolic keys to a "higher" understanding. Steeped in Plato and other Greek learning, the Gnostics held that the body and the physical world were irredeemably evil. Some even believed that the material world was the creation of a lesser god, designed to blind humans to their inner spiritual "spark" and its connection with the true God. Not surprisingly, the prominent second-century heresy hunter, Bishop Irenaeus of Lyon, charged that these works of "so-called gnosis" were "full of blasphemy." Yet the fact that he and other Christians devoted so much effort to exposing them is perhaps the strongest proof of the Gnostics' wide appeal.

Athanasius, whose church had, not long before, essentially become the religion of the Roman Empire, aimed to rid Egypt of the Gnostic texts. But his work wasn't entirely successful. At least a few rebellious monks decided to bury their condemned texts rather than destroy them.

Archbishop Athanasius ordered Christians to repudiate heretical texts.

A few of those documents were recovered in the 18th and 19th centuries. Yet until quite recently, the Gnostic writings were known to modern readers mainly through what the great heresy hunters had written about them.

Influential discovery. That began to change in 1945, when some farmers who lived near the northern Egyptian town of Nag Hammadi discovered a jar containing 13 leatherbound papyrus books at the base of a cave-riddled mountain. These books, later scholarly examination would reveal, contained 52 different texts reflecting the Gnostic perspective, most of which had never been seen by modern eyes. The first complete English edition of these works, *The Nag Hammadi Library*, edited by James Robinson of Claremont Graduate University, came out in 1978 and has had an enormous influence on the study of early Christianity.

The discovery of these works is itself a compelling story, particularly when supplemented by the more recent find of the Gospel of Judas, introduced to the modern world in 2006 by the National Geographic Society, the publisher of the first English translation. In the spring of 2007, an impressive new collection of Gnostic writings appeared, entitled *The Nag Hammadi Scriptures*, edited by Marvin Meyer of Chapman University. A capstone of sorts, it reflects the efforts of an international community of scholars that has been instrumental in translating and interpreting the Gnostic materials for a modern audience.

Among the promoters, none has been more influential than Elaine Pagels, now a professor of religion at Princeton University but a junior faculty member at Barnard College when she published her hugely popular 1979 book, *The Gnostic Gospels*. In fact, it is fair to say that Pagels's bestseller set the stage for the runaway success of *The Da Vinci Code*, which made millions on the premise that official Christianity repressed the whole truth about Jesus and his earliest followers. Simply put, *The Gnostic Gospels* was the right book at the right time. In an America still reeling from Watergate, still distrustful of authority and institutions, and still shaken by the liberating intensities of the 1960s, here was a book that argued that early Christianity contained a multitude of diverse interpretations and movements—or at least did until the leaders

Bishop Irenaeus of Lyon charged that these works of "so-called gnosis" were "full of blasphemy."

of the orthodox church succeeded in suppressing them as heresies.

Why were the teachings of the Gnostics such a great threat to the emerging orthodoxy? The reason, Pagels argued, was that Gnostic ideas challenged theological interpretations that underlay the structures of authority of the orthodox church. According to orthodox belief, Jesus bestowed ecclesiastical authority only on those male apostles who saw him after his Resurrection, thereby establishing the line of succession running from his inner circle of disciples, and particularly Peter, to the generations of bishops who would follow.

Women's roles. But the Gnostics, interpreting the Resurrection as a symbolic event, cited the canonical Gospels (Mark and John) as well as their own (the Gospel of Mary) to argue that Jesus appeared to others, including Mary Magdalene, and would continue to appear to those who are prepared through gnosis to receive him and learn his truth. To challenge the spiritual privilege of what the Gnostics called "the apostolic men" was to challenge the basis of clerical authority. Moreover, Pagels argued, to insist that women were among Jesus's closest confidants was to put into question the exclusively male character of the priesthood and many of the implicitly and explicitly sexist assumptions of what became orthodox Christianity. And that wasn't all. The Gnostic idea of the divinity—a sort of oversoul that contained both female and male aspects—challenged the very notion of the patriarchal deity of the Old Testament, the Yahweh that orthodox Christians wholeheartedly embraced.

Gnostics challenged the spiritual privilege claimed only for male apostles like Peter.

Most threatening to the orthodox position, though, was the Gnostics' interpretation of Jesus and the Christian message: To the Gnostics, or at least to many of them (there were various schools, with names like Sethians, Marcionites, Valentinians, and Thomas Christians), Jesus was not the son of Yahweh sent to redeem fallen humanity through his death and Resurrection; he was an avatar or voice of the oversoul sent to teach humans to find the sacred spark within. This was a view of Jesus that made priests and even churches peripheral, if not irrelevant, to salvation. Salvation was not the redemption of embodied creatures or the world they inhabited (bringing the Kingdom of God to this world) but freedom from the body and the physical world.

As Pagels presented them, the Gnostics came across as forerunners of modern spiritual seekers wary of institutional religion, literalism, and hidebound traditions. Along with several other scholars of early Christianity, including Michael Williams and Karen King, Pagels now rejects the label Gnostic as an imprecise name for the many different movements to which orthodox heresy hunters applied it. "I've come to think of them simply as the 'other' Christian gospels," Pagels says. While she insists her book is often misread as arguing that the "good guys lost," she does not deny that she intended to challenge Christian traditionalists, Protestant and Roman Catholic, on many points of theological and historical interpretation. In an accessible and popular way, Pagels's book (along with her later *Beyond Belief: The Secret Gospel of Thomas*) threw down the gauntlet.

She was not alone. James Robinson may make a more

modest case for the Gnostics, even to the point of saying that these "second-century Christian eggheads" missed "the center of Jesus's teaching." But he still argues that the Gnostics were an important example of the many strains of early Christianity and insists that they had a decisive influence on the shape of emerging orthodoxy, not least by forcing it to formulate its creeds and sharpen its positions. A prolific author and former Anglican bishop, N.T. Wright, has penned a stinging critique of the overselling of Gnosticism, *Judas and the Gospel of Jesus: Have We Missed the Truth About Christianity?* His is certainly not a minority position within early Christianity studies. But along with scholars like Luke Timothy Johnson (*The Creed: What Christians Believe and Why It Matters*), Philip Jenkins (*Hidden Gospels: How the Search for Jesus Lost Its Way*), and Ben Witherington (*What Have They Done With Jesus?*), Wright makes a strong counterargument to the claims of the Gnostic boosters.

The long view. Take, for instance, the proposition that Gnostic perspectives have only recently been rediscovered in all their rich and complex glory. Not so, says Wright. Joining historian Jenkins, he notes that those perspectives are set forth not only in pre-Nag Hammadi findings (the *Pistis Sophia* and the Gospel of Mary, for example) but also in the detailed and accurate descriptions of the orthodox heresy hunters such as Irenaeus, Hippolytus, and Tertullian that have long been available.

Arguing that the Gnostic perspective was never fully extinguished, Wright says that it has been particularly strong in the West for close to three centuries. "There's a sense," he says, "in which post-Enlightenment culture on both sides of the Atlantic has been implicitly Gnostic." America has a particularly strong case of the Gnostic bug, Wright asserts, because "the default position of American religion is discovering who you really are, as opposed to being saved by grace, which reaches you from somewhere else."

If the Gnostic perspective is not really that new, and if its seminal ideas are already planted in the heart of modern Western, and particularly American, culture, why are the defenders of orthodoxy so troubled by the arguments of modern Gnostic enthusiasts? Perhaps it is a matter of self-defense on the part of those who see delicate historical and theological truths on the verge of demolition.

Traditionalists see a creeping intellectual imperialism in many of the boldest claims made for the Gnostics and their works, as well as some intellectual sleight of hand. Wright wonders, for one, why progressives embrace the Gnostics when they were clearly more concerned with an elite few than with the mass of humanity. For that matter, the Gnostics' contempt for the world and their emphasis on their own individual salvation led them to ignore Jesus's highly political emphasis on bringing the Kingdom of God into this world. (In their rejection of the social gospel, Wright points out, the Gnostics were more like contemporary American fundamentalists than most liberal-minded Gnostic supporters would like to acknowledge.) And if Gnostics were really such proto-feminists, why, he asks, does the Gospel of Thomas have Jesus saying of Mary Magdalene, "Look, I shall guide her to make her male, so that she too may become a living spirit resembling you males"?

Despite such problematic passages, boosters of Gnosticism and many seekers after the "historical Jesus" often credit the Gospel of Thomas with as much authority as the canonical Gospels. Johnson, however, is not alone among critics in pointing out that Thomas has none of the narrative elements of the canonical Gospels. And he insists that it isn't accidental that the Gnostic writings are merely "gnomic and revelatory." Writing narratives, he argues in *The Real Jesus*, "inevitably involves materiality.... To have the good news revealed in a human story represents an affirmation of the body and of time, which are intrinsically attached to materiality.... But precisely that conviction is incompatible with the Gnostic perception of materiality as a ghastly error or malicious trick."

Boosters of Gnosticism often credit the Gospel of Thomas with as much authority as the canonical Gospels.

Gnostic defenders argue that not all Gnostics were extreme dualists who reviled the physical. Certainly, many modern-day Gnostics embrace the physical, within limits. Talking about such matters with Jordan Stratford, a Gnostic priest who lives in British Columbia, is a little like talking to a Buddhist: The body can be a distraction, he suggests, but it isn't evil.

Yet it is that looseness and flexibility when it comes to interpreting sacred texts that drives the orthodox so crazy. "A vision that embraces the truth of all traditions is the mark of the Gnostic," writes Johnson. "It follows that traditional Christianity is false insofar as it is exclusive and is improved to the degree that it is elevated to a more universal view." The Gnostic claim that the truth lies within fuels an argument so deep and old that it is hardly surprising that it finds expression in our contemporary culture wars. And it is unlikely that it will cease doing so in the culture wars to come. ●

By Jay Tolson

TRUTH OR TALE?

Elaborate forgeries of biblical authors are common

 iterary forgery was a common phenomenon in the ancient world. Discussions of it can be found in the writings of some of the best-known authors from antiquity. Among the Greeks and Romans there are references to and comments about it in authors as diverse as Herodotus, Cicero, Galen, and Plutarch. In the writing of recognized Christian authors, such as Irenaeus, Tertullian, Eusebius, and Augustine, forgery is also a familiar theme. Here, in an excerpt from Jesus, Interrupted: Revealing the Hidden Contradictions in the Bible (and Why We Don't Know About Them), Bart Ehrman, a professor of religious studies at the University of North Carolina–Chapel Hill and a bestselling author, describes how and why scholars have come to believe that several New Testament books have been misattributed, and he offers some reasons for why so many people wrote under assumed names.

It is sometimes argued by scholars of the New Testament that forgery was so common in the ancient world that no one took it seriously: Since the deceit could normally be easily detected, it was never really meant to fool anyone. I have spent the past couple of years examining the ancient discussions of forgery and have come to the conclusion that the only people who make this argument are people who haven't actually read the ancient sources.

Ancient sources took forgery seriously. They almost universally condemn it, often in strong terms. How widely was it condemned? Odd as it might seem, the practice of forgery is sometimes condemned

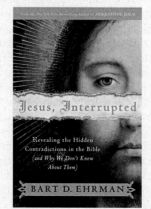

even in documents that are forged. Furthermore, the claim that no one was ever fooled is completely wrong. People were fooled all the time. I don't need to give a detailed account of the ancient discussion of forgery here; there is plenty of scholarship on the problem. But I can illustrate the point by giving one particularly telling anecdote. In second-century Rome, there was a famous physician and author named Galen. Galen tells the story that one day, as he was walking through the streets of Rome, he passed by a bookseller's stall. There he saw two men arguing over a certain book for sale, written in the name of ... Galen! One man was insisting that the book really was Galen's, and the other was equally vociferous in claiming that it could not be, since the writing style was completely different from Galen's. This, needless to say, warmed the cockles of Galen's heart, since he had not in fact written the book. But he was more than a little perturbed that someone was trying to sell a book under his name. And so he went home and composed a small book called How to Recognize the Books of Galen. We still have the book today.

Forgery was widely practiced, and it often worked. That it was not an accepted practice is clear from the terms that an-

cient authors used for it. Two of the most common terms for a forgery in Greek are *pseudon*, a lie, and *nothon*, a bastard child. This latter term is as harsh and unsavory in Greek as it is in English. It is often juxtaposed with the term *gnesion*, which means something like legitimate or authentic. From a wide range of ancient sources, it is clear that the intention of a literary forgery was to deceive readers into thinking that someone other than the actual author had written the book. But what motivated authors to do this? Why didn't they just write books using their own names? There were many motivations for pagan, Jewish, and Christian authors to forge literary texts. Here are 10 of the most common:

To make a profit. The two greatest libraries in the ancient world were located in the cities of Alexandria and Pergamum. Acquiring books for a library collection in antiquity was very different from today. Since books were copied by hand, different copies of the same book might differ, sometimes sizably, from one another, so the most important librarians preferred to have an original of a book, rather than a later copy that might have mistakes in it. According to Galen, this led entrepreneurial types to create "original" copies of the classics to sell to libraries.

To oppose an enemy. Sometimes a literary work would be forged in order to make a personal enemy look bad.

A Greek historian of philosophy, Diogenes Laertius, indicates that a philosopher named Diotemus forged and then circulated 50 obscene letters in the name of his philosophical nemesis Epicurus. This obviously did not do wonders for Epicurus's reputation. I have sometimes wondered if something of the sort is happening in one of the more peculiar forgeries of early Christianity. The fourth-century heresy hunter Epiphanius indicated that he had read a book allegedly used by a group of highly immoral Christian heretics known as the Phibionites. This book, *The Greater Questions of Mary*, allegedly contained a bizarre account of Jesus and Mary Magdalene, in which Jesus takes Mary up to a high mountain and in her presence pulls a woman out of his side (much as God made Eve from the rib of Adam) and begins having sexual intercourse with her. This strange tale is found nowhere outside of Epiphanius, who is famous for making up a lot of his "information" about heretics. I've often wondered whether he made this whole account up, forging a Phibionite book in order to make his heretical opponents look very bad indeed.

To oppose a particular point of view. If I'm right about Epiphanius, then part of his motivation would have been to oppose a view, the Phibionite heresy, that he found noxious. Similar motivations can be found in the cases of a large number of other Christian forgeries. 3 Corin-

thians, for example, was clearly written in the second century, as it opposes certain heretical views known from that time, which propose that Jesus was not a real flesh-and-blood human being and that his followers would not actually be resurrected in the flesh. According to this author, they would be resurrected. He states this view in no uncertain terms—while claiming to be the apostle Paul. It may seem odd to try to counteract a false teaching by assuming a false identity, but there it is. It happened a lot in the forgeries of the early Christian tradition.

One forger said in his defense that he had written his work "out of love" for the apostle Paul.

To defend one's own tradition as divinely inspired. There is an ancient collection of writings known as the Sibylline oracles. The Sibyl was reputed to be an ancient pagan prophetess, inspired by the Greek god Apollo. Our surviving oracles, however, are mostly written by Jews. In them, the prophetess, allegedly living long before the events she predicts, discusses the future events of history—and she is always right, since the actual author is living after these events—and confirms the validity of important Jewish beliefs and practices. Not to be outdone, later Christians took some of these oracles and inserted references to the coming of Christ in them, so that now this pagan prophetess accurately foresees the coming of the Messiah. What better testimony to the divine truthfulness of one's religion than the prophecies allegedly delivered by the inspired spokesperson of one's enemies?

Out of humility? It is commonly argued by scholars of the New Testament that members of certain philosophical schools would write treatises in the name of their master-teacher and sign his name to their own work as a gesture of humility, since one's own thoughts are simply the extension of what the master himself said. This is said to be particularly true of a group of philosophers known as the Pythagoreans, named after the great Greek philosopher Pythagoras. There is, however, serious dispute as to whether the Pythagorean philosophers who claimed to be Pythagoras actually did it out of humility: These Pythagoreans may have been inspired by other motives.

Out of love for an authority figure. In a similar vein, we do have one author from antiquity who claimed to have forged his work as an act of love and reverence. This is a most unusual situation, one in which a forger was caught red-handed. The story is told by the early third-century church father Tertullian, who indicates that the well-known stories of Paul and his female disciple Thecla, famous as a model disciple throughout the Middle Ages, were forged by a leader of a church in Asia Minor, and that he was discovered in the act and deposed from his church office as a result. In his self-defense, the forger claimed that he had written his work "out of love for Paul." It is not clear exactly what he meant by that, but it may mean that his devotion to Paul led him to invent a tale in Paul's name to capture some of what he took to be the apostle's most important teachings and views. Actually, the teachings and views found in the surviving Acts of Paul and Thecla are not at all what Paul taught: Among other things, we learn from this narrative that Paul proclaimed that eternal life would come not to those who believed in Jesus's death and Resurrection, as Paul himself proclaimed, but to those who followed Jesus in remaining sexually abstinent—even if they were married.

To see if they could get away with it. There were some ancient forgers who created their work simply in order to see if they could pull the wool over other people's eyes. The technical term for this is "mystification." The most fatuous instance, told by Diogenes Laertius, is of an author named Dionysius who set out to fool one of his sworn enemies, Heraclides of Pontus, by forging a play in the name of the famous tragedian Sophocles. Heraclides was fooled and quoted the play as authentic. Dionysius then uncovered his deceit—but Heraclides refused to believe him. And so Dionysius pointed out that if you took the first letters of several lines of the text and wrote

them out as words (an acrostic), they spelled the name of Dionysius's boyfriend. Heraclides claimed that it was just a coincidence, until Dionysius showed that later in the text were two other acrostics, one that spelled the message "an old monkey isn't caught in a trap; oh yes, he is caught at last, but it takes time," and another that said, "Heraclides is ignorant of letters and is not ashamed of his ignorance."

To supplement the tradition. Especially in early Christianity there were lots of instances in which forgers would provide "authoritative" writings that would supplement what was thought to be lacking in the tradition. For example, the author of Colossians 4:17 (Paul?) tells his readers that they are also to read the letter sent to the Christians in the town of Laodicea. We don't have an authentic letter of Paul to the Laodiceans, however. No surprise, then, that in the second century a couple of such letters turned up, forged in Paul's name. Another example: It is well known that the Gospels of the New Testament say virtually nothing about Jesus's early life.

IN THE EARLY FOURTH CENTURY,
AN ANTI-CHRISTIAN PAGAN
FORGERY WAS PRODUCED CALLED
THE ACTS OF PILATE.

This had some early Christians puzzled, and in the second century, accounts of Jesus as a boy started cropping up. The most famous of these was claimed to have been written by someone named Thomas, a name that means "the twin." It is an intriguing narrative of the adventures of the young Jesus, starting when he was a 5-year-old.

To counter other forgeries. One of the least studied phenomena of early Christian forgery is the production of forged texts designed to counter other forgeries. In the early fourth century, an anti-Christian pagan forgery was produced called the Acts of Pilate. Apparently, this narrative told the story of Jesus's trial and execution from a Roman point of view, to show that Jesus fully deserved what he got. This was a widely read document: The Roman Emperor Maximin Daia issued a decree that it was to be read by schoolboys learning their letters. Soon afterward, however, a Christian document that was also known as the Acts of Pilate made its appearance. In this account, Pilate is in complete sympathy with Jesus and fervently tries to release him as innocent of all charges. The Christian version appears to have been written to counter the pagan one. This phenomenon of Christian counterforgery appears to have been fairly widespread.

written by Peter to James in order to oppose Paul; and we have a number of apocalypses, for example, an Apocalypse of Peter (which very nearly made it into the canon) and an Apocalypse of Paul.

From a historical perspective, there is no reason to doubt that some forgeries very well could have made it into the canon. We have numerous forgeries outside the New Testament. Why not inside? I don't think one can argue that the church fathers, starting at the end of the second century, would have known which books really were written by apostles and which ones were not. How would they know? Or perhaps more to the point, how can we ourselves know? This might sound a little strange, but it is easier for us today to detect ancient forgeries than it was for people in the ancient world. The methods we use are the same as theirs. Like Galen, we consider the style in which a letter is written. Is it the same writing style that the author uses elsewhere? Or are there some features of the style that are completely unlike what the writer uses elsewhere?

Ancient critics who attempted to detect forgeries didn't have data banks and computers to crunch out detailed evaluations of vocabulary and style. They had to rely a lot on common sense and intuition. We have that, plus lots of data. Of the 27 books of the New Testament, only eight almost certainly were written by the authors to whom they are traditionally ascribed: the seven undisputed letters of Paul and the Revelation of John. My views about the authors of the New Testament are not radical within scholarship. Doubts about the authorship of writings that became the canon were raised in the early church, but in the modern period, starting in the 19th century, scholars have pressed the arguments home with compelling reasoning. Even now many scholars are loath to call the forged documents of the New Testament forgeries. But the reality is that by any definition of the term, that's what they are. ●

To provide authority for one's own views. This is the motivation that I think is by far the most common in early Christian forgeries. There were lots of Christians in the early centuries of the church who claimed numerous points of view, most of which came to be branded as heresies. Yet all of these Christians claimed to represent the views of Jesus and his disciples. How could you demonstrate that your views were apostolic, in order to, say, convince potential converts? The easiest way was to write a book, claim that it had been written by an apostle, and put it in circulation. Every group of early Christians had access to writings allegedly written by the apostles. Most of these writings were forgeries.

No one can reasonably doubt that a lot of the early Christian literature was forged. From outside the New Testament, for example, we have a large range of other gospels allegedly written by well-known early Christian leaders: Peter, Philip, Thomas, and James, the brother of Jesus, among others; we have a variety of apostolic Acts, such as the Acts of John and of Paul and Thecla; we have epistles, such as the letter to the Laodiceans, 3 Corinthians, an exchange of letters between Paul and the Roman philosopher Seneca, and a letter allegedly

Outside the New Testament, there is a gospel allegedly written by the apostle Philip.

From the book Jesus, Interrupted: Revealing the Hidden Contradictions in the Bible (and Why We Don't Know About Them) *by Bart D. Ehrman. Copyright © 2009 by Bart D. Ehrman. Reprinted by permission of HarperOne, an imprint of HarperCollins Publishers.*

SAINT PHILIP BY PETER PAUL RUBENS / RESTORED TRADITIONS

DIGGING FOR PROOF

Startling finds—and frauds—roil the archaeological world

ulldozers are the best archaeologists," quips James Tabor, a historian of Christian origins and ancient Judaism at the University of North Carolina–Charlotte. Construction and urban sprawl, more than anything else in the Mideast, he says, are responsible for the latest spate of discoveries about Jesus and his times.

With each new find comes thrilling speculation. Has Jesus's DNA been identified? Could a 2,000-year-old treasure list lead to a priceless trove of artifacts? Is an ancient tomb outside Jerusalem the final resting place of Jesus and his family? Could a new "gospel" overturn two millennia of religious teachings? "The public expects bombshells," says Lawrence H. Schiffman, a Dead Sea Scrolls scholar and vice provost for undergraduate education at New York's Yeshiva University. But such expectations are unrealistic and can obscure the true importance of many finds, he says.

Indeed, the desire for revelation can be so strong that it can blind people to the reality of elaborate frauds. When the Shroud of Turin last went on public display in the spring of 2010, for example, an estimated 2 million people lined up to see the cloth alleged to retain the ghostly image of Jesus. However, radiocarbon dating and detailed comparisons with material dating from the time of Christ have shown that the cloth that supposedly cradled Jesus after his crucifixion is in fact

a clever 14th-century hoax. Nevertheless, it remains an evocative relic, a testament to the long-held desire—not only of Christians but of scientists, historians, and scholars alike—to find some direct, tangible archaeological evidence directly connected to Jesus.

The history of this quest is riddled with smuggled treasure, clandestine meetings, and the lust for celebrity and fame that has led to vitriolic academic infighting, lawsuits, and even death threats. All of this, of course, is "wholly incompatible with scholarly investigation," says Margaret Barker, a British text scholar and expert in early Christianity. As the rate of discoveries has only seemed to accelerate in recent years, the task of identifying true artifacts seems ever more daunting. Examining the stories behind just a few of these recent finds helps explain why.

The Gospel of Judas

he fascination with the Gospel of Judas is not difficult to understand when one considers the potentially explosive, heterodox nature of a 1,700-year-old text supposedly recounting Judas Iscariot's side of the story of Christ (story, Page 66). The document itself, written by an unknown author, has a history that reads like a dime-store novel. What can safely be said of the document is that it was originally discovered sometime in the 1970s in Egypt, after which the fragile papyrus changed

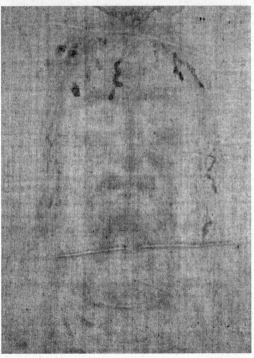

The Shroud of Turin was found to be a clever fake.

hands several times, becoming damaged along the way, and eventually landed in the possession of a Zurich-based antiquities dealer, Frieda Nussberger-Tchacos, in 2000.

Subsequent analysis, including carbon-14 dating by scientists at the University of Arizona, confirmed that the document was from roughly A.D. 280, give or take half a century. Chemical analysis of the iron gall and soot inks helped to confirm these findings. This gospel, like many others, is a copy written in Coptic (an ancient Egyptian language) of what is believed to be an original Greek text probably composed about A.D. 180. So if the authenticity of the Gospel of Judas is not in dispute, what's the controversy?

Some scholars, such as April DeConick, a professor of biblical studies at Rice University and author of *The Thirteenth Apostle*, offered translations that differed from the initial transcription by a group sponsored by the National Geographic Society, which suggested that Jesus chose Judas especially to betray him so that Jesus could be released from his bodily prison. DeConick's version, for example, makes Judas much less of a sympathetic character and more like the traditional betrayer. "What was originally published by National Geographic was not the entire text," she notes. Now that other fragments have been added, new and competing translations are being worked on, DeConick says.

No doubt part of the attendant controversy arose from academic sensitivity to what many scholars regard as sensationalist journalistic treatment of such artifacts. Some experts, for example, took issue with how the 2006 National Geographic documentary, *The Gospel of Judas*, portrayed the gospel as an attempt to vindicate Judas. It begins, "The secret account of the revelation that Jesus spoke in conversation with Judas Iscariot," as if promising to tell the real truth about what led to Jesus's crucifixion. "You will sacrifice the man that clothes me," Jesus later says to Judas. The overall implication is that Judas was the lone apostle who understood Jesus's true message and intention.

Despite the criticism by DeConick and others, National Geographic stands by its documentary. "One man's sensationalism is another man's big story," observes the Society's spokesperson, Betty Hudson. "Our job is not to tell people what it might mean," she says, "but to start an ongoing dialogue about what it might mean." To that end, she says, the Society convened a panel of experts of different viewpoints to analyze and debate the gospel, a discussion that National Geographic furthered through two books, a website where the Coptic pages were posted, and a magazine cover story.

Regarding the theological importance of the gospel, biblical scholars point out that many so-called secret accounts of Christ's story and other matters were circulating 150 years or more after the Crucifixion. Such Gnostic texts originated from various early or pre-Christian sects, many of which had mystical leanings, including multiple gods and differing stories about creation and the origins of evil, according to Schiffman. Many of these texts were well known in previous versions to early Christian leaders, but were rejected during the first centuries of the church. Schiffman believes the revelations of this particular text don't constitute the kind of discovery that could overturn thousands of years of doctrine today. "The Gospel of Judas, it's fascinating," he says, noting that it still intrigues scholars. In the end, though, many say it is unlikely to lead to a reinterpretation of the canonical Gospels. Experts may differ on its interpretation, but this account still ends with the familiar, cold fact: Judas sold Jesus to the Romans.

A fragment of the ancient papyrus text known as the Gospel of Judas.

The James Ossuary

ot much bigger than a breadbox, this limestone discovery has been the source of much conjecture and a lengthy court battle in Israel that *Archaeology* magazine in its March/April 2005 issue predicted would be the "trial of the century." The five-year criminal case, which began in September 2005 against an alleged forger and several suspected accomplices, ended in October 2010; a verdict is pending.

Purported to be the final resting place of James, the supposed brother of Jesus, the ossuary is a stone box of a type that was used at the time to house the bones of the deceased after the flesh had decomposed. Discoveries of genuine ossuaries dating from about the time of Christ are not uncommon; hundreds have been unearthed around Jerusalem over the past 40 years. However, the

James Ossuary bears the Aramaic inscription, "James, son of Joseph, brother of Jesus." This triumvirate of names has been hypothesized to mean this is the ossuary of Jesus's brother James, an early leader of the faithful after Christ's Crucifixion. If the inscription is genuine, it would be the earliest mention of Jesus on record.

Its owner, Oded Golan, is a Tel Aviv antiquities collector who, prosecutors allege, produced sophisticated forgeries—including this one. Golan continues to proclaim his innocence, but where and how the ossuary was found, and what happened to any bones within it, remain a mystery.

Initial scientific analysis and studies of the inscription by specialists in ancient writings indicated that the ossuary and its inscription were genuine, findings that the *Biblical Archaeology Review* published in 2002. At least one expert found there was no evidence of modern tools used to carve the inscription and attributed some inconsistencies in the patina to attempts at cleaning, according to Hershel Shanks, editor of the *Review*. There are no conclusive tests for dating stone, as there are for, say, papyrus, so researchers look for microbes and chemical elements of the coating or patina of the stone to estimate its age.

A second review, this time under the auspices of the Israel Antiquities Authority (IAA), declared the James Ossuary to be a fake. While the ossuary itself may be very

The controversial James Ossuary, displayed in 2002 at the Royal Ontario Museum in Toronto

old, the second part of the inscription referring to Jesus differed from the first, indicating it had been tampered with, the IAA asserted. The patina in some of the letters was also consistent with attempts at forgery, it said. News reports that Israeli authorities had found the ossuary sitting unprotected in a Tel Aviv bathroom—along with materials that allegedly could be used to fabricate ancient artifacts—seemed to close the issue for many. However, as the years went by, other researchers were enlisted. One concluded, from further tests of microorganisms and microfossils on the ossuary's patina and within the lettering, that the stone container and its inscription were consistent with relics from that time. There was no indication that the inscription was fake or recently minted. Since then, additional researchers have suggested that the James Ossuary has "geochemical fingerprints" that link it to the so-called Jesus Tomb (see below).

Experts agree that all three names were common at the time, so finding an ossuary with such an inscription does not necessarily mean that it is related to Christ. Statisticians, on the other hand, have argued that the appearance of all three names on a single ossuary has to be more than a coincidence. But it's not conclusive, either. After all the study and all the debate, Shanks says: "My expectation is the alleged forger will be acquitted. My own view is the inscription is authentic." Several scholars, however, believe that while the ossuary is ancient and of interest, some degree of forgery was involved.

Though the trial ended in October of last year, no verdict has been handed down yet. Whatever the legal results, they likely won't change scholars' opinions on either side. The controversy, Shanks notes, may have "forever tainted" the ossuary.

The Tomb of Jesus and the Jesus Nails

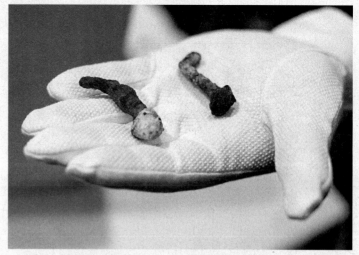
Some have speculated that these nails are from Jesus's crucifixion.

In 1980 a construction crew working in a neighborhood south of old Jerusalem accidentally uncovered another tomb containing 10 ossuaries. At the time, this serendipitous discovery didn't generate much attention. Only in 2007 did major controversy break out. That's when a documentary about the tomb was broadcast by the Discovery Channel. It was directed by Simcha Jacobovici, host of a popular series called *The Naked Archaeologist*, and produced by James Cameron, director of blockbuster feature films including *Titanic* and *Avatar*. The show was called *The Lost Tomb of Jesus*. And it got attention—lots of attention.

The main contention of the program—and of some biblical scholars like James Tabor, author of *The Jesus Dynasty*—is that the site is possibly Jesus of Nazareth's family tomb. The conclusion is based in part on what Tabor calls an "interesting cluster of names," including two nicknames, in Aramaic, Hebrew, and Greek found on six of the stone boxes: Jesus son of Joseph, two Marys, a Joseph, a Matthew, and Jude son of Jesus. Unlike other controversies, this one is not based on issues of provenance or the authenticity of the artifacts found. The tomb was originally excavated by the late Joseph Gat, an inspector under Amos Kloner, the district archae-

ologist for Jerusalem and Judea at the Department of Antiquities (later the IAA). For all intents and purposes, scholars do not dispute the inscriptions or what they say, either. The argument is about interpretation: Is it simply an ancient but common Jewish family tomb or the hidden resting place of Jesus of Nazareth?

"We got it from both sides," Tabor says. "There was a huge evangelical Christian response and one from the scholarly world." Understandably, the religious response was incredulous. If the hypothesis is true, it would appear to show that Jesus was married (DNA tests show this Jesus and one of the Marys were not directly related so they could have been husband and wife) and had a child. Also, because the tomb contained bones, it contravened important points in the Gospels. In response, proponents explained ways in which some of this could still be interpreted as consistent with the New Testament (a spiritual ascension rather than a physical one, for example). But academics had other criticisms.

THE SCIENCE OF AUTHENTICATION

Verifying whether an artifact is genuine can be a convoluted process involving multiple disciplines and numerous specialists ranging from metallurgists to physicists to paleographers. It can require an arsenal of expensive equipment as well. "There's a lot of technology, and it's enormously important" in determining whether an artifact is a true relic or a forgery, notes Hershel Shanks, editor of *Biblical Archaeology Review*.

Organic materials, such as linen or

wood, can be dated using accelerator mass spectrometers in the radiocarbon dating process. There are drawbacks, however. The process destroys the sample in order to measure its carbon-14 and carbon-12 content, and anything older than 50,000 years cannot be dated. Non-destructive tests can also be applied. A type of particle accelerator called a cyclotron, for example, has been used to determine the exact chemical composition of ink on centuries-old documents without destroying the originals.

Researchers at the University of

California–Davis, for example, used a cyclotron on a portion of the Dead Sea Scrolls to reveal that the black text was written in pure carbon soot ink. Furthermore, scanning electron microscopes can detect otherwise imperceptible tool marks on solid objects and provide detail about the chemical and crystalline properties of an item. All of this information can be used to confirm the age and source of an artifact, but the results aren't always unequivocal.

"New computer technology is very helpful because photos can be

Echoing much of what had been said against the James Ossuary, several researchers including Kloner contend that all the names found among the ossuaries of the 2,000-year-old tomb were common at the time. Others say that while that may be true, one Greek name for Mary (Mariamene) found on a single ossuary is rare. In the documentary it is suggested that Mariamene could be Mary Magdalene, while the other Mary could be the mother of Jesus. The inclusion of that name, together with the others, suggests Tabor, would be an amazing statistical coincidence if this is not Jesus's family tomb.

The protracted back and forth between academics probably isn't helped by the involvement of the documentary's director, Jacobovici. For many scholars, Jacobovici's investigative journalistic techniques have made him a lightning rod. "I come from the world of journalism and documentary films," Jacobovici says. "I've brought a different sensibility to the world of biblical archaeology, and it can touch a nerve."

The recent pronouncements about the so-called Jesus Nails are another case in point. In 1990, at a construction site in a Jerusalem park, a truck broke open the ceiling of yet another tomb. This one contained broken ossuaries, several artifacts (such as a bronze coin from A.D. 43), and an untouched ornately decorated ossuary bearing the inscription "Joseph, son of Caiaphas." According to experts, it refers to none other than the man who condemned Jesus, the Jewish High Priest Caiaphas. It is the earliest physical record of the figure mentioned in the New Testament. Since then, the IAA has confirmed that an ossuary containing the granddaughter of Caiaphas has also been

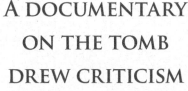

A DOCUMENTARY ON THE TOMB DREW CRITICISM FROM SCHOLARS AND BELIEVERS.

discovered. The excavation was overseen by archaeologist Zvi Greenhut and, after two years of study, the IAA confirmed the findings based on the inscriptions on the boxes and walls, various scientific tests, and the age and type of artifacts also found in the tomb. Among the latter were two iron nails. Shortly thereafter, the nails appeared to go missing or perhaps were misplaced.

Enter Jacobovici, who asked the IAA for a look at the Caiaphas nails and was told, he says, that they were missing. During the course of his research, Jacobovici discovered there were two undocumented Roman nails in the Tel Aviv University Anthropology Department. Could these two bent nails be the lost Caiaphas nails? (The only previously found nail known to have been used in a crucifixion is bent—and embedded in a heel bone that was found in another ossuary in 1968.) Following various clues, including the reported timing of the arrival of the nails at the anthropology department and the chalk-like substance on them, Jacobovici concluded these nails could be those missing from the Caiaphas tomb. He notes that there is historical reason to believe some people at the time thought nails from a crucifixion held special powers. So this might explain why they were buried with Caiaphas, leading Jacobovici and others to wonder whether they were the very nails used in the Crucifixion of Jesus.

Seeking to blunt the speculation, archaeologists have pointed out that no physical evidence exists to conclusively say the Roman nails were ever used in a crucifixion. They are smaller than the one known crucifixion nail, for example, and lack traces of bone. Greenhut has since tried to quell any further debate by indicating that

nhanced to make them more legible," notes Rice University's April DeConick. "Pieces can be puzzled together without having to disturb the aged manuscript." To bolster the evidence, researchers also look at the provenance, or history of ownership, of the item in question, as well as contextual historical clues. Establishing provenance is like maintaining a chain of evidence, which can be tricky if not impossible in the world of art and antiquities. Smugglers don't want to divulge the location of their finds, and double-dealing traders may embellish stories of discovery. Indeed, dealing in antiquities is illegal in some countries, often leading sellers to conceal

the actual provenance of some items, Shanks observes.

Differing opinions. Garnering contextual evidence can be even more difficult. Only a handful of experts may specialize in a certain type of script, for example, and opinions may differ. Furthermore, a researcher may find that there are only a half dozen or fewer similar samples for comparison. For biblical scholars, historians, and the faithful, much can rest on these findings. A newly discovered "gospel" can shed light not only on the beginnings of Christianity but also on parts of the Bible—confirming stories that have been in the canon for centuries. It can also

provide insight into daily life at the time, as the Dead Sea Scrolls have done. Each stone and nail contributes to the historical picture, confirming where King Herod lived, that the high priest Caiaphas existed, and that crucifixions took place in the manner described in the Gospels.

Through it all, archaeologists and scientists struggle to prevent their findings from becoming imbued with extreme religious views or hijacked to serve some ecclesiastic argument. They remain committed to an objective search for the truth. However, as recent rounds of findings and controversies show, that may be impossible when the subject is Jesus. –*JRQ* the nails in question were from a 1970s medical school collection, predating the Caiaphas excavation but still of unknown provenance. In a lengthy rebuttal to his critics, Jacobovici disputed this claim and reasserted they could still be the Roman iron used to crucify Christ. Regarding a consensus on the nails, Tabor merely says, "The jury is still out on that."

The Jordan Codices

A mysterious set of 1,800-to-2,000-year-old sealed metal books, revealed to exist about the time of the Jesus Nails controversy, has generated a firestorm of criticism from the academic community. As described in various March 2011 media reports and interviews with British biblical scholar David Elkington and his wife and collaborator, Jennifer, the 50 or more lead and copper books, or codices, range in size from just over a square inch to that of a hardcover book. The metal books reputedly date from only a few years after Jesus's Crucifixion and were uncovered in Jordan at a site said to be near the area where James and his followers took refuge from the Romans. The codices also drew particular attention because they are made of metal rather than the more commonly found parchment. Some sample lead pages have clearly been cast rather than etched and then sealed by metal rings, which recalls to many people the references in the New Testament's Book of Revelation about a book whose seals could be broken only by Jesus. The news created a tidal wave of excitement. Then came the flood of criticism.

Before bringing the books to public attention, Elkington says he sought the opinion of experts, including Peter Thonemann, a lecturer in ancient history at Oxford University, to whom he sent an image of at least one copper page he thought seemed dubious. Thonemann determined that one decipherable Greek phrase in the photo—"without grief, farewell! Abgar, also known as Eision"—was in fact lifted from a Roman tombstone on display in the Jordan Archaeological Museum in Amman. According to Thonemann, there were other issues, too. Conclusion: The Jordan Codices are a hoax. Elkington says other books from the collection appear to be authentic, but when he later went public with a sampling of lead pages that seemed to be genuine, Thonemann went public as well, deriding the codices as fake in a *Times Literary Supplement* article. Photos circulated online. Bloggers jumped into the discussion, and Elkington found himself on a "roller coaster of criticism and skepticism.... We've had our phone hacked and had our

THE METAL BOOKS REPUTEDLY DATE FROM ONLY A FEW YEARS AFTER JESUS'S CRUCIFIXION.

E-mail hacked," he says, "and we've had death threats." Elkington suggests it may be because some people fear the texts contradict the Gospels. "We're talking here about people's faith," he says.

Like many other discoveries, the provenance of the lead and copper pages is, to say the least, obscure. Elkington says he first saw pictures of the codices through friends who had contacts in the Mideast. He then made arrangements to see the books firsthand in Israel in 2009 at a secret meeting with a Bedouin whom Elkington describes as their "guardian" but whose background, and the way he came into possession of the smuggled artifacts, have been questioned in press accounts. Elkington says he went public with the discoveries this year hoping to prevent them from being sucked into the black market and disappearing forever in some private collection.

So far, Elkington says, initial metallurgic tests yet to be made public on more than 15 lead pages have shown them to be roughly 1,800 to 2,000 years old. He adds that the results of further independent tests confirming these results will be released in the near future. Still, the possibility of metallurgic authentication hasn't swayed academic opinion. The IAA, for example, has postulated that ancient lead could have been used to create modern fakes. Unfortunately, very few experts have had an opportunity to analyze the books firsthand. One scholar enlisted by Elkington, who has seen hundreds of photographs and two lead items from the collection, is Margaret Barker. "I am certain that some of the stuff in the hoard is of more recent origin," she says, and it may be that only the bits that have been tested so far are old. Regarding all the lead codices, "I would be very interested in having them properly tested," she says. Until that happens, "we're all in limbo."

Though the release of more test results has been promised, prevailing academic opinion has adjudicated that the codices are forgeries. Undaunted, Elkington is working on getting the metal books repatriated to the Jordanian government so that a full analysis can be done. "I can't blame people for being skeptical," he says, "but let's not jump the gun. Let's see all the evidence." .

The Dead Sea Scrolls

I f we were purists about provenance, we wouldn't have the Dead Sea Scrolls," says Schiffman, referring to the scrolls' tortuous history. They were first discovered in caves near the site of the ancient community of Qumran (about 15 miles east of Jerusalem)

by a Bedouin shepherd in 1947 and peddled on the antiquities market for years. But the importance of the flaking and fading documents—1,000 years older than any previously known biblical texts—wasn't recognized for several years, and some scholars initially argued they were a hoax. (Carbon-14 analysis later showed them to be authentic.) After an ad was placed in the *Wall Street Journal* by an antiquities dealer who had collected several of the scrolls, they were purchased by intermediaries in New York for the Israeli government in 1954 and returned to Jerusalem. After the 1967 war, the Israelis took control of the Rockefeller Museum in Jerusalem, previously under Jordanian control, and found themselves in possession of a large cache of additional scrolls. To this day the ownership of the ancient documents is contested (Jordan continues to demand that they be returned), and there are still several fragments of the priceless texts in private collectors' hands.

Of course, after such historic finds, archaeologists were eager to see if more texts lay hidden away, waiting to be discovered. What is now known as Cave 1 was discovered in 1949, and over the next seven years, archaeological digs uncovered a total of 10 more caves that housed more than 900 documents. These texts comprised roughly 350 different works written by multiple authors in Hebrew, Aramaic, and Greek. Radiocarbon dating of the linen wrappers and cyclotron tests on the ink have shown the scrolls to be authentic.

A worker prepares a display of ossuaries that some say are from the tomb of Jesus's family.

Experts have not established for certain who wrote the various books, which include copies of books of the Old Testament, Jewish biblical texts, rules for community behavior, and commentaries on sacred texts. One curious document, a copper scroll, lists over 60 treasures—gold, silver, and even more scrolls—with instructions on where to find them. However, references to ancient geographic landmarks remain obscure and scholars have been unable to determine the meaning of some of the vocabulary.

Nonetheless, even if nothing more is found, the Dead Sea Scrolls are the most important set of documents yet discovered relating to the roots of modern Judaism and Christianity. And scholars are still trying to piece together the full significance of the collection. With the scrolls largely controlled by a small group of scholars, first in Jordan and then in Israel after the 1967 war, the little information that trickled out produced intense frustration among academics around the world. For nearly 40 years, many other scholars were denied access to the artifacts, thwarting wider study. Finally, in 1991 the *Biblical Archaeology Review* printed what was essentially a bootlegged copy of pictures of the unpublished documents. (The source has never been identified.) This led to a copyright lawsuit against editor Hershel Shanks. He lost in an Israeli court and says he had to pay roughly $100,000 in judgment and legal fees. Still, the release of the remaining scroll images opened the academic flood-

Could the ossuaries from this cave mark Jesus's family tomb?

gates, allowing people worldwide to see them.

Today, the documents are about to undergo their most intense scientific scrutiny yet. In August 2011, the IAA was set to begin photographing the entire collection for the first time since the 1950s, using a high-resolution, multi-spectrum customized camera system developed in part by MegaVision, an imaging company based in Santa Barbara, Calif. Using special LED panels to limit the amount of light the fragments are exposed to, the MegaVision system will shoot images at different light wavelengths. Experts hope this will reveal symbols and text that have been invisible to the naked eye for some two millennia. It's a time-consuming process that could take several years.

According to John Cox, the production manager at MegaVision, 28 images will be shot of each of the thousands of fragments. When the project is completed, the entire set of scrolls, together with translations and historical information, will be hosted on the Web by Google for anyone to study. The hope is that by allowing experts and translators around the world to see all the text and to search across the thousands of images, scholars will develop new insights into the scrolls and shed fresh light on the history of Judaism and Christianity.

The Search Goes On

There are still discoveries to be made, as previously untouched archaeological areas submit to the march of urban expansion in the Mideast. Even sites that have been worked over for 60 years, like the caves where the Dead Sea Scrolls were found and the nearby community of Qumran, could yield new artifacts. Of course, with new finds will come new controversies and perhaps more funding for archaeologists looking for answers. Schiffman, though, cautions that there are no straightforward answers regarding many artifacts. "We used to say [the authors of] the scrolls believed the world was divided into good and evil," he explains. But now researchers know there are "about six different theories about evil in the scrolls," echoing a religious debate that took place thousands of years ago. So how does he believe people should interpret this kind of news? "I encourage people to read it—and enjoy." ●

By John R. Quain

THE ENTIRE SET OF SCROLLS WILL BE HOSTED ON THE WEB BY GOOGLE FOR ANYONE TO STUDY.

KANJI
LOOK AND LEARN

512 Kanji with Illustrations and Mnemonic Hints

イメージで覚える[げんき]な漢字512

ワークブック
W O R K B O O K

坂野永理
Eri Banno

池田庸子
Yoko Ikeda

品川恭子
Chikako Shinagawa

田嶋香織
Kaori Tajima

渡嘉敷恭子
Kyoko Tokashiki

the japan times

[著者紹介]

坂野　永理　岡山大学言語教育センター教授

池田　庸子　茨城大学留学生センター教授

品川　恭子　カリフォルニア大学サンタバーバラ校東アジア学科講師

田嶋　香織　関西外国語大学外国語学部非常勤講師

渡嘉敷　恭子　関西外国語大学外国語学部教授

KANJI LOOK AND LEARN　ワークブック

2009 年 6 月 20 日　初版発行
2017 年12月 20 日　第 17 刷発行
著　者：坂野永理・池田庸子・品川恭子・田嶋香織・渡嘉敷恭子
発行者：堤丈晴
発行所：株式会社 ジャパンタイムズ
　　　　〒108-0023 東京都港区芝浦 4 丁目 5 番 4 号
　　　　電話 （03）3453-2013 （出版営業部）
ISBN978-4-7890-1350-5

First edition: June 2009
17th printing: December 2017

Illustrations: Noriko Udagawa
Photos: Kyodo News (p. 132 and p. 154)
Layout design and typesetting: DEP, Inc.
Cover design: Nakayama Design Office
　　　　　　　Gin-o Nakayama and Kenji Sugiyama

Published by The Japan Times, Ltd.
5-4, Shibaura 4-chome, Minato-ku, Tokyo 108-0023, Japan
Phone: 03-3453-2013
http://bookclub.japantimes.co.jp/

ISBN978-4-7890-1350-5

Printed in Japan

ワークブックの内容と使い方

このワークブックは『KANJI LOOK AND LEARN ― イメージで覚える［げんき］な漢字512』のテキストに沿って、32課で構成されています。

テキストでは、1課16字ずつ学習します。ワークブックでは、これを各課それぞれ（1）（2）の2回に分けて学習していきます。

問題は（1）も（2）も同じ構成で、Iが漢字の練習表、IIが単語の読み方と例文、IIIが漢字の穴埋め問題です。

I 漢字の練習表

各漢字には、練習するマスが5つあります。まず、テキストに載っている筆順を意識して、薄く書かれている漢字をなぞってみます。モデルを見ながら、大きさやバランスに注意して、同じような形に書く練習をしましょう。あとは、覚えられるまで、自分のノートで練習してください。

II 単語の読み方と例文

テキストの語彙リストで網がけになっているものが並んでいます。まず、それぞれの単語の読み方を「Reading」のマスに書き入れましょう。そして例文を読んでみます。例文の中にまだ導入されていない漢字や語彙が入る場合は、ルビがついています。

読めない単語があった場合は、もう一度テキストをよく見て、しっかり読み方を覚えておきましょう。

III 漢字の穴埋め問題

IIで学習した語彙が文の中に組み込まれていますから、まず文全体を読んでみましょう。文の意味がわかったら、次に、ひらがなの上の＿＿＿に漢字、漢字の上の〰〰に読み方を書き入れます。新出の漢字語彙は太字で示してあります。それ以外に復習の漢字も練習できるようにしてあります。何度も繰り返し練習することで、漢字の書き方、読み方を完全にマスターしましょう。

応用練習

各課の最後に応用練習があります。ここでは（1）と（2）で学習した漢字を総合的に練習します。多様な形式の問題や文章に取り組むことにより、漢字の定着を図ります。

なお、別冊に、IIの単語と例文の読み方、およびIIIと応用練習の解答があります。

About This Workbook

This workbook consists of 32 lessons based on the lessons presented in the companion textbook, *Kanji Look and Learn*.

In the textbook, sixteen kanji are studied in each lesson. The lessons in this workbook are subdivided into two parts that generally cover eight kanji each. Both parts (1) and (2) of each lesson comprise a kanji practice table (section I), vocabulary reading exercises with example sentences (section II), and a kanji fill-in-the-blank task (section III).

(I) Kanji practice table

Five practice squares are provided for each kanji. First, trace over the character's form in the first square, following the stroke order shown in the textbook, and then practice writing the character in the other four squares. Be sure to give your characters the proper sizing and balance, using the model character as a guide. Continue practicing to write the kanji in a note-book until you have it firmly planted in your memory.

(II) Vocabulary reading & example sentences

The table in this section lists the shaded vocabulary of the corresponding textbook lesson. First, write each word's reading in the Reading column, and then read the example sentence provided for it. Some sentences contain kanji and words not yet studied, so their readings are given in *hiragana* subtext for your convenience.

If you have trouble reading any of the target words, go over it again in the textbook in order to solidly learn its reading.

(III) Kanji fill-in-the-blank task

In this task, you need to write the vocabulary covered by section II in the blanks of each sentence. First, read through the sentence to grasp its meaning, and then write the appropriate kanji or the reading of kanji in the underlined blank. The kanji vocabulary studied in that lesson are shown in bold type. The sentences also provide practice in the kanji and words learned in earlier lessons. Practicing the target kanji and vocabulary over and over will enable you to completely master how to read and write them.

Applied exercises

Each lesson ends with applied exercises for general review of parts (1) and (2). In order to ensure firm retention of the target kanji, the exercises have been designed in various formats (including reading material containing the kanji).

An answer key lists the readings of section II vocabulary and example sentences, and the answers to the section III exercises and the applied exercises.

もくじ Contents

Part 1

第1課 — 第10課
<small>だい か だい か</small>
（漢字番号 1-160）
<small>かん じ ばん ごう</small>

Ⅰ 漢字を練習しましょう。　Practice the following kanji.
かんじ　れんしゅう

一	一	一	一	一	一	六	六	六	六	六	六
二	二	二	二	二	二	七	七	七	七	七	七
三	三	三	三	三	三	八	八	八	八	八	八
四	四	四	四	四	四	九	九	九	九	九	九
五	五	五	五	五	五	十	十	十	十	十	十

Ⅱ 漢字の読み方を勉強しましょう。　Study the readings of the following kanji.
かんじ　よ　かた　べんきょう

Numbers

Word	Reading	Meaning	Word	Reading	Meaning
一	いち	1	十	じゅう	10
二	に	2	二十	にじゅう	20
三	さん	3	三十	さんじゅう	30
四	よん／し	4	四十	よんじゅう	40
五	ご	5	五十	ごじゅう	50
六	ろく	6	六十	ろくじゅう	60
七	しち／なな	7	七十	ななじゅう	70
八	はち	8	八十	はちじゅう	80
九	きゅう／く	9	九十	きゅうじゅう	90

Counter for small items

Word	Reading	Meaning	Word	Reading	Meaning
一つ	ひとつ	1	四つ	よっつ	4
二つ	ふたつ	2	五つ	いつつ	5
三つ	みっつ	3	六つ	むっつ	6

七つ	ななつ	7	九つ	ここのつ	9
八つ	やっつ	8	十	とお	10

Ⓘ 漢字と読み方を書きましょう。 Write kanji and the readings.

A. Example : 5 ＿五＿ （ ご ）

1. 3 ＿三＿ （ さん ）
2. 6 ＿六＿ （ ろく ）
3. 9 ＿九＿ （ きゅう ）
4. 1 ＿一＿ （ いち ）
5. 8 ＿八＿ （ はち ）
6. 10 ＿十＿ （ じゅう ）
7. 7 ＿七＿ （ なな/しち ）
8. 2 ＿二＿ （ に ）
9. 4 ＿四＿ （ よん/し ）

B. Example :  ＿一つ＿ （ ひとつ ）

1.  ＿三つ＿ （ みっつ ）
2.  ＿八つ＿ （ やっつ ）
3.  ＿二つ＿ （ ふたつ ）
4.  ＿九つ＿ （ ここのつ ）
5.  ＿七つ＿ （ ななつ ）
6.  ＿四つ＿ （ ようっつ ）
7.  ＿六つ＿ （ むっつ ）
8.  ＿五つ＿ （ いつつ ）
9.  ＿十つ＿ （ とお ）

Ⅰ 漢字を練習しましょう。　Practice the following kanji.
かんじ　れんしゅう

百	百	百	百	百	百	円	円	円	円	円	円
千	千	千	千	千	千	口	口	口	口	口	口
万	万	万	万	万	万	目	目	目	目	目	目

Ⅱ 漢字の読み方を勉強しましょう。　Study the readings of the following kanji.
かんじ　よ　かた　べんきょう

Numbers

Word	Reading	Meaning	Word	Reading	Meaning
百	ひゃく	100	千	せん	1,000
二百	にひゃく	200	二千	にせん	2,000
三百	さんびゃく	300	三千	さんぜん	3,000
四百	よんひゃく	400	四千	よんせん	4,000
五百	ごひゃく	500	五千	ごせん	5,000
六百	ろっぴゃく	600	六千	ろくせん	6,000
七百	ななひゃく	700	七千	ななせん	7,000
八百	はっぴゃく	800	八千	はっせん	8,000
九百	きゅうひゃく	900	九千	きゅうせん	9,000

一万	いちまん	10,000	六万	ろくまん	60,000
二万	にまん	20,000	七万	ななまん	70,000
三万	さんまん	30,000	八万	はちまん	80,000
四万	よんまん	40,000	九万	きゅうまん	90,000
五万	ごまん	50,000	十万	じゅうまん	100,000
			百万	ひゃくまん	1,000,000

Other words

Word	Reading	Meaning
百円	ひゃくえん	one hundred yen
千円	せんえん	one thousand yen
口	くち	mouth
目	め	eye

Ⅲ 漢字の読み方を書きましょう。 Write the readings of kanji.

1. 八百六十
(はちひゃくろくじゅう)

2. 二千五百
(にせんごひゃく)

3. 四千九百
(よんせんきゅうひゃく)

4. 一万三千
(いちまんさんせん)

5. 四百五十円
(よんひゃくごじゅうえん)

6. 八千三百円
(はっせんさんびゃくえん)

7. 十万五千円
(じゅうまんごせんえん)

8. 七万六千円
(ななまんろくせんえん)

9. 目 と 口
(め) (くち)

Ⅳ 漢字を書きましょう。 Write the followings in kanji.

1. 1,200 　一千二百

2. 590 　五百九十

3. 73,000 　七万三千

4. 4,800 　四千八百

5. 65,000 　六万五千

6. 340 　三百四十

7. 8,600 　八千六百

8. 970 　九百七十

9. 　八百円
はっぴゃくえん

10. 　十万円
じゅうまんえん

11. 　口
くち

12. 　目
め

13. 　百万
ひゃくまん

Ⅰ メニューを見て、値段を書きましょう。　Look at the menu and write the prices.
み　ねだん　か

てんぷらうどん
wheat flour noodles with
deep-fried shrimps

ざるそば
cold buckwheat noodles

てんぷらうどん	九百円	
月見そば	六百円	
定食	七百円	
牛丼	八百円	
ざるそば	五百円	
ビール	三百円	
ジュース	二百円	

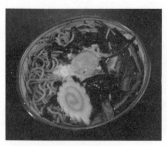

月見そば
つきみ
buckwheat noodles
topped with an egg

定食
ていしょく
set menu

牛丼
ぎゅうどん
beef bowl

Example：てんぷらうどん ＿＿＿¥900＿＿＿

1. ジュース　　　¥＿200＿＿＿

2. 月見そば　　　¥＿600＿＿＿
　　つき み

3. 牛丼　　　　　¥＿800＿＿＿
　ぎゅうどん

4. ざるそば　　　¥＿500＿＿＿

5. ビール　　　　¥＿300＿＿＿

6. 定食　　　　　¥＿700＿＿＿
　ていしょく

Ⅰ 漢字を練習しましょう。 Practice the following kanji.

日	日	日	日	日	日	木	木	木	木	木	木
月	月	月	日	日	日	金	金	金	金	金	金
火	火	火	火	火	火	土	土	土	土	土	土
水	水	水	水	水	水	曜	曜	曜	曜	曜	曜

Ⅱ 単語の読み方を勉強しましょう。 Study the readings of the following words.

Days of the week

Word	Reading	Meaning
日曜日	にちようび	Sunday
月曜日	げつようび	Monday
火曜日	かようび	Tuesday
水曜日	すいようび	Wednesday
木曜日	もくようび	Thursday
金曜日	きんようび	Friday
土曜日	どようび	Saturday
曜日	ようび	day of the week

Month

Word	Reading	Meaning
一月	いちがつ	January
二月	にがつ	February
三月	さんがつ	March
四月	しがつ	April
五月	ごがつ	May
六月	ろくがつ	June
七月	しちがつ	July
八月	はちがつ	August
九月	くがつ	September
十月	じゅうがつ	October
十一月	じゅういちがつ	November
十二月	じゅうにがつ	December

Other words

Word	Reading	Meaning	Example Sentence
月	つき	moon; month	月を見ました。
火	ひ	fire	あれは火です。
水	みず	water	水を飲みます。
木	き	tree	木があります。
お金	おかね	money	お金がありません。

Ⅲ 漢字の読み方を書きましょう。　Write the readings of kanji.

1. 火曜日
（ かようび ）

2. 金曜日
（ きんようび ）

3. 月曜日
（ げつようび ）

4. 土曜日
（ どようび ）

5. 木曜日
（ もくようび ）

6. 水曜日
（ すいようび ）

7. 日曜日
（ にちようび ）

8. 二月
（ にがつ ）

9. 七月
（ なながつ ）

10. 四月
（ しがつ ）

11. 九月
（ くがつ ）

12. 十一月
（ じゅういちがつ ）

13. 五月
（ ごがつ ）

14. 一月
（ いちがつ ）

15. 三月
（ さんがつ ）

16. 十二月
（ じゅうにがつ ）

17. 六月
（ ろくがつ ）

18. 八月
（ はちがつ ）

19. 十月
（ じゅうがつ ）

20. お金
（ おかね ）

21. あれは月です。
（ あれはつきです ）

22. 水を飲みます。
（ みずをのみます ）

23. 火は熱いです。
（ ひはあついです ）

24. 木があります。
（ きがあります ）

Ⅳ 漢字を書きましょう。　Write the followings in kanji.

1. 五月
ごがつ

2. 十月
じゅうがつ

3. 四月
しがつ

4. 六月
ろくがつ

5. 九月
くがつ

6. 七月
しちがつ

7. 三月
さんがつ

8. 十二月
じゅうにがつ

9. 土曜日
どようび

10. 金曜日
きんようび

11. 月曜日
げつようび

12. 火曜日
かようび

13. 水曜日
すいようび

14. 木曜日
もくようび

15. 日曜日
にちようび

16. お金 があります。
おかね

17. 水 を飲みます。
みず

18. 月 を見ました。
つき

19. あの 木 は大きいです。
き

20. 火 は熱いです。
ひ

だい　か

① 漢字を練習しましょう。　Practice the following kanji.
かん じ　れんしゅう

本	本	本	本	本	本	時	時	時	時	時	時
人	人	人	人	人	人	半	半	半	半	半	半
今	今	今	今	今	今	刀	刀	刀	刀	刀	刀
寺	寺	寺	寺	寺	寺	分	分	分	分	分	分

② 単語の読み方を勉強しましょう。　Study the readings of the following words.
たん ご　よ　かた　べんきょう

Hours

Word	Reading	Meaning	Word	Reading	Meaning
一時	いちじ	one o'clock	七時	しちじ	seven o'clock
二時	にじ	two o'clock	八時	はちじ	eight o'clock
三時	さんじ	three o'clock	九時	くじ	nine o'clock
四時	よじ	four o'clock	十時	じゅうじ	ten o'clock
五時	ごじ	five o'clock	十一時	じゅういちじ	eleven o'clock
六時	ろくじ	six o'clock	十二時	じゅうにじ	twelve o'clock

③ 単語の読み方を書いて、文を読みましょう。
たん ご　よ　かた　か　　ぶん　よ

Write the readings of the words and read the sentences.

Word	Reading	Meaning	Example Sentence
本	ほん	book	本を読みます。
日本	にほん	Japan	今、日本にいます
一本	いっぽん	one (long object)	ビールを一本飲みました。
二本	にほん	two (long objects)	えんぴつを二本ください。
三本	さんぼん	three (long objects)	かさが三本あります。

人	ひと	person	あの人は親切な人です。
日本人	にほんじん	Japanese people	田中さんは日本人です。
一人	ひとり	one person	弟が一人います。
二人	ふたり	two people	姉が二人います。
三人	さんにん	three people	家族は三人です。
一人で	ひとりで	alone	一人でデパートに行きました。
今	いま	now	今、十月です。
今月	こんげつ	this month	今月、日本に行きます。
今日	きょう	today	今日は暑いです。
(お)寺	おてら	temple	この寺は大きいです。
～時	じ	… o'clock	今、一時です。
～時半	じはん	half past …	三時半に大学に行きます。
五分	ごふん	five minutes	今、一時五分です。
十分	じっぷん	ten minutes	十分待ってください。
半分	はんぶん	half	ピザを半分食べました。
分かる	わかる	to understand	日本語が分かります。

Ⅳ 漢字と読み方を書きましょう。　Write kanji and the readings.

Example：　07:30　　　七時半　　　（　　しちじはん　　）

1.　06:10　　六時十分　　（ろくじじっぷん　　）

2.　04:05　　四時五分　　（よじごふん　　　）

3.　09:30　　九時半分　　（くじ はんぶん　　）

Ⓥ ひらがなを漢字にかえましょう。

Rewrite the *hiragana* with an appropriate mix of kanji and *hiragana*.

1. えんぴつを＿＿＿＿＿＿＿＿とペンを＿＿＿＿＿＿＿＿ください。
　　　　　　　　いっぽん　　　　　　　　　　にほん

2. 弟が＿＿＿＿＿＿＿＿と兄が＿＿＿＿＿＿＿＿います。
　　おとうと　　ひとり　　　あに　　　ふたり

3. ＿＿＿＿＿＿＿＿、＿＿＿＿＿＿＿＿に行きました。
　　　　ひとりで　　　　　　おてら

4. ＿＿＿＿＿＿＿＿は＿＿＿＿＿＿＿＿です。
　　　こんげつ　　　　　はちがつ

5. ＿＿＿＿＿＿＿＿、＿＿＿＿＿＿＿＿を読みました。
　　　きょう　　　　　　ほん　　　　　よ

6. 花を＿＿＿＿＿＿＿＿買いました。
　　はな　　さんぼん　　　か

7. 子供が＿＿＿＿＿＿＿＿います。
　　こども　　さんにん

8. あの＿＿＿＿＿＿＿＿は＿＿＿＿＿＿＿＿です。
　　　　ひと　　　　　にほんじん

9. 宿題を＿＿＿＿＿＿＿＿しました。
　　しゅくだい　はんぶん

10. ＿＿＿＿＿＿＿＿、＿＿＿＿＿＿＿＿語が少し＿＿＿＿＿＿＿＿。
　　　　いま　　　　　　にほん　　　ご　　すこ　わかります

Ⅰ 絵を見て、下線に正しい漢字を書きましょう。
え み かせん ただ かんじ か

Look at the picture and fill in the blanks with the appropriate kanji.

Example : えんぴつが＿＿＿一本＿＿＿あります。

1. 人が＿＿二人＿＿います。　　2. たまごが＿＿七つ＿＿あります。

3. にんじんが＿＿三本＿＿あります。　4. りんごが＿＿四つ＿＿あります。

5. 男の人が＿三人＿います。　　6. ワインが＿一本＿あります。
おとこ

7. トマトが＿二つ＿あります。　　8. ボールが＿六つ＿あります。

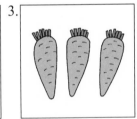

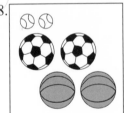
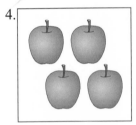

Ⅱ 次の質問に漢字を使って答えましょう。
つぎ しつもん かんじ つか こた

Answer the following questions using kanji.

1. 今、何時ですか。
　　なんじ

十一時 十六分です

2. 兄弟 (brothers and sisters) が何人いますか。
　きょうだい　　　　　　　　　なんにん

二います

3. えんぴつが何本ありますか。
　　　　　　なんぼん

三本あります

Ⅰ 漢字を練習しましょう。　Practice the following kanji.

上	上	上	上	上	上	工	工	工			
下	下	下	下	下	下	左	左	左			
中	中	中	中	中	中	前	前	前			
外	外	外	外	外		後	後	後			
右	右	右									

Ⅱ 単語の読み方を書いて、文を読みましょう。
Write the readings of the words and read the sentences.

Word	Reading	Meaning	Example Sentence
上	うえ	up; above	本はテレビの上です。
上げる		to raise	手を上げます。
下	した	down; below	かさはいすの下です。
下げる		to lower	手を下げます。
中		middle; inside	ペンはかばんの中です。
外	そと	outside	外は寒いです。
右	みぎ	right	ペンは電話の右です。
左	ひだり	left	ノートは電話の左です。
前		before; front	バス停はスーパーの前です。
後ろ		back; behind	山田さんは田中さんの後ろです。
〜の後		after ...	クラスの後、何をしますか。
後で		later	後で電話します。

Ⅲ ひらがなを漢字に、漢字をひらがなにかえましょう。

Rewrite the *hiragana* with an appropriate mix of kanji and *hiragana*.
Rewrite the kanji with *hiragana*.

1. ＿＿＿＿＿はテーブルの＿＿＿＿＿です。
   本　　　　　　　　　　　うえ

2. ねこは＿＿＿＿＿、＿＿＿＿＿にいます。
   　　　　今　　　　　そと

3. ＿＿＿＿＿＿はかばんの＿＿＿＿＿にあります。
   おかね　　　　　　　なか

4. ＿＿＿＿＿＿はあのビルの＿＿＿＿＿＿です。
   お寺　　　　　　　うしろ

5. 手を＿＿＿＿＿＿ください。＿＿＿＿＿＿ください。
   て　あげて　　　　　　　さげて

6. 新聞はベッドの＿＿＿＿＿です。　　7. クラスの＿＿＿＿＿、うちへ帰ります。
   しんぶん　　　した　　　　　　　　　　　　　あと　　　　　　　かえ

8. 駅の＿＿＿＿＿に本屋があります。＿＿＿＿＿にホテルがあります。
   えき　みぎ　　ほんや　　　　　ひだり

9. デパートの＿＿＿＿＿で＿＿＿＿＿＿待ちました。　10. ＿＿＿＿＿＿電話します。
   まえ　　　ごふん　　ま　　　　　　　あとで　　でんわ

Ⅳ 絵を見て、下線に正しい漢字を書きましょう。
   え　み　かせん　ただ　かんじ　か

Look at the picture and fill in the blanks with the appropriate kanji.

1. 本はテーブルの ＿＿＿＿＿＿＿ です。

2. 時計はテレビの ＿＿＿＿＿＿＿ です。
   と けい

3. さいふはかばんの ＿＿＿＿＿＿＿ です。

4. リモコンはテレビの ＿＿＿＿＿＿＿ です。

5. CDはステレオの ＿＿＿＿＿＿＿ です。

6. めがねはテレビの ＿＿＿＿＿＿＿ です。

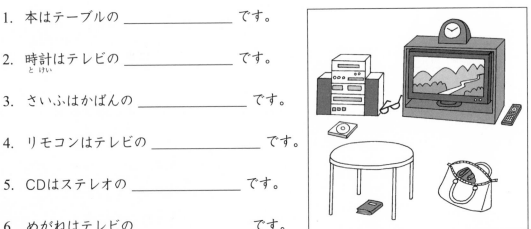

だい　か

Ⅰ 漢字を練習しましょう。　Practice the following kanji.
かんじ　れんしゅう

午	午	午	午	午	午	西	西	西		
門	門	門	門	門	門	南	南	南		
間	間	間	間			北	北	北		
東	東	東								

Ⅱ 単語の読み方を書いて、文を読みましょう。
たんご　よ　かた　か　ぶん　よ

Write the readings of the words and read the sentences.

Word	Reading	Meaning	Example Sentence
午前		A.M.	午前一時です。
午後		P.M.; in the afternoon	午後六時半です。
午前中		in the morning	クラスは午前中にあります。
門		gate	車は門の後ろです。 くるま
間		between	本屋は銀行とホテルの間です。 ほんや　ぎんこう
時間		time	時間がありません。
〜時間		… hours	二時間勉強しました。 べんきょう
東		east	日本は中国の東にあります。 ちゅうごく
東口		east exit	今、東口にいます。
中東		the Middle East	中東に行きます。 い
西		west	京都は東京の西です。 きょうと　とうきょう
西口		west exit	西口に来てください。 き
南		south	九州は南にあります。 きゅうしゅう
南口		south exit	南口はどこですか。
東南アジア		Southeast Asia	東南アジアから来ました。 き
北		north	北海道は北にあります。 ほっかいどう
北口		north exit	北口で待ちます。 ま

Ⅲ ひらがなを漢字に、漢字をひらがなにかえましょう。

Rewrite the *hiragana* with an appropriate mix of kanji and *hiragana*.
Rewrite the kanji with *hiragana*.

1. _____ _____ _____ _____
　　 ひがし　　　　にし　　　　みなみ　　　　きた

2. _____と_____は、
　　 げつようび　　　　　　もくようび

　　 _____も_____もクラスがあります。
　　　　ごぜん　　　　　　ごご

3. この駅には_____と_____があります。
　　　　　　　　 ひがしぐち　　　　にしぐち

4. _____、 ～～～～～～～～ _____アジアに行きます。
　　 こんげつ　　　　　一人で　　　　　とうなん

5. A： ここは_____ですか。
　　　　　　みなみぐち

　　 B： いいえ、_____ですよ。
　　　　　　　　　　きたぐち

6. _____にはどんな国がありますか。
　　 ちゅうとう

7. _____は忙しいです。あまり_____がありません。
　　 ごぜんちゅう　　　　　　　　　　　　じかん

8. 銀行とホテルの_____に公園があります。
　　　　　　　　　　あいだ

9. _____の_____の ～～～～～ で_____待ちました。
　　 おてら　　　もん　　　　前　　　　にじかん

Ⅰ 反対の意味の言葉を漢字で書きましょう。Give antonyms of the following words in kanji.
はんたい いみ ことば かんじ か

Example：南 ⇔ ＿北＿　　1. 後ろ ⇔ ＿＿＿＿＿　　2. 左 ⇔ ＿＿＿＿＿

3. 上 ⇔ ＿＿＿＿＿　　4. 中 ⇔ ＿＿＿＿＿　　5. 東 ⇔ ＿＿＿＿＿

Ⅱ 地図を見て、下から正しい漢字を選んで書きましょう。
ちず み した ただ かんじ えら か

Look at the maps and choose the appropriate kanji for the blanks.

東	西	南	北

1. 青森は岩手と秋田の ＿北＿＿＿ です。
あおもり いわて あきた 　東

2. 福島は宮城と山形の ＿＿＿＿＿ です。
ふくしま みやぎ やまがた

3. 山形は宮城の ＿＿＿＿＿ です。
やまがた みやぎ

4. 岩手は秋田の ＿＿＿＿＿ です。
いわて あきた

5. 大分は熊本の ＿＿＿＿＿ です。
おおいた くまもと

6. 佐賀は福岡の ＿＿＿＿＿ です。
さが ふくおか

7. 宮崎は大分の ＿＿＿＿＿ です。
みやざき おおいた

8. 福岡は熊本の ＿＿＿＿＿ です。
ふくおか くまもと

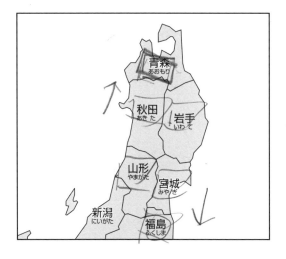

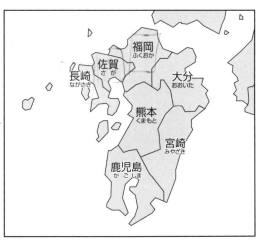

Ⅰ 漢字を練習しましょう。　Practice the following kanji.

田	田	田	田	田	田	学	学	学	学	学	学
力	力	力	力	力	力	生	生	生	生	生	生
男	男	男	男	男	男	先	先	先	先	先	先
女	女	女	女	女	女	何	何	何	何	何	何
子	子	子	子	子	子						

Ⅱ 単語の読み方を書いて、文を読みましょう。
Write the readings of the words and read the sentences.

Word	Reading	Meaning	Example Sentence
田中さん	たなかさん	Mr./Ms. Tanaka	あの人は田中さんです。
力	ちから	power	彼女は力が強いです。
男の人	おとこのひと	man	あの男の人は日本人です。
女の人	おんなのひと	woman	あそこに女の人がいます。
男の子	おとこのこ	boy	男の子が五人います。
女の子	おんなのこ	girl	あの女の子はだれですか。
学生	がくせい	student	田中さんは学生です。
生まれる	うまれる	to be born	1980年に子供が生まれました。
生きる	いきる	to live	ねこは三十年生きました。
先生	せんせい	teacher	先生はどこですか。
先月	せんげつ	last month	先月、日本に来ました。

何	なに/なん	what	何を食べましたか。 それは何ですか。
何か	なにか	something	何かしませんか。
何人	なんにん	how many people	学生は何人いますか。
何時	なんじ	what time	今、何時ですか。

Ⅲ ひらがなを漢字に、漢字をひらがなにかえましょう。

Rewrite the *hiragana* with an appropriate mix of kanji and *hiragana*.
Rewrite the kanji with *hiragana*.

1. ＿＿＿＿＿、＿＿＿＿＿が＿＿＿＿＿＿＿。
　　せんげつ　　　おとこのこ　　　　うまれました

2. A：＿＿＿＿、＿＿＿＿をしますか。　B：＿＿＿＿＿出かけます。
　　今日　　　なに　　　　　　　　　　　　ごご

3. A：今、＿＿＿＿＿ですか。　B：＿＿＿＿＿です。
　　　　なんじ　　　　　　　　　九時

4. ＿＿＿の＿＿＿に＿＿＿＿＿＿がいますね。あの人は＿＿＿＿＿さんです。
　門　　まえ　　おとこのひと　　　　　　　　たなか

5. あの＿＿＿＿＿＿は＿＿＿＿が強いです。
　　　おんなのこ　　　ちから

6. A：日本語の＿＿＿＿＿は＿＿＿＿＿いますか。　B：＿＿＿＿＿います。
　　　　せんせい　　　なんにん　　　　　　　　ふたり

7. 百歳まで ＿＿＿＿＿＿＿＿＿です。
　　　　　　いきたい

8. 大学に＿＿＿＿＿が＿＿＿＿＿＿います。
　　　がくせい　　いちまんにん

9. ＿＿＿＿＿に、＿＿＿＿＿の＿＿＿＿＿＿に会いました。
　火曜日　　　　日本人　　おんなのひと

10. A：＿＿＿＿＿買いましたか。　B：はい。かさを＿＿＿＿＿買いました。
　　なにか　　　　　　　　　　　　　　　　一本

Ⅰ 漢字を練習しましょう。　Practice the following kanji.

父	父	父				毎	毎	毎			
母	母	母				王	王	王			
年	年	年				国	国	国			
去	去	去									

Ⅱ 単語の読み方を書いて、文を読みましょう。
Write the readings of the words and read the sentences.

Word	Reading	Meaning	Example Sentence
父		my father	父は五十歳です。
お父さん		father	お父さんの仕事は何ですか。
父の日		Father's Day	父の日は六月にあります。
母		my mother	母は日本人です。
お母さん		mother	お母さんはどの人ですか。
母の日		Mother's Day	母の日は五月にあります。
～年生		… year student	妹は三年生です。
～年		… year(s)	日本語を一年勉強しています。
今年		this year	今年、日本に行きます。
年		year	今年はいい年でした。
去年		last year	去年、子供が生まれました。
毎日		every day	毎日、クラスがあります。
毎月		every month	毎月、お金を送ります。
毎年		every year	毎年、東南アジアに行きます。

国		country	来月、国に帰ります。
外国		foreign country	外国に住みたいです。
中国		China	日本は中国の東です。

Ⅲ ひらがなを漢字に、漢字をひらがなにかえましょう。

Rewrite the *hiragana* with an appropriate mix of kanji and *hiragana*.
Rewrite the kanji with *hiragana*.

1. ＿＿＿＿＿＿＿＿＿、＿＿＿＿＿＿＿＿＿にネクタイをあげます。
  まいとし　　　　　ちちのひ

2. ＿＿＿＿＿＿＿、＿＿＿＿＿＿＿＿＿＿＿＿＿アジアへ行きました。
  きょねん　　　　一人で　　　　　　東南

3. ＿＿＿＿＿＿＿＿、＿＿＿＿＿＿＿から日本語のクラスがありますか。
  まいにち　　　　なんじ

4. 私は大学＿＿＿＿＿＿＿＿＿です。
  よねんせい

5. ＿＿＿＿＿＿＿＿はどんな＿＿＿＿＿＿でしたか。
  ことし　　　　　とし

6. その＿＿＿＿＿＿＿＿は＿＿＿＿＿＿ ＿＿＿＿＿＿に住んでいます。
  おんなのひと　　　にねん　ちゅうごく

7. ＿＿＿＿＿＿＿＿＿の＿＿＿＿＿＿＿＿の仕事は＿＿＿＿＿ですか。
  たなかさん　　　　おとうさん　　　　何

8. ＿＿＿＿＿＿＿に、＿＿＿＿＿＿＿＿に＿＿＿＿＿あげますか。
  ははのひ　　　　おかあさん　　　なにか

9. ＿＿＿＿＿＿＿から＿＿＿＿＿に行きます。
  日曜日　　　　がいこく

10. ＿＿＿＿＿の＿＿＿と＿＿＿に＿＿＿＿手紙を書きます。
  くに　　ちち　　はは　　まいつき

① 次の質問に漢字を使って答えましょう。 Answer the following questions using kanji.

1. 今年の母の日は何月何日ですか。

2. あなたは何年に生まれましたか。

3. きのう、何時に寝ましたか。

4. 去年、外国に行きましたか。

5. あなたの日本語の先生は男の人ですか。

6. あなたの日本語のクラスには女の人が何人いますか。

② 私の家族

> 私の家族は三人です。父と母と私です。父はオーストラリア人で、母は中国人です。私は中国で生まれました。私は去年、日本に来ました。今、日本の大学の学生です。

質問に答えましょう。 Answer the questions in Japanese.

1. この人の家族は何人ですか。

2. お父さんは中国人ですか。

3. この人はどこで生まれましたか。

4. この人はいつ日本に来ましたか。

Ⅰ 漢字を練習しましょう。　Practice the following kanji.
かんじ　れんしゅう

見	見	見			良	良			
行	行				食	食			
米	米				飲	飲			
来	来				会	会			

Ⅱ 単語の読み方を書いて、文を読みましょう。
たんご　よ　かた　か　　　　ぶん　よ
Write the readings of the words and read the sentences.

Word	Reading	Meaning	Example Sentence
見る		to see	テレビを見ます。
見せる		to show	パスポートを見せてください。
見える		can be seen	ここから山が見えます。 やま
行く		to go	今月、中国へ行きます。
（お）米		rice	スーパーでお米を買いました。 か
来る		to come	田中さんは来るでしょう。
来ます		to come	一月に日本に来ました。
来ない		not to come	田中さんは来ないでしょう。
来年		next year	来年、外国へ行きます。
食べる		to eat	パンを食べます。
飲む		to drink	毎日コーヒーを飲みます。
会う		to meet	先生に会いました。

Ⅲ　ひらがなを漢字に、漢字をひらがなにかえましょう。

Rewrite the *hiragana* with an appropriate mix of kanji and *hiragana*.
Rewrite the kanji with *hiragana*.

1. あの車の＿＿＿＿＿に＿＿＿＿＿＿＿＿＿がいます。＿＿＿＿＿＿＿＿＿か。
　　　　　　なか　　　　　　女の人　　　　　　　　　みえます

2. メニューを＿＿＿＿＿＿＿ください。
　　　　　　　　みせて

3. ＿＿＿＿＿、＿＿＿＿＿へ＿＿＿＿＿＿＿。
　　らいねん　　にほん　　　　いきます

4. ＿＿＿＿＿の＿＿＿＿＿に＿＿＿＿＿で＿＿＿＿＿＿＿。
　　金曜日　　じゅうじはん　　東口　　　あいましょう

5. ＿＿＿＿、彼は＿＿＿＿＿でしょう。でも明日は＿＿＿＿＿と思います。
　　今日　　かれ　　こない　　　　　　あした　　　くる　　　　おも

6. 友だちと、映画を＿＿＿＿＿、コーヒーを＿＿＿＿＿＿＿＿＿。
　　とも　　えいが　　みて　　　　　　　　のみました

7. ＿＿＿＿＿＿はよく＿＿＿＿を＿＿＿＿＿＿。
　　にほんじん　　　こめ　　　たべます

8. ＿＿＿＿＿は＿＿＿＿＿　＿＿＿＿＿か。
　　学生　　　　なんにん　　　きます

9. 祖父は＿＿＿＿歳まで＿＿＿＿＿＿＿＿。
　　そふ　　ひゃく　さい　　いきました

10. その店は＿＿＿＿＿を出て＿＿＿＿へ＿＿＿＿＿です。
　　　みせ　　にしぐち　　で　　みぎ　　　　五分

11. プレゼントは＿＿＿＿＿です。私が＿＿＿＿＿、＿＿＿＿＿を出します。
　　　　　　さんぜんえん　　　わたし　　はんぶん　　　お金　　だ

Ⅰ 漢字を練習しましょう。 Practice the following kanji.

耳	耳	耳			立	立	立			
聞	聞	聞			待	待	待			
言	言	言			周	周	周			
話	話	話			週	週	週			

Ⅱ 単語の読み方を書いて、文を読みましょう。
Write the readings of the words and read the sentences.

Word	Reading	Meaning	Example Sentence
耳		ear	うさぎは耳が長いです。
聞く		to listen	九時からラジオを聞きます。
聞こえる		can be heard	音楽が聞こえます。
言う		to say	何と言いましたか。
話す		to speak	日本語を話します。
話		talk; story	父の話を聞きました。
会話		conversation	先生との会話は楽しいです。
立つ		to stand	立ってください。
待つ		to wait	ちょっと待ってください。
今週		this week	今週は忙しいです。
来週		next week	来週は母の日です。
先週		last week	先週、中国へ行きました。
毎週		every week	毎週テニスをします。
一週間		one week	一週間ホームステイをしました。

Ⅲ ひらがなを漢字に、漢字をひらがなにかえましょう。
Rewrite the *hiragana* with an appropriate mix of kanji and *hiragana*.
Rewrite the kanji with *hiragana*.

1. あの＿＿＿＿＿＿＿＿＿＿は＿＿＿＿＿が大きいです。
　　　　　男の人　　　　　　みみ　　　おお

2. ＿＿＿＿＿＿、＿＿＿と＿＿＿といっしょに旅行に＿＿＿＿＿＿＿。
　　らいしゅう　　父　　　母　　　　りょこう　　　　いきます

3. ＿＿＿＿＿＿の＿＿＿＿を＿＿＿＿＿＿＿＿。
　　せんせい　　はなし　　　ききました

4. ＿＿＿＿＿＿＿＿に一度、日本語の＿＿＿＿＿＿＿のクラスがあります。
　　いっしゅうかん　　いちど　　　　ご　かいわ

5. ＿＿＿＿＿＿＿は＿＿＿＿＿＿＿＿＿＿アルバイトがあります。
　　こんしゅう　　　　　毎日

6. よく＿＿＿＿＿＿＿＿＿＿でした。もう一度＿＿＿＿＿＿＿ください。
　　　きこえません　　　　　　いちど　　いって

7. ＿＿＿＿＿＿＿、＿＿＿＿＿＿＿にサッカーをします。
　　まいしゅう　　どようび

8. ＿＿＿＿＿＿＿に日本人の友だちと＿＿＿＿＿＿＿、＿＿＿＿＿＿＿＿。
　　もくようび　　　　　とも　　会って　　　　　はなしました

9. ＿＿＿＿＿＿＿ください。ちょっと＿＿＿＿＿＿＿ください。
　　たって　　　　　　　　　まって

10. ＿＿＿＿＿＿＿、＿＿＿＿＿＿＿が＿＿＿＿＿＿＿＿＿＿。
　　せんしゅう　　おんなのこ　　　　生まれました

11. ＿＿＿＿＿＿＿、映画を＿＿＿＿＿＿＿＿＿＿＿＿＿。
　　毎月　　　　えいが　　二本　　　　みます

Ⅰ 下の漢字を使って文を作りましょう。
した かんじ つか ぶん つく

Write appropriate verbs using the following kanji, and complete the sentences.

食	飲	見	立	聞	会	話	行

Example： すしを＿＿＿食べます＿＿＿。

1. テレビを＿＿＿＿＿＿＿＿＿＿＿。　　2. コーヒーを＿＿＿＿＿＿＿＿＿＿＿。

3. 友だちに＿＿＿＿＿＿＿＿＿＿＿。　　4. ラジオを＿＿＿＿＿＿＿＿＿＿＿。
とも

5. 東京へ＿＿＿＿＿＿＿＿＿＿＿。　　6. 日本語を＿＿＿＿＿＿＿＿＿＿＿。
とうきょう　　　　　　　　　　　　　　　ご

Ⅱ アンさんの週末
しゅうまつ

　先週、日本人の友だちの家へ行きました。土曜日の午前十時ごろ駅で友だちと
会って、いっしょに行きました。家では友だちのお父さんとお母さんが待ってい
ました。弟さんもいました。十歳の男の子です。私は「はじめまして」と言いま
した。お母さんは英語の先生で、英語を話しますが、お父さんと弟さんはぜんぜ
ん話しません。私は二人の話があまりわかりませんでした。夜、てんぷらとすし
を食べました。とてもおいしかったです。お酒も飲みました。午後八時半ごろ帰
りました。

質問に答えましょう。　Answer the questions in Japanese.
しつもん こた

1. アンさんは何時に友だちと会いましたか。
とも

2. 友だちの家にだれがいましたか。
とも いえ

3. アンさんは弟さんに何と言いましたか。
おとうと

4. 友だちのお母さんの仕事は何ですか。
とも しごと

5. 夜、何を食べましたか。何を飲みましたか。
よる

Ⅰ 漢字を練習しましょう。　Practice the following kanji.

大	大	大				新	新	新			
小	小	小				古	古	古			
高	高	高				元	元	元			
安	安	安				気	気	気			

Ⅱ 単語の読み方を書いて、文を読みましょう。

Write the readings of the words and read the sentences.

Word	Reading	Meaning	Example Sentence
大きい		big	私の国は大きいです。
大学		college	毎日、大学へ行きます。
大学生		college student	マイクさんは大学生です。
大人		adult	大人が三人います。
小さい		small	この辞書は小さいです。
小学生		elementary school student	弟は小学生です。
高い		high; expensive	このカメラは高かったです。
安い		cheap	このスーパーは安いです。
新しい		new	新しい車が欲しいです。
新聞		newspaper	新聞を読みます。
古い		old	この寺はとても古いです。
元気な		fine; energetic	母は元気です。
気をつける		to be careful	気をつけてください。

Ⅲ ひらがなを漢字に、漢字をひらがなにかえましょう。
Rewrite the *hiragana* with an appropriate mix of kanji and *hiragana*.
Rewrite the kanji with *hiragana*.

1. つくえの＿＿＿＿＿＿に＿＿＿＿＿＿＿ ＿＿＿＿＿＿があります。
　　　　　　上　　　　　　ふるい　　　ほん

2. あそこに＿＿＿＿＿＿＿＿＿ ＿＿＿＿＿＿があります。＿＿＿＿＿＿＿＿＿か。
　　　　　おおきい　　　　き　　　　　　　　　　　　みえます

3. このコンピューターは ＿＿＿＿＿＿＿＿、＿＿＿＿＿＿＿＿です。
　　　　　　　　　　　　あたらしくて　　　　ちいさい

4. ＿＿＿＿＿＿＿＿＿、＿＿＿＿＿＿＿で、＿＿＿＿＿＿＿を読みました。
　　ごぜんちゅう　　　だいがく　　　　しんぶん　　　　　よ

5. あの店は＿＿＿＿＿＿ですが、この店は＿＿＿＿＿＿です。
　　　　みせ　　たかい　　　　　　　　みせ　　やすい

6. ＿＿＿＿＿＿＿＿＿＿はもう＿＿＿＿＿＿＿です。子供じゃありません。
　　だいがくせい　　　　　　　おとな　　　　　　こども

7. あの＿＿＿＿＿＿＿＿＿の＿＿＿＿＿＿＿＿＿は＿＿＿＿＿＿＿です。
　　　しょうがくせい　　　　おとこのこ　　　　　げんき

8. ＿＿＿＿＿からも＿＿＿＿＿＿からも車が来ます。＿＿＿＿＿＿をつけてください。
　　前　　　　　　後ろ　　　　　　くるま　　　　　　き

9. 山本さんは＿＿＿＿＿＿＿に＿＿＿＿＿＿＿と＿＿＿＿＿＿＿＿＿いました。
　　やまもと　　　　　七時　　　　　来る　　　　　いって

10. その＿＿＿＿＿は＿＿＿＿＿＿＿＿＿ずっとそこに＿＿＿＿＿＿＿＿＿いました。
　　　　ひと　　　　にじかん　　　　　　　　　　　たって

11. ＿＿＿＿＿の部屋から＿＿＿＿＿＿＿が＿＿＿＿＿＿＿＿＿＿＿＿＿。
　　下　　　　　へや　　　　かいわ　　　　　　聞こえました

Ⅰ 漢字を練習しましょう。　Practice the following kanji.

多	多	多				長	長	長			
少	少	少				明	明	明			
広	広	広				好	好	好			
早	早	早				友	友	友			

Ⅱ 単語の読み方を書いて、文を読みましょう。

Write the readings of the words and read the sentences.

Word	Reading	Meaning	Example Sentence
多い		many	この大学は女の人が多いです。
少し		a little	パンを少し食べました。
少ない		few	ご飯が少ないです。
広い		wide; spacious	このアパートは広いです。
早い		early	日本語のクラスは朝早いです。
早く		early	朝、早く起きました。
長い		long	あの人は髪が長いです。
明るい		bright	この部屋は明るいです。
明日		tomorrow	明日、先生に会います。
好きな		favorite	サッカーが好きです。
大好きな		very favorite	アイスクリームが大好きです。
友だち		friend	友だちと話します。

Ⅲ　ひらがなを漢字に、漢字をひらがなにかえましょう。
　　Rewrite the *hiragana* with an appropriate mix of kanji and *hiragana*.
　　Rewrite the kanji with *hiragana*.

1.　＿＿＿＿＿＿宿題をしました。でも＿＿＿＿＿＿、終わりません。
　　　すこし　しゅくだい　　　　　　　おおくて　　　　　お

2.　この部屋は＿＿＿＿＿＿、＿＿＿＿＿＿です。
　　　　へ や　　　ひろくて　　　　　あかるい

3.　西さんの＿＿＿＿＿＿は髪が＿＿＿＿＿です。
　　　にし　　　お母さん　　　かみ　　ながい

4.　＿＿＿＿＿、＿＿＿＿＿起きて、＿＿＿＿に出かけましょう。
　　　あした　　　はやく　　お　　　そと　　　　で

5.　A：日本の食べ物が＿＿＿＿＿ですか。　　B：はい、＿＿＿＿＿＿です。
　　　　　　　もの　　すき　　　　　　　　　　　　だいすき

6.　駅の＿＿＿＿＿は店が＿＿＿＿＿ですが、＿＿＿＿＿＿はにぎやかです。
　　　えき　みなみぐち　みせ　すくない　　　　　北口

7.　＿＿＿＿＿＿の日本語のクラスは朝＿＿＿＿＿です。
　　　さんねんせい　　　　　ご　　　あさ　はやい

8.　クラスの＿＿＿＿、＿＿＿＿の所で＿＿＿＿＿を＿＿＿＿＿＿＿。
　　　　　あと　　　門　　ところ　ともだち　　　　　待ちました

9.　田中さんは＿＿＿＿＿＿クラスに＿＿＿＿＿と言っていました。
　　　　　こんしゅう　　　　　来ない

10.　きのうから＿＿＿＿＿の＿＿＿＿＿が痛いです。
　　　　ひだり　　　みみ　　　いた

① 反対の意味の言葉を漢字で書きましょう。Give antonyms of the following words in kanji.
はんたい いみ ことば かんじ か

1. 古い ⇔ _____
2. 大きい ⇔ _____
3. 安い ⇔ _____
4. 短い ⇔ _____
   みじか
5. 暗い (dark) ⇔ _____
   くら
6. 遅い ⇔ _____
   おそ

② 手紙
   て がみ

りかさん、お元気ですか。

私は四月に日本に来ました。今、京都の大学で勉強しています。京都には、古
わたし きょうと べんきょう きょうと
いお寺がたくさんあります。でも新しいビルもたくさんあって、おもしろい所で
ところ
す。外国人も多いので、いろいろな国のレストランがあります。少し高いですが、
おいしいです。

大学の寮は大きいです。私の部屋は広くて明るいです。月曜日から金曜日まで
りょう へや
大学へ行きます。日本語のクラスは九時から十二時まで、毎日三時間あります。
ご
クラスは長いですが、楽しくて大好きです。
たの
では、体に気をつけてください。
からだ

8月20日

マイク・ハドソン

寮　dormitory
りょう

質問に答えましょう。　Answer the questions in Japanese.
しつもん こた

1. 京都には何がありますか。
   きょうと

2. 寮の部屋はどんな部屋ですか。
   りょう へや へや

3. 日本語のクラスは何時から何時までですか。
   ご

① 漢字を練習しましょう。　Practice the following kanji.

入	入	入			村	村	村		
出	出	出			雨	雨	雨		
市	市	市			電	電	電		
町	町	町			車	車	車		

② 単語の読み方を書いて、文を読みましょう。
Write the readings of the words and read the sentences.

Word	Reading	Meaning	Example Sentence
入る	はいる *hairu*	to enter	先月テニスクラブに入りました。
入れる	いれる *ireru*	to put something in	本をかばんに入れます。
入り口/入口	いりぐち *iriguchi*	entrance	入り口はあそこにあります。
入学する	にゅうがく *nyuugaku*	to enter a school	去年大学に入学しました。
出る	でる *deru*	to exit	外に出てください。
出かける	でかける *dekakeru*	to go out	母と出かけました。
出す	だす *dasu*	to take something out	かばんから本を出します。
出口	でぐち *deguchi*	exit	トイレは出口の左です。
つくば市	つくばし	Tsukuba City	大学はつくば市にあります。
市長	しちょう	mayor	新しい市長は女の人です。
町	まち	town	大きい町に住んでいます。
村	むら	village	山に小さい村があります。
雨	あめ	rain	土曜日は雨でした。

電気	でんき	electricity	電気をつけます。
電話	でんわ	telephone	父に電話をしました。
車	くるま	car	車でその町に行きます。
電車	でんしゃ	train	電車が来ました。

Ⅲ ひらがなを漢字に、漢字をひらがなにかえましょう。

Rewrite the *hiragana* with an appropriate mix of kanji and *hiragana*.
Rewrite the kanji with *hiragana*.

1. ＿＿＿＿＿の＿＿＿＿＿から＿＿＿＿＿ください。
　　東　　　　いりぐち　　　　はいって

2. かばんからセーターを＿＿＿＿＿、本を＿＿＿＿＿。
　　　　　　　　　　　だして　　　　　いれます

3. 大学はつくば＿＿＿にあります。＿＿＿＿＿＿＿＿＿しました。
　　　　　　　し　　　　　　　先月　　　にゅうがく

4. ＿＿＿＿＿は＿＿＿＿＿が降っていました。
　　月曜日　　　あめ

5. ＿＿＿＿でその＿＿＿に＿＿＿＿＿＿＿。
　　くるま　　　　むら　　　行きました

6. ＿＿＿＿に行ってから、＿＿＿＿＿に＿＿＿＿＿をかけました。
　　まち　　　　　　　ともだち　　　でんわ

7. ＿＿＿＿＿＿から＿＿＿＿を消してください。
　　でかけます　　　　でんき

8. ＿＿＿＿の＿＿＿を＿＿＿＿＿＿＿。
　　しちょう　はなし　　ききましょう

9. ＿＿＿＿を降りて、8番＿＿＿から＿＿＿ください。
　　でんしゃ　お　　ばん　でぐち　　でて

Ⅰ 漢字を練習しましょう。　Practice the following kanji.

馬	馬	馬				店	店	店			
駅	駅	駅	駅			銀	銀	銀			
社	社	社				病	病	病			
校	校	校				院	院	院			

気 長 長

Ⅱ 単語の読み方を書いて、文を読みましょう。
Write the readings of the words and read the sentences.

Word	Reading	Meaning	Example Sentence
馬	うま	horse	馬に乗ったことがあります。
駅	えき	station	駅の北口で会いましょう。
会社	かいしゃ	company	毎日、電車で会社に行きます。
社会	しゃかい	society	今はネット社会です。
社長	しゃちょう	company president	社長と話をしました。
学校	がっこう	school	学校で友だちに会いました。
高校	こうこう	high school	高校に入学しました。
中学校	ちゅうがっこう	junior high school	田中さんは中学校の先生です。
小学校	しょうがっこう	elementary school	小学校は駅の東にあります。
校長	こうちょう	principal	父は小学校の校長です。
店	みせ	shop	その店は安いです。
銀行	ぎんこう	bank	銀行でお金を出します。
病気	びょうき	illness	病気になりました。

病院	びょういん	hospital	社長は午後、病院へ行きます。
入院する	にゅういん	to be hospitalized	母は一年入院しています。
大学院	だいがくいん	graduate school	九月から大学院で勉強します。
大学院生	だいがくいんせい	graduate student	あの男の人は大学院生です。

Ⅲ ひらがなを漢字に、漢字をひらがなにかえましょう。

Rewrite the *hiragana* with an appropriate mix of kanji and *hiragana*.
Rewrite the kanji with *hiragana*.

1. 小学校 の友だちは今、会社 の社長 です。
   しょうがっこう　　　　かいしゃ　　しゃちょう

2. 私の父 は中学校 の こうちょう です。
   わたし　ちち　　ちゅうがっこう　　こうちょう

3. 大学院 に入って 、日本 社会 について勉強します。
   だいがくいん　はいって　にほん　しゃかい　　べんきょう

4. 店 は、銀行 の 西 にあります。
   みせ　　ぎんこう　　西

5. 高校 は駅 からバスで五分 です。
   こうこう　えき　　　　五分

6. その女の子 は馬 が、大好き です。
   女の子　　うま　　だいすき

7. あの人は先生 じゃありません。大学院生 です。
   せんせい　　　だいがくいんせい

8. 母が病気 で入院 していますから、毎日病院 に行きます。
   びょうき　にゅういん　　　　びょういん

9. 村 には学校 が二つ あります。
   むら　　がっこう　　二つ

Ⅰ　1から4は何ですか。下の ☐ から選びましょう。
えら

What are 1-4? Choose the answer from the box.

| a. college   b. high school   c. bank   d. elementary school   e. hospital   f. station |

1.　　　　　　　　2.　　　　　　　　3.　　　　　　　　4.

市民病院 　　小学校 　　銀行 　　大学

(e)　　　　　(d)　　　　　(c)　　　　　(a)

Ⅱ　どこに着きますか。日本語で書きましょう。
つ　　　　　　　ご　か

Read the following directions and write the places in Japanese.

Example : 駅の西口から五分です。 ➡ _____病院_____

1.　駅の北口を出て、まっすぐ十分行きます。　　　➡ 会社_____

2.　駅の南口を出て、五分行きます。　　　　　　　➡ 高校_____

3.　駅の東口を出て、十五分行きます。小学校の前です。➡ 店_____

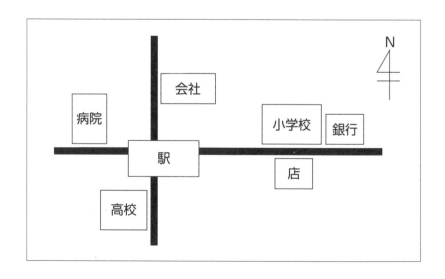

I 漢字を練習しましょう。　Practice the following kanji.

休	休	休				買	買	買			
走	走	走				売	売	売			
起	起	起				読	読	読			
貝	貝	貝				書	書	書			

II 単語の読み方を書いて、文を読みましょう。
Write the readings of the words and read the sentences.

Word	Reading	Meaning	Example Sentence
休む	やすむ	to rest; to be absent	病気で学校を休みました。
休み	やすみ	holiday; absence	土曜日は学校が休みです。
走る	はしる	to run	駅まで走ります。
起きる	おきる	to get up	毎日七時に起きます。
起こす	おこす	to wake someone up	明日は早く起こしてください。
貝	かい	shellfish	きれいな貝を見つけました。
買う	かう	to buy	駅で新聞を買いました。
売る	うる	to sell	古い車を売ります。
読む	よみ	to read	十時まで本を読みました。
書く	かく	to write	今週レポートを書きます。

Ⅲ ひらがなを漢字に、漢字をひらがなにかえましょう。

Rewrite the *hiragana* with an appropriate mix of kanji and *hiragana*.
Rewrite the kanji with *hiragana*.

1. ＿＿＿＿＿の日も＿＿＿＿＿＿＿＿＿＿＿＿。
　　やすみ　　　　　はやく　　　　おきます

2. その＿＿＿＿＿＿＿＿＿＿＿を＿＿＿＿＿＿ください。
　　　　大きい　　　　　かい　　　　みせて

3. コンビニで＿＿＿＿を＿＿＿＿＿＿＿＿＿。
　　　　　　　水　　　　かいました

4. ＿＿＿＿の＿＿＿で＿＿＿＿＿＿を＿＿＿＿＿。
　　でんしゃ　　なか　　　　新聞　　　　よみます

5. ＿＿＿＿は＿＿＿＿＿＿＿に＿＿＿＿＿ください。
　　あした　　　　六時半　　　　おこして

6. ＿＿＿＿の＿＿＿＿＿＿＿は、＿＿＿＿＿を＿＿＿＿＿＿。
　せんしゅう　　すいようび　　　　学校　　　やすみました

7. あの＿＿＿で、＿＿＿＿を＿＿＿＿＿＿います。
　　　みせ　　　　米　　　　うって

8. ＿＿＿、＿＿＿＿＿に手紙を＿＿＿＿＿。
　　まいとし　　ちちのひ　　てがみ　　かきます

9. ＿＿＿、＿＿＿＿＿に三十分＿＿＿＿＿。
　　まいにち　　ごぜんちゅう　　　　はしります

10. りんごは＿＿＿＿＿で＿＿＿＿＿です。
　　　　　　五つ　　　ろっぴゃくえん

11. ＿＿＿＿は＿＿＿＿が＿＿＿＿＿＿です。
　　今月　　　雨　　　すくない

気

Ⅰ　漢字を練習しましょう。　Practice the following kanji.
かん　じ　　れんしゅう

勉

持

勉

帰	帰	帰	帰	帰		強	強	強		
勉	勉	勉				持	持	持		
弓	弓	弓				名	名	名		
虫	虫	虫				語	語	語		

Ⅱ　単語の読み方を書いて、文を読みましょう。
たん　ご　　よ　かた　か　　　　ぶん　よ

　Write the readings of the words and read the sentences.

Word	Reading	Meaning	Example Sentence
帰る	かえる	to return	父はいつも七時に帰ります。
虫	むし	insect	山にいろいろな虫がいます。 やま
強い	つよい	strong	今日は風が強いです。 かぜ
勉強する	べんきょうする	to study	毎日一時間勉強します。
持つ	もつ	to hold	今、一万円持っています。
お金持ち	おかねもち	rich person	あの社長はお金持ちです。
気持ち	きもち	feeling	いい天気で気持ちがいいです。 てんき
名前	なまえ	name	あの人の名前は田中です。
日本語	にほんご	Japanese language	日本語を少し話します。
中国語	ちゅうごくご	Chinese language	中国語を勉強したいです。

Ⅲ ひらがなを漢字に、漢字をひらがなにかえましょう。

Rewrite the *hiragana* with an appropriate mix of kanji and *hiragana*.
Rewrite the kanji with *hiragana*.

1. ＿＿＿＿して＿＿＿＿の辞書を＿＿＿＿。
   にゅうがく　　ちゅうごくご　　　　じしょ　　かいました

2. たくさん＿＿＿がいて＿＿＿＿が悪くなりました。
   　　　　　　むし　　　　　　きもち　　　　　わる

3. ＿＿＿＿から、＿＿＿＿の＿＿＿＿で＿＿＿＿します。
   今年　　　　がいこく　　だいがくいん　　べんきょう

4. その＿＿＿＿の＿＿＿＿はひろしです。
   　　おとこのこ　　　なまえ

5. ＿＿＿＿は＿＿＿＿＿＿＿に＿＿＿＿。
   友だち　　　去年　　　くに　　かえりました

6. あの＿＿＿は、＿＿＿が＿＿＿です。
   　　がくせい　　ちから　　つよい

7. ＿＿＿は＿＿＿で、たくさん＿＿＿を＿＿＿います。
   しゃちょう　おかねもち　　　　　　車　　もって

8. この＿＿＿に＿＿＿の先生が＿＿＿います。
   　　がっこう　　にほんご　　　　三人

9. ＿＿＿＿はもう＿＿＿です。
   だいがくせい　　おとな

10. ＿＿＿＿＿＿＿ごろ、外はもう＿＿＿です。
    ごぜん　　ろくじ　　　　　　あかるい

11. ここに＿＿＿を＿＿＿ください。
    　　おかね　　入れて

Ⅰ 下の漢字を使って、あなたの明日のスケジュールを書きましょう。
　　かんじ つか　　　　　　　　　　　　　　　　　　　　　　　か

Make your schedule for tomorrow using kanji below.

食 行 飲 会 聞 話 休 走 買 読 書 帰 勉強 起

Example : ___3___ 時 _____本を読む_____

___7___ 時 起る。　　　　　　　　___12:25___ 時 イ木すむ
___8___ 時 あさごはんを食。　　　___そ3:50___ 時 スポーツ行をます
___8:45___ 時 学校を行をます。　　___26:15___ 時 うちを帰ります
___8:55___ 時 生青は聞をます。　　___～8:00___ 時 ばんごはんを食べ

Ⅱ アンさんの日記

十月八日（土）　雨

　今日は休みだったので、九時ごろ起きた。朝ご飯を食べて、新聞を読んだ。あ
　　　　　　　　　　　　　　　　　　　　　　あさ　はん　　　　しんぶん
まりおもしろいニュースはなかった。その後、雨が降っていたが、三十分走った。
　　　　　　　　　　　　　　　　　　　　　ふ
学校の前で日本語の先生に会って、少し話した。先生は「来週テストがある」と
言っていた。日本語のクラスはテストが多くて大変だ。家に帰って、二時間ぐら
　　　　　　　　　　　　　　　　　　　たいへん　いえ
い新しい漢字を勉強した。
　　　　かんじ

　午後、本屋でまんがを買った。千円だった。日本のまんがはとてもおもしろい。
　　　　ほんや
店でコーヒーを飲んで、そのまんがを読んだ。この店のコーヒーは少し高いが、
おいしい。ケーキも食べた。五時ごろ帰って、国の友だちに手紙を書いた。
　　　　　　　　　　　　　　　　　　　　　　　　　　　てがみ

質問に答えましょう。　Answer the questions in Japanese.
しつもん こた

1.　この日の天気はどうでしたか。あついです。
　　　　　てんき

2.　アンさんは新聞を読んで、その後、何をしましたか。

3.　どこで先生に会いましたか。

4.　先生に会ってから、家で何をしましたか。先生です
　　　　　　　　　　いえ

5.　本屋で何をしましたか。はい
　　ほんや

Ⅰ　漢字を練習しましょう。　Practice the following kanji.

春	春	春			朝	朝	朝			
夏	夏	夏			昼	昼	昼			
秋	秋	秋			夕	夕	夕			
冬	冬	冬			方	方	方			

Ⅱ　単語の読み方を書いて、文を読みましょう。
Write the readings of the words and read the sentences.

Word	Reading	Meaning	Example Sentence
春	はる	spring	春が好きです。
春休み	はるやすみ	spring vacation	春休みは来週からです。
夏	なつ	summer	今年の夏は暑いです。
夏休み	なつやすみ	summer vacation	夏休みになりました。
秋	あき	autumn; fall	日本の秋はきれいです。
冬	ふゆ	winter	ここの冬は寒いです。
冬休み	ふゆやすみ	winter vacation	冬休みにスキーに行きます。
朝	あさ	morning	朝、新聞を読みます。
毎朝	まいあさ	every morning	毎朝、八時に起きます。
今朝	けさ	this morning	今朝、駅で先生に会いました。
昼	ひる	noon; daytime	今、昼の一時です。
昼間	ひるま	daytime	昼間は暖かいです。
昼休み	ひるやすみ	lunch break	昼休みは一時間です。
〜方	かた	way of …ing	この字の読み方は何ですか。
夕方	ゆうがた	early evening	夕方、出かけます。

Ⅲ ひらがなを漢字に、漢字をひらがなにかえましょう。
かんじ　　　　　　かんじ

Rewrite the *hiragana* with an appropriate mix of kanji and *hiragana*.
Rewrite the kanji with *hiragana*.

1. <u>いち</u> には <u>四つ</u> の季節があります。
　　一年　　　　　　よっつ　　　　きせつ

　<u>春</u> と <u>夏</u> と <u>秋</u> と <u>冬</u> です。
　はる　　　なつ　　　あき　　　ふゆ

2. <u>今朝</u> は <u>早く</u> <u>起きました</u> 。
　けさ　　　はやく　　おきました

3. <u>毎朝</u>、<u>日本語</u> の本を <u>読みます</u> 。
　まいあさ　　にほんご　　　　よみます

4. <u>夏休み</u> は、<u>春休み</u> や <u>冬休み</u> より
　なつやすみ　　　はるやすみ　　　ふゆやすみ

　<u>ながい</u> です。
　　長い

5. <u>朝</u> と <u>昼間</u> は人が <u>多かった</u> ですが、
　あさ　　ひるま　　　　おおかった

　<u>夕方</u> には <u>少なく</u> なりました。
　ゆうがた　　　すくなく

6. <u>昼休み</u> は <u>じゅうにじ</u> から <u>一時間</u> です。
　ひるやすみ　　　十二時　　　　いちじかん

7. この漢字の <u>読み方</u> が分からないので、先生に <u>聞きます</u> 。
　　かんじ　　よみかた　　　　　　　　　　　　ききます

8. <u>きんようび</u> の <u>昼</u> 、
　　金曜日　　　　ひる

　<u>車</u> で <u>ぎんこう</u> へ行きます。
　くるま　　　銀行

Ⅰ 漢字を練習しましょう。　Practice the following kanji.

晩	晩	晩				足	足	足			
夜	夜	夜				体	体	体			
心	心	心				首	首	首			
手	手	手				道	道	道			

Ⅱ 単語の読み方を書いて、文を読みましょう。
Write the readings of the words and read the sentences.

Word	Reading	Meaning	Example Sentence
晩	ばん	night	きのうの晩、雨が降りました。
今晩	こんばん	tonight	今晩、レポートを書きます。
毎晩	まいばん	every night	毎晩八時ごろ、帰ります。
夜	よる	night	夜、父から電話がありました。
今夜	こんや	tonight	今夜は月がきれいです。
夜中	よなか	midnight; middle of the night	たいてい夜中まで勉強します。
心	こころ	heart	彼は心が広い人です。
安心する	あんしんする	to be relieved	彼が元気なので安心しました。
手	て	hand	手が冷たいです。
下手な	へた	poor at	歌が下手です。
上手な	じょうず	good at	日本語が上手になりたいです。
足	あし	foot; leg	田中さんは足が大きいです。
足りる	たりる	to be sufficient	お金が足りません。
足す	たす	to add	お風呂に水を足してください。
体	からだ	body	母は体が小さいです。

首	くび	neck	今朝から首が痛いです。
道	みち	road	この道は広いです。

Ⅲ ひらがなを漢字に、漢字をひらがなにかえましょう。

Rewrite the *hiragana* with an appropriate mix of kanji and *hiragana*.
Rewrite the kanji with *hiragana*.

1. 今晩＿＿＿、中学校＿＿＿の友だちに合います＿＿＿。
   こんばん　　ちゅうがっこう　　　　　　あいます

2. 夜中＿＿＿にちち＿＿＿から話電＿＿＿がありました。
   よなか　　　父　　　でんわ

3. 今夜＿＿＿、外＿＿＿で食べる＿＿＿つもりです。
   こんや　　そと　　たべる

4. きのうの晩＿＿＿運動したので、手＿＿＿と足＿＿＿と
   ばん　うんどう　　　　て　　　あし

   首＿＿＿が痛くなりました。
   くび　　いた

5. 日本語が下手＿＿＿なので上手＿＿＿になりたいです。
   へた　　　じょうず

6. 東さんのお父さん＿＿＿は、心＿＿＿がひろい＿＿＿人です。
   ひがし　おとうさん　　こころ　　広い

7. 塩が足りない＿＿＿ので、スープに塩を足す＿＿＿ください。
   しお　たりない　　　　しお　　たして

8. 夜＿＿＿、子供がかえって＿＿＿きて、安心する＿＿＿しました。
   よる　こども　帰って　　あんしん

9. 毎晩＿＿＿、この道＿＿＿を走ります＿＿＿。
   まいばん　　みち　　　はしります

10. 休＿＿＿に気＿＿＿をつけてください。
    からだ　　気

46　第9課(2)

Ⓘ 漢字の中でグループに入らないものを一つ選びましょう。
かんじ えら
Choose one kanji which does not belong to the others.

1.（ 首 （道） 足 手 体 ）　　2.（ 夜 朝 昼 （今） 晩 ）

3.（ 冬 （夕） 秋 夏 春 ）　　4.（ （馬） 町 村 市 国 ）

Ⓘ さくらちゃんの一日

さくらちゃんの一日	さくらちゃんの小学校の一年	

　　南さくらちゃん（七歳）は小学校の二
　　　　　　　　　さい
年生です。とても元気な女の子です。さ
くらちゃんは毎朝六時半に起きて、朝ご
飯を食べます。近所の友だちといっしょ
はん　　　　　きんじょ
に、歩いて学校へ行きます。学校までの
　　ある
道は車が多いので気をつけて歩きます。
　　　　　　　　　　　　　ある

さくらちゃんの小学校の一年		
春	四月	新しい学年になる がくねん
夏	七〜八月	夏休み（五週間）
秋	十月	運動会 うんどうかい
冬 （春）	十二〜一月 三〜四月	冬休み（二週間） 春休み（二週間）

クラスは八時半に始まります。十二時に教室で昼ご飯を食べます。昼休みに友だ
　　　　　　　はじ　　　　　　　　　きょうしつ　　はん
ちと遊んだ後、みんなで教室を掃除します。午後のクラスは三時に終わります。
　　あそ　　　　　きょうしつ　そうじ　　　　　　　　　　　　　お
　　火曜日は早く家に帰って、夕方ピアノのレッスンへ行きます。一年生の時はま
　　　　　　　いえ
だ下手でしたが、少し上手になりました。毎晩、七時ごろ晩ご飯を食べます。夜、
宿題をして、九時半ごろ寝ます。
しゅくだい　　　　　　　ね

近所　neighborhood　　学年　school year　　運動会　sports day
きんじょ　　　　　　　がくねん　　　　　　うんどうかい

正しいものには○、正しくないものには×を書きましょう。
ただ　　　　　　ただ　　　　　　　　か
Mark ○ if the statements are true. Mark × if not true.

1.（ ○ ）さくらちゃんは毎朝六時半に起きます。

2.（ ○ ）さくらちゃんは一人で学校へ行きます。

3.（ × ）さくらちゃんは木曜日にピアノのレッスンへ行きます。

4.（ ○ ）さくらちゃんは五週間の夏休みがあります。

Ⅰ 漢字を練習しましょう。 Practice the following kanji.
かんじ　れんしゅう

山	山	山				空	空	空			
川	川	川				海	海	海			
林	林	林				化	化	化			
森	森	森				花	花	花			

Ⅱ 単語の読み方を書いて、文を読みましょう。
たんご　よ　かた　か　　ぶん　よ
Write the readings of the words and read the sentences.

Word	Reading	Meaning	Example Sentence
山	やま	mountain	日本には山がたくさんあります。
山道	やまみち	mountain road	この山道を行きましょう。
山田さん	やまだ	Mr./Ms. Yamada	山田さんは元気です。
川	かわ	river	川の水を飲みました。
小川さん	おがわ	Mr./Ms. Ogawa	小川さんは外国で生まれました。
林	はやし	small forest; grove	お寺の前に林があります。
森	もり	forest	男の子が一人で森に入りました。
森田さん	もりた	Mr./Ms. Morita	森田さんは入院しました。
空	そら	sky	空がとても青いです。あお
空気	くうき	air	空気がきれいです。
海	うみ	sea	海で泳ぎましょう。およ
北海道	ほっかいだ	Hokkaido	北海道は北にあります。
化学	かがく	chemistry	化学のクラスが好きです。
花	はな	flower	きれいな花を一本買いました。
花見	はなみ	flower viewing	先週、花見をしました。

Ⅲ ひらがなを漢字に、漢字をひらがなにかえましょう。

Rewrite the *hiragana* with an appropriate mix of kanji and *hiragana*.
Rewrite the kanji with *hiragana*.

1. 日本には＿＿＿山＿＿＿と＿＿＿川＿＿＿がたくさんあります。
　　　　　　　　やま　　　　　かわ

2. ＿＿どようび＿＿に＿＿＿山田＿＿さんと＿＿森田＿＿さんと
　　　　土曜日　　　　　　やまだ　　　　　　もりた

　＿＿＿小川＿＿さんが＿＿く来ました＿＿＿。
　　　　おがわ　　　　　　　　来ました

3. この＿＿虫＿＿は＿＿＿森＿＿や＿＿＿林＿＿にいます。
　　　　　むし　　　　もり　　　　　はやし

4. ＿＿＿空＿＿と＿＿海＿＿はきれいで、＿＿＿空気＿＿もおいしいです。
　　　　そら　　　うみ　　　　　　　　　くうき

5. ＿＿夏休み＿＿、＿＿＿北海道＿＿へ行って、＿＿うま＿＿に乗りました。
　　　なつやすみ　　　　　ほっかいどう　　　　　　馬　　　　の

6. ＿＿高校＿＿で＿＿化学＿＿を＿＿勉強＿＿しました。
　　　こうこう　　　　かがく　　　　べんきょう

7. ＿＿ははのひ＿＿に＿＿花＿＿をあげました。
　　　母の日　　　　　はな

8. ＿＿会衆＿＿、＿＿会社＿＿の人と＿＿花見＿＿をします。
　　らいしゅう　　　かいしゃ　　　　　はなみ

9. この＿＿山道＿＿は狭いので、＿＿気＿＿をつけてください。
　　　　やまみち　　　せま　　　　　き

Ⅰ 漢字を練習しましょう。　Practice the following kanji.
かんじ　れんしゅう

天	天	天	天	天	天	黒	黒	黒	黒	黒	黒
赤	赤	赤	赤	赤	赤	色	色	色	色	色	色
青	青	青	青	青	青	魚	魚	魚	魚	魚	魚
白	白	白	白	白	白	犬	犬	犬	犬	犬	犬

Ⅱ 単語の読み方を書いて、文を読みましょう。
たんご　よ　かた　か　　　　ぶん　よ
Write the readings of the words and read the sentences.

Word	Reading	Meaning	Example Sentence
天気	てんき	weather	いい天気なので、出かけます。
赤	あか	red	赤ワインをよく飲みます。
赤い	あかい	red	私の電話は赤いです。
赤ちゃん	あかちゃん	baby	赤ちゃんが泣いています。
青	あお	blue	青が好きです。
青い	あおい	blue	青い海が見えます。
青空	あおぞら	blue sky	今日はきれいな青空です。
白	しろ	white	赤と白のかさを持っています。
白い	しろい	white	白い花を買いました。
黒	くろ	black	黒が好きです。
黒い	くろい	black	黒い車を持っています。
色	いろ	color	どんな色が好きですか。
魚	さかな	fish	この店の魚はおいしいです。
犬	いぬ	dog	犬を飼っています。
子犬	こいぬ	puppy	その子犬はとても小さいです。

Ⅲ ひらがなを漢字に、漢字をひらがなにかえましょう。

Rewrite the *hiragana* with an appropriate mix of kanji and *hiragana*.
Rewrite the kanji with *hiragana*.

1. ___火曜日___ はいい ___天気___ で、きれいな ___青空___ でした。
  かようび　　　　　　てんき　　　　　　　　　　　あおぞら

2. ___赤ちゃん___ が ___病気___ になりました。
  あかちゃん　　　　びょうき

3. ___南___ の島の ___うみ___ には ___赤___ や ___青___ の ___魚___ がいます。
  みなみ　　しま　海　　　　あか　　　あお　　　さかな

4. ___色___ の中で ___白___ と ___黒___ が ___好き___ です。
  いろ　　　　　しろ　　　くろ　　　　すき

5. この ___黒い___ ___犬___ の ___名前___ はポチです。
  くろい　　　いぬ　　なまえ

6. ___赤い___ シャツを着ている人が ___山田___ さん、
  あかい　　　　　　　　き　　　　　　　山田

  ___青い___ スカーフをしている人が ___小川___ さんです。
  あおい　　　　　　　　　　　　　　　小川

7. ___二週間___ 前、 ___子犬___ が ___生まれました___ 。
  にしゅうかん　　　　こいぬ　　　うまれました

8. ___山道___ で ___白い___ ___花___ を見つけました。
  やまみち　　　しろい　　　はな

9. ___入口___ は ___北___ にあります。
  いりぐち　　きた

Ⅰ 下の国の国旗の色をぬりましょう。 Color in the pictures of the national flags.
こっ き

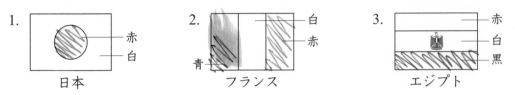

1. ── 赤
   ── 白
   日本

2. ── 白
   ── 赤
   青
   フランス

3. ── 赤
   ── 白
   ── 黒
   エジプト

Ⅱ 北海道

　　北海道はぼくの一番好きな所です。東京から北海道の札幌まで飛行機で二時間
　　　　　　　　　いちばん　　　ところ　　　とうきょう　　　　　　　さっぽろ　　ひこうき
ぐらいです。北海道は大きくて道も広いので、レンタカーを借りたほうがいいで
　　　　　　　　　　　　　　　　　　　　　　　　　　か
す。北海道には森や林や湖など自然がたくさんあります。空気もとてもきれいで
　　　　　　　　　　　みずうみ　しぜん
す。また、アイヌの村があって、アイヌの文化について知ることができます。
　　　　　　　　　　　　　　　　　　　　ぶんか　　し
　　夏は暑くなくて、たいてい天気がいいので、旅行にいい季節です。きれいな花
　　あつ　　　　　　　　　　　　　　　　　りょこう　　きせつ
を見ることができます。冬は長いです。雪がたくさん降るので、スキーやスノー
　　　　　　　　　　　　　　　　　　　　　　ふ
ボードができます。二月に札幌では雪祭りがあります。このお祭りはとても有名
　　　　　　　　　さっぽろ　　ゆきまつ　　　　　　まつ　　　　　ゆうめい
で、毎年たくさんの人が見に来ます。また、冬にはおいしい魚が食べられます。
　まいねん

湖　lake　　　自然　nature　　　また　also　　　アイヌ　an ethnic group indigenous to Hokkaido
みずうみ　　　し ぜん
文化　culture　　季節　season　　　祭り　festival
ぶん か　　　　き せつ　　　　　　　まつ

質問に答えましょう。 Answer the questions in Japanese.
しつもん　こた

1. 東京から札幌まで飛行機でどのぐらいかかりますか。
　 とうきょう　さっぽろ　　ひ こう き

2. どうして北海道ではレンタカーを借りたほうがいいですか。
　　　　　　　　　　　　　　　　か

3. 北海道にはどんな自然がありますか。
　　　　　　　　　し ぜん

4. 北海道の夏はどんな天気ですか。

5. いつ有名なお祭りがありますか。
　　ゆう めい　　まつ

Part 2

第11課 — 第20課
（漢字番号 161-320）

Ⅰ 漢字を練習しましょう。

料	料	料				牛	牛	牛		
理	理	理				豚	豚	豚		
反	反	反				鳥	鳥	鳥		
飯	飯	飯				肉	肉	肉		

Ⅱ 単語の読み方を書いて、文を読みましょう。

単　語	読み方	意　味	例　文
料理	りょうり	cooking; dish	母の料理が食べたいです。
ご飯	ごはん	cooked rice; meal	今晩、山田さんとご飯を食べます。
朝ご飯	あさごはん	breakfast	毎朝、八時に朝ご飯を食べます。
昼ご飯	おひるごはん	lunch	大学で昼ご飯を食べました。
晩ご飯	ばんごはん	dinner	今日の晩ご飯は魚です。
牛	うし	cow; bull	北海道に牛がたくさんいます。
豚	ぶた	pig	あの豚は大きいです。
鳥	とり	bird	森で赤い鳥を見ました。
小鳥	ことり	little bird	小鳥はかわいいです。
肉	にく	meat	日本の肉は高いです。
牛肉	ぎゅうにく	beef	牛肉が好きです。
豚肉	ぶたにく	pork	豚肉はあまり食べません。
鳥肉	とりにく	chicken	あの店で鳥肉を買います。

とり

Ⅲ ひらがなを漢字に、漢字をひらがなにかえましょう。
かんじ　　　かんじ

1. おじさんの家には＿＿＿＿＿と＿＿＿＿＿と＿＿＿＿＿がいます。
   いえ　　　　　うし　　　　　ぶた　　　　　うま

2. 私の家には＿＿＿＿＿と＿＿＿＿＿がいます。
   わたし　いえ　　　とり　　　　いぬ

3. ＿＿＿＿＿、＿＿＿＿＿さんと＿＿＿＿＿を＿＿＿＿＿。
   今週　　　　もりた　　　　ひるごはん　　　たべました

4. あの＿＿＿＿＿で＿＿＿＿＿と＿＿＿＿＿を＿＿＿＿＿います。
   店　　　とりにく　　　ぎゅうにく　　　うって

5. ＿＿＿＿＿に、スープを＿＿＿＿＿。
   あさごはん　　　　　　　　のみました

6. ＿＿＿＿＿を＿＿＿＿＿、＿＿＿＿＿しました。
   にく　　　　かって　　　りょうり

7. ＿＿＿＿＿、＿＿＿＿＿の声が＿＿＿＿＿。
   朝　　　　ことり　　こえ　　　きこえます

8. 私は＿＿＿＿＿が＿＿＿＿＿じゃありません。
   わたし　ぶたにく　　好き

9. ＿＿＿＿＿は＿＿＿＿＿からなので、早く＿＿＿＿＿。
   ばんごはん　　しちじはん　　　　　はや　　かえります

10. ＿＿＿＿＿の＿＿＿＿＿はおいしくなかったです。
    びょういん　ごはん

11. ＿＿＿＿＿がいい日は、＿＿＿＿＿で＿＿＿＿＿を釣ります。
    てんき　　　　　かわ　　　魚　　　　っ

Ⅰ 漢字を練習しましょう。

茶	茶	茶				切	切	切			
予	予	予				作	作	作			
野	野	野				未	未	未			
菜	菜	菜				味	味	味			

Ⅱ 単語の読み方を書いて、文を読みましょう。

単　語	読み方	意　味	例　文
お茶	おちゃ	Japanese tea	父は毎日お茶を飲みます。
茶色	ちゃいろ	brown	茶色のジャケットを買いました。
長野	ながの	Nagano	長野は山が多いです。
野菜	やさい	vegetable	野菜は体にいいです。
切る	きる	to cut	肉と野菜を切ってください。
切手	きって	postage stamp	切手を三枚ください。
大切な	たいせつ	precious	小川さんは大切な友だちです。
作る	つくる	to make	晩ご飯を作りました。
手作り	てづくり	handmade	これは手作りのケーキです。
未来	みらい	future	この国の未来は明るいです。
味	あじ	taste	この料理は味がうすいです。

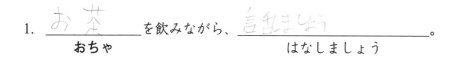

Ⅲ ひらがなを漢字に、漢字をひらがなにかえましょう。
　　　かんじ　　　かんじ

1. ___お茶___ を飲みながら、___話しましょう___。
　　　おちゃ　　　　　　　　　　　はなしましょう

2. ___長野___ の ___冬___ は寒いです。
　　　ながの　　　　ふゆ　　　さむ

3. ___茶色___ のくつと ___白い___ シャツを買いました。
　　　ちゃいろ　　　　　　しろい

4. ___野菜___ を ___切手___、サラダを ___作りました___。
　　　やさい　　　　きって　　　　　　　　つくりました

5. この ___りょうり___ は ___味___ がありません。
　　　　　料理　　　　　あじ

6. 郵便局で ___切手___ を買って、手紙を ___出しました___。
　　ゆうびんきょく　きって　　　　　　てがみ　　　出しました

7. ___大切___ な人に ___手作り___ のチョコレートをあげます。
　　　たいせつ　　　　てづくり

8. ___未来___ には、___何___ があるでしょうか。
　　　みらい　　　　なに

9. ___森___ へ行って、___長い___ ___山道___ を歩きました。
　　　森　　　　　　ながい　　　山道　　　ある

10. ___黒い___ ジーンズは ___高かった___ ので、買いませんでした。
　　　くろい　　　　　　　　たかかった

11. ___今晩___ は ___月___ が ___見えません___。
　　　こんばん　　　つき　　　みえません

Ⅰ 下の漢字でこの課の漢字を作りましょう。

Which new kanji from this lesson includes the following kanji?

例. 未 → 味

1. 予 → 野
2. 反 → 坂
3. 月 → 作
4. 米 → 菜
5. 刀 → 切

Ⅱ 季節の料理

　日本には四つの季節があり、その季節に食べる料理があります。春は山菜を食べます。山菜は、山などにある草で、天ぷらなどにして、食べます。夏は暑くて、元気がなくなります。そんな時はうなぎを食べます。昔から、うなぎを食べると力が出ると言います。うなぎは、ご飯の上にのせて食べます。また、夏は、冷たい料理をよく食べます。そうめんはその一つです。そうめんは白い麺で、つゆにつけて食べます。秋はまつたけがおいしいです。まつたけはとても高くて、一本五千円くらいです。冬には温かいなべ料理を食べます。鳥肉や豚肉などの肉や魚、野菜やとうふを切って、大きいなべの中に入れて煮ます。そのなべから好きな物を小さい皿に取って食べます。晩ご飯に家族や友だちといっしょに食べると楽しいです。

山菜	wild plants	草	grass	うなぎ	eel	のせる	to put on	麺	noodle
つゆ	sauce for noodle		つける	to dip		まつたけ	pine mushroom	なべ	pan
煮る	to simmer								

1〜4の食べ物の名前を【　】から選んで、表に季節を書きましょう。

Choose the names of the food 1 to 4 and write their seasons in the table.

【　山菜　・　そうめん　・　まつたけ　・　なべ料理　】

	1.	2.	3.	4.
名前				
季節	なつ	ふゆ	あき	はる

（だい）（か）

I 漢字を練習しましょう。
（かんじ）（れんしゅう）

音	音	音				転	転	転			
楽	楽	楽				乗	乗	乗			
歌	歌	歌				写	写	写			
自	自	自				真	真	真			

II 単語の読み方を書いて、文を読みましょう。
（たんご）（ぶん）

単語	読み方	意味	例文
音	おと	sound 音	音を少し大きくしてください。
音楽	おんがく	music 音楽	車の中で音楽を聞きます。
楽しい	たのしい	enjoyable 楽しい	夏休みは楽しかったです。
楽しみ	たのしみ	fun 楽しみ	春休みが楽しみです。
歌	うた	song 歌	山田さんは歌が上手です。
歌う	うたう	to sing 歌う	日本の歌を歌いました。
歌手	かしゅ	singer 歌手	有名な歌手が町に来ました。
自分	じぶん	oneself 自分	自分のお金で車を買いました。
自転車	じてんしゃ	bicycle 自転車	自転車を持っています。
乗る	のる	to ride 乗	毎日、自転車に乗ります。
写す	うつす	to copy 写	友だちのノートを写しました。
写真	しゃしん	photograph 写真	お寺の前で写真を撮りました。
真ん中	まんなか	center	町の真ん中にタワーがあります。

（たんご）（い み）（れいぶん）

Ⅲ ひらがなを漢字に、漢字をひらがなにかえましょう。

1. <u>歌</u>が<u>大好き</u>なので、<u>歌手</u>になりたいです。
うた　　だいすき　　　　　　かしゅ

2. <u>らいしゅう</u>の<u>花見</u>が<u>楽しみ</u>です。
来週　　　　　　はなみ　　たのしみ

3. <u>大きい</u>声で<u>歌い</u>ましょう。
おおきい　　こえ　うたい

4. <u>楽しい</u><u>音楽</u>を<u>聞きたい</u>です。
たのしい　おんがく　ききたい

5. 大きい<u>音</u>で<u>よなか</u>に<u>起きました</u>。
おと　　夜中　　おきました

6. <u>ほっかいどう</u>で、<u>写真</u>をたくさん撮りました。
北海道　　　　　しゃしん　　　　　と

7. <u>休み</u>の日は、よく<u>自転車</u>で<u>出かけます</u>。
やすみ　　　　　じてんしゃ　でかけます

8. バスに<u>乗って</u>、<u>山</u>へ行きます。
のって　　やま

9. <u>小学校</u>は<u>まち</u>の<u>真ん中</u>にあります。
しょうがっこう　町　　まんなか

10. 友だちの宿題を<u>写さない</u>で、<u>自分</u>でしてください。
しゅくだい　うつさない　　　じぶん

11. もっと<u>水</u>を<u>足して</u>ください。
みず　　たして

Ⅰ 漢字を練習しましょう。

台	台	台			羊	羊	羊		
央	央	央			洋	洋	洋		
映	映	映			服	服	服		
画	画	画			着	着	着		

Ⅱ 単語の読み方を書いて、文を読みましょう。

単 語	読み方	意 味	例 文
～台	たい/だい	counter for machines	家にパソコンが三台あります。
映画	えいが	movie	きのうの夜、古い映画を見ました。
羊	ひつじ	sheep	あそこに黒い羊がいます。
服	ふく	clothes	あの店で服を売っています。
洋服	ようふく	Western clothes	洋服をたくさん持っています。
着る	きる	to wear	森さんは青いシャツを着ています。
上着	うわぎ	jacket	茶色の上着を持って行きます。
下着	したぎ	underwear	新しい下着を買いました。
着く	つく	to arrive	十時に長野に着きます。

Ⅲ ひらがなを漢字に、漢字をひらがなにかえましょう。

1. 白転車 を 二台 持 います。
   じてんしゃ　　　　にだい　　　　もって

2. 大学 で、中学 の 映画 を見ました。
   だいがく　　　ちゅうごく　　えいが

3. 羊 の 肉 で 料理 を 着くりました。
   ひつじ　　　肉　　　料理　　　　つくりました

4. あの 洋着 は はちちえん です。
   ようふく　　　八千円

5. 新じ 上着 はちょっと 小が です。
   あたらしい　うわぎ　　　　　　ちいさい

6. はは は 下着 の 会社 に勤めています。
   母　　　したぎ　　　かいしゃ　　つと

7. その 歌手 は八時に東京に 着きます。
   かしゅ　　　　　　とうきょう　　つきます

8. 女の子 は 赤 服 を 着て います。
   おんなのこ　　あかい　　ふく　　きて

9. 雨 だったので、本 を 読んで 、 おんがく を聞きました。
   あめ　　　　　　ほん　　よんで　　　おんがく

10. せいもう 、 しゃちょう は 入院 しました。
    先月　　　　　　社長　　　　にゅういん

11. 赤ちゃん が げんき で 安心 しました。
    あかちゃん　　元気　　　あんしん

① 下の言葉を漢字で書いて、文を作りましょう。
ことば かんじ ぶん つく

Write the following words using kanji and complete the sentences.

えいが おんがく うた ふく じてんしゃ やさい

1. ___ふく___ を着ます。 2. ___うた___ を歌います。

3. ___えいが___ を見ます。 4. ___おんがく___ を聞きます。

5. ___じてんしゃ___ に乗ります。 6. ___やさい___ を切ります。

② 日本人の趣味
しゅ み

「あなたの趣味は何ですか」——この質問を日本人の20代の男女452人に聞き
しゅ み しつもん だい
ました。趣味は「映画を見ること」という人は184人で、一番多かったです。「本
しゅ み いちばん
を読むこと」という人は177人、「音楽を聞くこと」という人は173人でした。
「買い物」は164人で「旅行」より多かったです。趣味が「ネットサーフィン」とい
か もの りょこう しゅ み
う人は「パソコン」という人より少し多かったです。「ドライブ」と「寝ること」
ね
と「おしゃべり」の中では、「おしゃべり」が一番人気がありました。
いちばんにん き
これから始めたい趣味も聞きました。一番多かった趣味は「スポーツ」、二番
はじ しゅ み いちばん しゅ み にばん
目は「料理」、三番目は「スキューバダイビング」でした。
め りょうり さんばんめ

おしゃべり chat 人気がある popular
にん き

(参考：コブスオンライン
きんこう
http://cobs.jp/com/20report/bn/031119/index.html)

下の表を完成させましょう。 Complete the rankings below.
ひょう かんせい

A. あなたの趣味は何ですか。 しゅ み		B. これから始めたい趣味は 何ですか。 はじ しゅ み
1. 映画を見ること	6. ネットサーフィン	1. スポーツ
2. 本をよむこと	7. パソコン	2. りょうり
3. 音楽をきくこと	8. ドライブ	3. スキューバダイビング
4. かじもの	9. 寝ること ね	
5. 旅行 りょこう	10. おんがくづくり	

Ⅰ 漢字を練習しましょう。

家	家	家			兄	兄	兄		
矢	矢	矢			姉	姉	姉		
族	族	族			弟	弟	弟		
親	親	親			妹	妹	妹		

Ⅱ 単語の読み方を書いて、文を読みましょう。

単 語	読み方	意 味	例 文
家	いえ	house	家は駅の近くです。
家族	かぞく	family	家族は四人です。
親	おや	parent(s)	親によく電話します。
親切な	しんせつ	kind	親切な人に会いました。
兄	あに	my older brother	兄は銀行員です。
お兄さん	おにいさん	older brother	お兄さんは何歳ですか。
姉	あね	my older sister	姉は大学院生です。
お姉さん	おねえさん	older sister	お姉さんはどこに住んでいますか。
弟	おとうと	younger brother	弟は高校生です。
兄弟	きょうだい	siblings	兄弟が何人いますか。
妹	いもうと	younger sister	妹が一人います。

Ⅲ ひらがなを漢字に、漢字をひらがなにかえましょう。

1. ___弟___は___小学校生___です。
   おとうと　　しょうがくせい

   ___らいねん___、___中学校___へ行きます。
   来年　　　　ちゅうがっこう

2. ___毎年___、___夏___に___家族___と旅行します。
   まいとし　　なつ　　かぞく　　　りょこう

3. A：___兄弟___がいますか。
   きょうだい

   B：はい。___姉___が___ふたり___います。
   あね　　　二人

4. A：___お姉さん___は___大学生___ですか。
   おねえさん　　だいがくせい

   B：いいえ、___大学院生___です。
   だいがくいんせい

5. ___兄___は今___ひとりで___外国___に住んでいます。
   あに　　　一人で　　　がいこく　　　す

6. 子供の時は___毎朝___、___親___に___起こして___もらいました。
   こども　　まいあさ　　おや　　おこして

7. ___たなかさん___の___兄弟さん___はとても___親切___です。
   田中さん　　おにいさん　　　しんせつ

8. これから___家___に___帰って___、___勉強___します。
   いえ　　かえって　　べんきょう

9. 時々、___妹___の___ようふく___を借りて、___着て___います。
   ときどき　いもうと　　洋服　　　か　　きて

Ⅰ 漢字を練習しましょう。

私	私	私			住	住	住		
夫	夫	夫			糸	糸	糸		
妻	妻	妻			氏	氏	氏		
主	主	主			紙	紙	紙		

Ⅱ 単語の読み方を書いて、文を読みましょう。

単 語	読み方	意 味	例 文
私	わたし	I	私は学生です。
夫	おっと	my husband	夫は会社に勤めています。
妻	つま	my wife	妻は出かけています。
主人	しゅじん	my husband	主人は音楽が好きです。
住む	すむ	to live	今、親と住んでいます。
糸	いと	thread	洋服に糸がついています。
氏名	しめい	full name	ここに氏名を書いてください。
紙	かみ	paper	白い紙を買ってきてください。
手紙	てがみ	letter	友だちから手紙が来ました。

Ⅲ ひらがなを漢字に、漢字をひらがなにかえましょう。

1. ___国___の___ともだち___から___てがみ___が___きました___。

2. ___しめい___と___でんわ___番号を___かいて___ください。

3. ___つま___は子供の___ふく___を___てづくり___します。

4. ___おっと___は___うた___とピアノが___じょうず___です。

5. ___しゅじん___と___えいが___を___み___に___いきました___。

6. この___いと___を___切って___ください。

7. ___かみ___とえんぴつを___持って___来てください。

8. ___わたし___は___冬休み___に___長野___でスキーをするつもりです。

9. ___いもうと___は東京に___すんでいて___、___しゃしん___の勉強をしています。

10. ___ごはん___の___うえ___に、___牛肉___をのせて食べました。

11. マフラーをしているので、___みみ___と___首___が暖かいです。

Ⅰ ①～⑨の( )の中に漢字を書きましょう。
かんじ

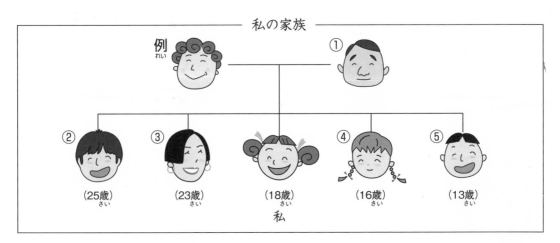

― 私の家族 ―

例
れい

①

②（25歳）
さい

③（23歳）
さい

（18歳）
さい
私

④（16歳）
さい

⑤（13歳）
さい

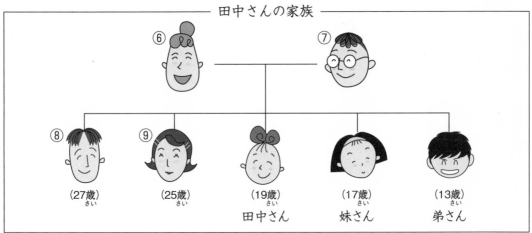

― 田中さんの家族 ―

⑥

⑦

⑧（27歳）
さい

⑨（25歳）
さい

（19歳）
さい
田中さん

（17歳）
さい
妹さん

（13歳）
さい
弟さん

私の家族

例（ 母 ）　①（ 父 ）　②（ 兄 ）
れい

③（ 姉 ）　④（ 妹 ）　⑤（ 弟 ）

田中さんの家族

⑥（ 母 ）　⑦（ 父 ）　⑧（ 兄 ）

⑨（ 姉 ）

Ⅱ 対談：ジョンさんとマリアさんが家族について話しています。
たいだん

ジョン：マリアさんはいつ日本に来たんですか。

マリア：三年前です。私の夫は日本人なんです。夫はイタリアの大学でデザインの勉強をしていて、その時に知り合いました。三年前に結婚して、日本に来ました。ジョンさんは日本語がお上手ですが、日本に長く住んでいるんですか。

ジョン：私は日本に来て、もう十年です。私が中学校の一年生の時、日本に来ました。

マリア：ご家族で日本に来たんですか。

ジョン：家では、親と話す時は日本語です。弟と妹がいるんですが、弟と話す時は英語で話しますが、二人とも日本に来た時はまだ小学生だったので、英語より日本語のほうが上手ですよ。

マリア：そうですか。ご家族は今も日本に住んでいるんですか。

ジョン：ええ。でも、母は去年アメリカに帰りました。この間、母から手紙が来て、人は親切だし、食べ物はおいしいし、日本が懐かしいと言っていましたよ。マリアさんのご家族はイタリアですか。

マリア：はい。両親と兄はミラノに住んでいます。姉はローマです。日本の生活は楽しいですが、時々イタリアに帰りたくなりますね。

対談　conversation　　知り合う　to get acquainted　　懐かしい　longed-for
たいだん　　　　　　　　し　あ　　　　　　　　　　　　　　なつ

質問に答えましょう。
しつもん　こた

1. マリアさんはご主人とどこで知り合いましたか。
し　あ

2. ジョンさんが初めて日本に来た時、何年生でしたか。
はじ

3. 家でジョンさんは何語を話しますか。

4. ジョンさんのお母さんからの手紙に何と書いてありましたか。

5. マリアさんのお兄さんとお姉さんは、どこに住んでいますか。

① 漢字を練習しましょう。

教	教	教	教			字	字	字			
室	室	室				式	式	式			
羽	羽	羽	羽			試	試	試			
習	習	習	習			験	験	験			
漢	漢	漢									

② 単語の読み方を書いて、文を読みましょう。

単　語	読み方	意　味	例　文
教える	おしえる	to teach	中国語を教えてください。
教会	きょうかい	church	日曜日に教会で歌を歌います。
教室	きょうしつ	classroom	化学の教室はここです。
羽	はね	wing; feather	この鳥は羽が大きいです。
習う	ならう	to learn	料理を習っています。
字	じ	character	林さんは字が上手です。
漢字	かんじ	Chinese character	漢字の勉強は楽しいです。
入学式	にゅうがくしき	entrance ceremony	四月三日に入学式があります。
試験	しけん	examination	来週、試験があります。

Ⅲ ひらがなを漢字に、漢字をひらがなにかえましょう。

1. _____ _____は_____です。
　　　あたらしい　　　きょうしつ　　　　ひろい

2. この_____は_____が_____です。
　　　　　鳥　　　　　　はね　　　　　　あおい

3. _____は_____が_____です。
　　　わたし　　　　　じ　　　　　へた

4. 子供の時、_____日曜日に、_____で_____に行きました。
　　こども　　　　毎週　　　　　　　　　かぞく　　きょうかい

5. _____、日本語の_____のクラスで_____があります。
　　あした　　　　　　　　かいわ　　　　　　　　しけん

6. この_____の_____が_____。
　　　　かんじ　　　　　よみかた　　　　　わかりません

7. _____の_____は_____八日です。
　　だいがく　　　にゅうがくしき　　　しがつ　　ようか

8. 日本で、_____と_____を_____。
　　　　お茶　　　　　お花　　　　　ならいました

9. 友だちの_____は_____を_____います。
　　　　おかあさん　　　　ちゅうごくご　　　　おしえて

10. 来年の_____、_____に_____します。
　　　　はる　　　しょうがっこう　　　　入学

11. _____の_____を飼っています。_____散歩に行きます。
　　ちゃいろ　　　いぬ　　　か　　　　ゆうがた　　　さんぽ

Ⅰ 漢字を練習しましょう。

宿	宿	宿				質	質	質		
題	題	題				問	問	問		
文	文	文				説	説	説		
英	英	英								

Ⅱ 単語の読み方を書いて、文を読みましょう。

単　語	読み方	意　味	例　文
宿題	しゅくわだい	homework ✗	今日は漢字の宿題があります。
文学	ぶんがく	literature	専門はロシア文学です。
作文	さくぶん	composition	クラスで作文を書きました。
文化	ぶんか	culture	大学で日本文化を教えています。
英語	えご	English ✗	中学校で英語を習います。
問題	もんたごい	problem; question	日本には多くの問題があります。 この問題の答えは何ですか。
質問	しんぶん	question ✗	先生に質問があります。
説明	せつめい	explanation	英語で説明してください。
小説	しょうせつ	novel	小説を読むのが好きです。

しつもんん

Ⅲ ひらがなを漢字に、漢字をひらがなにかえましょう。

1. よく、外国の＿＿＿＿＿を＿＿＿＿＿＿＿。
    　　　　　　しょうせつ　　　　　かいます

2. ＿＿＿＿＿＿＿＿＿の＿＿＿＿、＿＿＿＿＿をしました。
    　晩ご飯　　　　　　あと　　しゅくだい

3. ＿＿＿＿＿する時は、＿＿＿＿＿、大きい声で＿＿＿＿＿ください。
    　しつもん　　　　　　立って　　　こえ　　　　いって

4. ＿＿＿＿＿を書くのがあまり＿＿＿＿＿ではありません。
    　さくぶん　　　　　　　　すき

5. 私の専門は＿＿＿＿＿で、＿＿＿＿の専門はフランス＿＿＿＿＿です。
    　せんもん　化学　　　あに　　せんもん　　　　ぶんがく

6. ＿＿＿＿＿の人がATMの使い方を＿＿＿＿＿してくれました。
    　ぎんこう　　　　　　　つか　　せつめい

7. 友だちの＿＿＿＿＿＿＿は＿＿＿＿＿を＿＿＿＿＿＿。
    　　　　おねえさん　　　　えいご　　　はなします

8. これは日本の＿＿＿＿＿の大きな＿＿＿＿＿です。
    　　　　　しゃかい　　　　　もんだい

9. ＿＿＿＿＿お寺や神社は日本の＿＿＿＿＿ ＿＿＿＿＿の一つです。
    　ふるい　　　　じんじゃ　　たいせつな　ぶんか

10. この＿＿＿＿＿にはたくさんの＿＿＿＿や＿＿＿＿がいます。
    　　　村　　　　　　　　うし　　　羊

11. ＿＿＿＿＿に郵便局へ＿＿＿＿＿を買いに行きました。
    　ひるやすみ　　ゆうびんきょく　切手

Ⅰ 下の言葉を漢字で書いて、文を作りましょう。
した ことば かんじ か ぶん つく

> しゅくだい　せつめい　もんだい　しょうせつ　しつもん　ぶんか

1. ＿＿＿＿＿＿＿を読むのが好きです。

2. 私の＿＿＿＿＿＿＿に答えてください。
こた

3. この会社は＿＿＿＿＿＿＿が多くて大変です。
たいへん

4. 今日は＿＿＿＿＿＿＿がないので、遊びに行きます。
あそ

5. 分からないので、＿＿＿＿＿＿＿してください。

Ⅱ お知らせのメール：日本語の先生からメールが来ました。
し

✉ 件名：日本語クラスについて
けんめい

皆さん
みな
今日のクラスで説明しましたが、休んだ人が多かったので、もう一度説明します。
1. 教室について：来週月曜日のクラスは217教室であります。火曜日から金曜日
きょうしつ
は205教室です。
2. 宿題について：日本の文化と自分の国の文化について作文を書いてください。
習った漢字をたくさん使って書いてください。締め切りは来週の水曜日です。
3. 試験について：来週金曜日に日本語の試験があります。会話の試験と書く試験
です。会話は一人10分ぐらいです。私が質問するので、日本語で答えてくだ
さい。書く試験は30分ぐらいです。英語から日本語に訳す問題も出します。
では、来週クラスで会いましょう。

森めぐみ (morime@kanjidaisuki.ac.jp)

お知らせ　announcement　　件名　subject　　締め切り　deadline　　訳す　to translate
し　　　　　　　　　　　　けんめい　　　　　　し　き　　　　　　　　　　やく

質問に答えましょう。
しつもん こた

1. 来週木曜日の日本語クラスはどこでありますか。

2. 何について作文を書きますか。

3. 日本語の試験はいつですか。

4. 話す試験はどんな試験ですか。

I 漢字を練習しましょう。

遠	遠	遠				寒	寒	寒			
近	近	近				重	重	重			
者	者	者				軽	軽	軽			
暑	暑	暑				低	低	低			

II 単語の読み方を書いて、文を読みましょう。

	単 語	読み方	意 味	例 文
X	遠い	とおい	far	大学は駅から遠いです。
	遠く	とおく	far place	家族は遠くにいます。
X	近い	ちかい	near	病院はここから近いです。
	近く	ちかく	nearby	学校の近くに住んでいます。
X	学者	がくしや	scholar	学者はその質問に答えました。
	作者	さくしや	author	この本の作者は大学生です。
	暑い	あつい	hot	夏は暑いです。
	寒い	さむい	cold	冬はとても寒いです。
	重い	おもい	heavy	このかばんは重いです。
X	軽い	かるい	light	この自転車は軽いです。
X	低い	ひくい	low	父は背が低いです。

Ⅲ ひらがなを漢字に、漢字をひらがなにかえましょう。

1. ＿＿＿＿＿＿＿＿は＿＿＿＿＿＿＿＿＿＿＿に＿＿＿＿＿＿＿＿＿＿います。
   きょうだい　　　　とおい　　　　町　　　　　　すんで

2. ＿＿＿＿＿＿＿＿＿＿は＿＿＿＿＿から＿＿＿＿＿＿ので＿＿＿＿＿＿＿＿＿で行きます。
   　　会社　　　　　　いえ　　　　ちかい　　　　　じてんしゃ

3. この本の＿＿＿＿＿＿＿に会って、いろいろ＿＿＿＿＿＿＿してみたいです。
   　　　　さくしゃ　　　　　　　　　しつもん

4. 沖縄は＿＿＿＿＿＿＿は＿＿＿＿＿＿＿、＿＿＿＿＿＿はあまり＿＿＿＿＿＿ありません。
   おきなわ　　夏　　　あつくて　　　冬　　　　　　さむく

5. そのかばん、＿＿＿＿＿＿＿＿＿ですね。＿＿＿＿＿＿＿＿＿＿＿＿＿か。
   　　　　　おもそう　　　　　　　　もちましょう

6. ＿＿＿＿＿の＿＿＿＿＿＿のカフェで、＿＿＿＿＿＿＿の
   　えき　　　ちかく　　　　　　　試験

   ＿＿＿＿＿＿＿＿＿＿＿＿をしました。
   　　　勉強

7. このコンピューターは＿＿＿＿＿＿＿＿＿＿＿、＿＿＿＿＿＿＿＿＿です。
   　　　　　　　　　小さくて　　　　　かるい

8. 私の＿＿＿＿＿＿は背が＿＿＿＿＿＿ですが、＿＿＿＿＿＿は背が＿＿＿＿＿＿です。
   　　姉　　　せ　ひくい　　　　　　妹　　　　せ　たかい

9. ＿＿＿＿＿＿＿に＿＿＿＿＿＿＿、＿＿＿＿＿＿へ行きたいです。
   でんしゃ　　　のって　　　　とおく

10. ＿＿＿＿＿＿＿＿はその＿＿＿＿＿＿＿＿＿について話しました。
    がくしゃ　　　　　　問題

11. その＿＿＿＿＿＿＿＿＿にはテレビが＿＿＿＿＿＿＿＿＿あります。
    きょうしつ　　　　　　二台

Ⅰ 漢字を練習しましょう。

台風

弱	弱	弱			豆	豆	豆		
悪	悪	悪			短	短	短		
暗	暗	暗			光	光	光	光	
太	太	太			風	風	風		

Ⅱ 単語の読み方を書いて、文を読みましょう。

単　語	読み方	意　味	例　文
弱い	よわい	weak	妹は力が弱いです。
悪い	わるい	bad	たばこは体に悪いです。
暗い	くらい	dark	この教室は暗いです。
太い	ふとい	thick	このペンは太いです。
太る	ふとる	to gain weight	たくさん食べたので太りました。
豆	まめ	bean	豆のスープを作りました。
短い	みじかい	short	短い作文を書きました。
光	ひかり	light	窓から光が入ります。
光る	ひかる	to shine	星が光っています。
風	かぜ	wind	今日は風が強いです。
台風	たいふう	typhoon	もうすぐ台風が来るそうです。

Ⅲ ひらがなを漢字に、漢字をひらがなにかえましょう。

1. _ごご（午後）_ から _天気（てんき）_ が _悪く（わるく）_ なるそうです。

2. 少し _暗（くらい）_ ので、_電気（でんき）_ をつけてください。

3. すもうとり (Sumo wrestler) は _体（からだ）_ が大きくて _足（あし）_ も _太い（ふとい）_ です。

4. _弱（よわい）_ _光（ひかり）_ が木の _あいだ（間）_ から見えます。

5. _肉（にく）_ と _やさい（野菜）_ と _豆（まめ）_ でおいしい _料理（りょうり）_ を作ります。

6. 友だちに _光い（みじかい）_ _てがみ（手紙）_ を _書きました（かきました）_ 。

7. _はしる（走る）_ のをやめて、_すこし（少し）_ _太もした（ふとりました）_ 。

8. _夜（よる）_ 、_くっき（空）_ には星が _光って（ひかって）_ います。

9. 山の上は _風（かぜ）_ が _弓色い（つよい）_ です。_気（き）_ をつけてください。

10. _あき（秋）_ は _台風（たいふう）_ が _多い（おおい）_ です。

11. 私の _たのしみ（楽しみ）_ はカラオケで _歌（うたう）_ ことです。

12. _青空（あおぞら）_ の下で _花見（はなみ）_ をしながら _昼ご飯（ひるごはん）_ を食べました。

15

第15課 応用練習

① 反対の意味の言葉を漢字で書きましょう。　Write antonym using kanji.

1. 近い ⇔ _____
2. 寒い ⇔ _____
3. 重い ⇔ _____

4. 強い ⇔ _____
5. 明るい ⇔ _____
6. 細い ⇔ _____

7. 長い ⇔ _____
8. 高い山 ⇔ _____

② 「気」のつく言葉

　　日本語には「気」を使った言葉がたくさんあります。みなさんがよく知っている言葉には「元気」「天気」「気をつけてください」などがあるでしょう。「気」という漢字はもともと人の息という意味でした。でも今はいろいろな意味と使い方があります。例えば「あの人は気が短い」というと、「いつも急いでいて、ゆっくり待ったりすることができない人」という意味です。反対に「気が長い人」というのは「ゆっくり待つことができる人」という意味です。「気が弱い人」は人のことを気にして、自分の考えをはっきり言えません。その反対が「気が強い」です。他にも「試験があるので気が重い」「レポートを出したので気が軽くなった」など多くの使い方があります。いろいろな使い方を辞書で調べてみるとおもしろいですよ。

もともと　originally　　息　breath　　気にする　to mind　　考え　idea　　他　others

【　】の中の正しいものを選びましょう。

1. あの人は一年も手紙の返事を待っている。気が【　短い　・　長い　】人だ。

2. 宿題をしなかったので、授業に行くのは気が【　軽い　・　重い　】。

3. 彼女は気が【　強くて　・　弱くて　】、自分の考えを変えない。

① 漢字を練習しましょう。
かんじ　れんしゅう

運	運	運			使	使	使		
動	動	動			送	送	送		
止	止	止			洗	洗	洗		
歩	歩	歩			急	急	急		

② 単語の読み方を書いて、文を読みましょう。
たんご　　　　　　　　　　ぶん

単　語 たんご	読み方	意　味 いみ	例　文 れいぶん
運ぶ	はこぶ	to carry	この荷物を運んでください。 にもつ
運転	うんてん	driving	車の運転が下手です。
運転手	うんてんしゅ	driver	父はバスの運転手です。
動く	うごく	to move	この車は電気の力で動きます。
運動	うんどう	physical exercise	毎日運動をしています。
自動車	じどうしゃ	automobile	家には自動車が二台あります。
止まる	とまる	(something) stops	車は店の前で止まりました。
止める	とめる	to stop (something)	音楽を止めてください。
中止	ちゅうし	cancellation	雨でハイキングを中止しました。
歩く	あるく	to walk	会社まで歩いて行きます。
使う	つかう	to use	漢字を使って作文を書きます。
送る	おくる	to send	両親は妹に服を送りました。 りょうしん

洗う	あらう	to wash	手を洗ってから食べましょう。
お手洗い	おてあらい	bathroom	お手洗いはどこですか。
急に	きゅうに	suddenly	急に電車が止まりました。
急ぐ	いそぐ	to hurry	雨が降りそうなので、急ぎます。
急行	きゅうこう	express (train)	次の駅で急行に乗ってください。

Ⅲ ひらがなを漢字に、漢字をひらがなにかえましょう。

1. ___運動___ はバスを ___止めました___ 。
   うんてんしゅ　　　　　　　とめました

2. ___自動車___ を ___使って___ 、 ___重い___ 荷物を ___運びます___ 。
   じどうしゃ　　　　つかって　　　おもい　　　　　　はこびます

3. ___歩いた___ り ___走った___ りして、毎日 ___運動___ しています。
   あるいた　　　　はしった　　　　　　　　　うんどう

4. ___動かない___ で、ここで ___待って___ いてください。
   うごかない　　　　　　　　　　まって

5. ___急行___ が ___来る___ 前に、 ___お手洗い___ に行きました。
   きゅうこう　　　　くる　　　　　　おてあらい

6. ___風___ が強くなってきたので、 ~~花見~~ を ___中止___ しました。
   かぜ　　　　　　　　　　　　　　花見　　　ちゅうし

7. ~~ご飯~~ を食べる前に ___手___ を ___洗いましょう___ 。
   ご飯　　　　　　　　て　　　あらいましょう

8. ___急ぐ___ 時は、速達 (express mail) で ___送った___ ほうがいいですよ。　50
   いそぐ　　　　　そくたつ　　　　　おくった

9. ___運転___ している時、 ___急に___ ___止まる___ と危ないです。
   うんてん　　　　　　きゅうに　とまる　　　あぶ

Ⅰ 漢字を練習しましょう。

開	開	開			思	思	思		
閉	閉	閉		・	知	知	知		
押	押	押			考	考	考		
引	引	引			死	死	死		

Ⅱ 単語の読み方を書いて、文を読みましょう。

単　語	読み方	意　味	例　文
開く	あく	(something) opens	銀行は九時に開きます。
開ける	あける	to open (something)	暗いのでカーテンを開けます。
開く	ひらく	to open (something)	教科書を開いてください。
閉まる	しまる	(something) closes	店は六時に閉まります。
閉める	しめる	to close (something)	寒いので、窓を閉めます。
押す	おす	to push; to press	ここを押すと、電気がつきます。
引く	ひく	to pull	これを引くと、電気がつきます。
引き出し	ひきだし	drawer	引き出しにペンが入っています。
思う	おもう	to think	森田さんは来ないと思います。
思い出す	おもいだす	to recall	家族のことを思い出しました。
思い出	おもいて	memory	旅行はいい思い出になりました。
知る	しる	to know	あの先生を知っていますか。

知らせる	しらせる (handwritten)	to notice	家族に知らせてください。
考える	かんがえる (handwritten)	to think	この問題について考えました。
考え	かんがえ (handwritten)	idea	あなたの考えを書いてください。
死ぬ	しぬ (handwritten)	to die	台風で人が死にました。

Ⅲ ひらがなを漢字に、漢字をひらがなにかえましょう。

1. ここを＿＿＿＿＿（押す・handwritten）と、ドアが＿＿＿＿＿（開きます・handwritten）。
   おす　　　　　　　　　　あきます

2. ＿＿＿＿＿（自分・handwritten）の＿＿＿＿＿（考え・handwritten）を＿＿＿＿＿（説明・handwritten）しようと＿＿＿＿＿（思います・handwritten）。
   自分　　　　かんがえ　　　せつめい　　　　　おもいます

3. ＿＿＿＿＿（引出し・handwritten）にあった＿＿＿＿＿（写真・handwritten）を見て、
   ひきだし　　　　　　　しゃしん

   ＿＿＿＿＿（楽しかった・handwritten）ことを＿＿＿＿＿（思い出しました・handwritten）。
   楽しかった　　　　　　　　　　　　おもいだしました

4. ＿＿＿＿＿（暑い・handwritten）ので、窓を＿＿＿＿＿（開けて・handwritten）、カーテンを＿＿＿＿＿（閉めて・handwritten）ください。
   あつい　　　　　　まど　あけて　　　　　　　　しめて

5. この＿＿＿＿＿（所説・handwritten）の＿＿＿＿＿（さくしゃ・handwritten）を＿＿＿＿＿（知って・handwritten）いますか。
   しょうせつ　　　　　作者　　　　　　しって

6. ＿＿＿＿＿（ことり・handwritten）が＿＿＿＿＿（知だ・handwritten）ことを＿＿＿＿＿（えみ・handwritten）に＿＿＿＿＿（知らせました・handwritten）。
   小鳥　　　　しんだ　　　　　　弟　　　　しらせました

7. ＿＿＿＿＿（春休・handwritten）の＿＿＿＿＿（思い・handwritten）について＿＿＿＿＿（作文・handwritten）を書きました。
   はるやすみ　　　おもいで　　　　　　さくぶん

8. ＿＿＿＿＿（来年・handwritten）、店＿＿＿（店・handwritten）を＿＿＿＿＿（引こう・handwritten）と＿＿＿＿＿（考えて・handwritten）います。
   らいねん　　みせ　　　ひらこう　　　かんがえて

9. ここを＿＿＿＿＿（引・handwritten）と、ブラインドが＿＿＿＿＿（知まります・handwritten）。
   ひく　　　　　　　　　しまります

Ⅰ 写真を見て、a〜fから選びましょう。
しゃしん えら

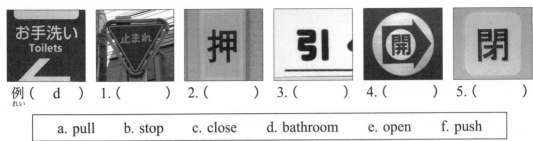

例 (d) 1. ( ) 2. ( ) 3. ( ) 4. ( ) 5. ( )
れい

| a. pull | b. stop | c. close | d. bathroom | e. open | f. push |

Ⅱ 東京と大阪
とうきょう おおさか

　私は東京の出身です。大学を卒業してから、大阪の会社に就職して、今は大阪
　　とうきょう しゅっしん　　　　そつぎょう　　　おおさか　　しゅうしょく　　　　　おおさか
に住んでいます。東京と大阪でいろいろと違うことにびっくりしました。
　　　　　とうきょう おおさか　　　　ちが

　大阪駅に着いて、エスカレーターに乗った時、私は左側に立ちました。すると
　おおさか　　　　　　　　　　　　　　　　　ひだりがわ
後ろの人が私を押して、急いで歩いていきました。よく見ると、急ぐ人は左を歩
いて、急がない人は右に立っています。東京とは反対です。また、車を運転して
　　　　　　　　　　　　　　　　とうきょう　　はんたい
いる時、黄色の信号で止まると、後ろの車にクラクションを鳴らされました。大
　　　きいろ しんごう　　　　　　　　　　　　　　な　　　　　　　　おお
阪の友だちによると「黄色は急いで行け」という意味なのだそうです。「自分ど
さか　　　　　　　　きいろ　　　　　　　　いみ
こから来たん？」と聞かれて、私は「さあ、知りません」と答えてしまいました。
　　　　　　　　　　　　　　　　　　　　　こた
後で、大阪では「自分」が「あなた」の意味だと聞きました。知らないことが多く
　　おおさか　　　　　　　　　　いみ
て、最初は東京に帰りたいと思いました。でもこの頃はぼちぼち慣れてきて、大
　　さいしょ とうきょう　　　　　　　　　　　ごろ　　　　な　　　　　おお
阪っておもろいなと思います。
さか

出身　coming from　　就職する　to get a job　　信号　traffic light　　クラクション　a horn
しゅっしん　　　　　しゅうしょく　　　　　　　　しんごう
鳴らす　to honk　　ぼちぼち＝少し／まあまあ (in Osaka dialect)
な
おもろい＝おもしろい (in Osaka dialect)

質問に答えましょう。
しつもん こた

1. 大阪で、急ぐ人はエスカレーターのどちら側を歩きますか。
　 おおさか　　　　　　　　　　　　　　　がわ

2. 大阪の友だちは黄色の信号の時はどうしたらいいと言いましたか。
　 おおさか　　　　　きいろ しんごう

3. 「自分どこから来たん？」を標準 (standard) の日本語で書いてください。
　　　　　　　　　　　　　　　ひょうじゅん

4. この人は大阪について今どう思っていますか。
　　　　　おおさか

① 漢字を練習しましょう。

医	医	医			研	研	研		
始	始	始			究	究	究		
終	終	終			留	留	留		
石	石	石			有	有	有		

② 単語の読み方を書いて、文を読みましょう。

単　語	読み方	意　味	例　文
医者	じしゃ	doctor	姉は医者です。
医学	いがく	medical science	医学を勉強しています。
始まる	はじまる	(something) begins	十時から入学式が始まります。
始める	はじめる	to begin (something)	今から試験を始めます。
終わる	おわる	to come to an end	夏休みが終わりました。
終わり	おわり	end	来月の終わりに会社をやめます。
石	いし	stone	この石は重くて持てません。
研究	けんきゅう	research	日本文学を研究しています。
研究者	けんきゅうしゃ	researcher	彼は有名な文学の研究者です。
研究室	けんきゅうしつ	research room	研究室はここから遠いです。
留学する	りゅうがく	to study abroad	九月からイギリスに留学します。
留学生	りゅうがくせい	international student	あの留学生はインドから来ました。
有名な	ゆうめいな	famous	あれは有名なお寺です。

Ⅲ ひらがなを漢字に、漢字をひらがなにかえましょう。

1. よんがつ の おわり に日本に りゅうがく して、
   （四月）

   けんきゅう を はじめました 。
   （研究）

2. 川 のそばで、きれいな 色 の 石 をたくさん拾いました。
   かわ　　　　　　　　　　　　　　いろ　　いし　　　　　　ひろ

3. 大学院 で 医学 を勉強しようと お思います 。
   だいがくいん　　いがく　　　　　　　　　　　おもいます

4. 試験は 来週 の月曜日に 始まって 、木曜日に 終わります 。
   （来週）　　　　　　　　はじまって　　　　　おわります

5. その 質問 に 研究者 が答えました。
   しつもん　　けんきゅうしゃ　　こた

6. この びょういん には 有名 な 医者 がいます。
   （病院）　　　　　　ゆうめい　　いしゃ

7. 研究室 には 留学生 が多いので 英語 で話します。
   けんきゅうしつ　りゅうがくせい　　　　　　えいご

8. 山田 さんの家はとても 遠くて 、 でも三十分かかります。
   （山田）　　　　　　　とおくて　きゅうこう

9. インターネットを 使って 、ロシア 文学 について調べました。
   つかって　　　　（文学）　　　しら

10. この荷物は 明るい ので、 小学生 でも 運ぶ ことができます。
    にもつ　　　かるい　　　　しょうがくせい　　はこぶ

11. 体 が 弱い ので、あまり 運動 できません。
    （体）　　よわい　　　　　うんどう

① 漢字を練習しましょう。
かんじ れんしゅう

産	産	産				員	員	員			
業	業	業				士	士	士			
薬	薬	薬				仕	仕	仕			
働	働	働				事	事	事			

② 単語の読み方を書いて、文を読みましょう。
たんご ぶん

単　語 たんご	読み方	意　味 いみ	例　文 れいぶん
生産	せいさん	production	この村では米を生産しています。
産業	さんぎょう	industry	その町は自動車産業で有名です。
工業	こうぎょう	manufacturing industry	この国の主な産業は工業です。 おも
薬	くすり	medicine	晩ご飯の前に薬を飲みます。
働く	はたらく	to work	妹は病院で働いています。
会社員	かいしゃいん	office worker	父は会社員です。
店員	てんいん	store clerk	あの店員は親切です。
銀行員	ぎんこういん	bank employee	兄は銀行員です。
仕事	しごと	job	日曜日も仕事がありました。
事	こと	thing	夏にいろいろな事をしました。
火事	かじ	fire	近くで火事がありました。
食事	しょくじ	meal	明日、外で食事をしましょう。

Ⅲ ひらがなを漢字に、漢字をひらがなにかえましょう。

1. となりの家が＿＿＿＿＿火事＿＿＿＿＿になって、＿＿＿急いで＿＿＿＿＿外＿＿＿に出ました。
   かじ　　　　　　　　　　いそいで　　　　そと

2. ＿＿＿食事＿＿＿の後に＿＿＿薬＿＿＿を＿のんで＿＿＿＿ください。
   しょくじ　　　　　　くすり　　　　飲んで

3. 日本の＿＿＿音楽＿＿＿　＿＿＿産業＿＿＿はアジアの＿＿＿こく＿＿＿にも進出しています。
   おんがく　　　　さんぎょう　　　　　国　　　　しんしゅつ

4. 中国は＿＿び＿＿の＿＿＿生産＿＿＿が世界一だと＿＿＿問きました＿＿＿。
   米　　　　せいさん　　せかいいち　　　ききました

5. ＿＿やね＿＿は＿＿＿金行員＿＿＿で、
   姉　　　　　ぎんこういん

   ＿＿＿毎晩＿＿＿遅くまで＿＿＿仕＿＿＿をしています。
   まいばん　　おそ　　　しごと

6. ＿＿妻＿＿はデパートの＿＿＿店員＿＿＿で、＿＿＿洋服＿＿＿を＿うって＿＿＿います。
   つま　　　　　　　てんいん　　　ようふく　　　売って

7. 父は＿＿＿会社員＿＿＿で、＿＿＿台風＿＿＿が来ても＿＿やすみません＿＿。
   かいしゃいん　　　たいふう　　　　　　休みません

8. その町は＿＿＿工業＿＿＿が盛んで、＿＿＿自動車＿＿＿を＿作って＿＿います。
   こうぎょう　　さか　　　じどうしゃ　　　つくって

9. 日本の＿＿＿文化＿＿＿ついてどんな＿＿＿事＿＿＿を＿いて＿＿いますか。
   ぶんか　　　　　　　こと　　知って

10. ＿＿私＿＿は大学の＿＿＿研究室＿＿＿で＿働がて＿＿います。
    わたし　　　　けんきゅうしつ　　はたらいて

11. ＿＿知んだ＿＿　＿＿しゅじん＿＿とはいい＿＿お思で＿＿がたくさんあります。
    しんだ　　　　　主人　　　　　　おもいで

① 「手」「員」「者」の中から一つ選んで、言葉を作りましょう。

1. 会社＿＿員＿＿　　2. 運転＿者＿＿　　3. 銀行＿＿員＿＿

4. 歌＿手＿＿　　　　5. 医＿手＿＿　　　6. 研究＿者＿＿

② 卒業の後の進路

> 　山下さんと東さんは同じ大学の学生です。二人は友達で、三年生まではサークルに入ったり、アルバイトをしたりして大学生活を楽しんでいました。四年生の今、卒業の後の進路について考えています。
>
> 　山下さんは大学でバイオの研究をしています。将来はバイオ産業の会社で仕事をしたいと思っているので、卒業の後も大学院に入って研究を続けるつもりです。九月に大学院の試験を受けるので、毎日勉強しています。
>
> 　東さんは三年生の秋から就職活動を始めました。それまで茶色だった髪を黒くして、リクルートスーツを買って、毎日、試験や面接を受けに行っています。暑い日もスーツを着て、会社を訪問するのは大変だと言っています。東さんは卒業した後は、銀行員になりたいと考えていますが、銀行で働きたい人は多いので、他の会社にも履歴書を送っているそうです。
>
> 　三月に二人の大学生活は終わります。その後、二人はそれぞれの道を進みます。

進路　a way　　サークル　circle　　バイオ産業　biotechnology　　就職活動　job-hunting
リクルートスーツ　a suit for job-hunting　　面接　interview　　訪問する　to visit
履歴書　resume　　それぞれ　each

質問に答えましょう。

1. 山下さんは大学で何を勉強していますか。

2. 山下さんは九月に何をしますか。

3. 東さんは面接を受ける前に、何をしましたか。

4. 東さんは卒業した後、どうしたいと思っていますか。

I 漢字を練習しましょう。

図	図	図			借	借	借		
官	官	官			代	代	代		
館	館	館			貸	貸	貸		
昔	昔	昔			地	地	地		

II 単語の読み方を書いて、文を読みましょう。

単　語	読み方	意　味	例　文
長官	ちょうかん	director general	長官は外国に行っています。
図書館	としょかん	library	図書館で働いています。
映画館	えいが かん	movie theater	映画館は人が多いです。
大使館	たいしかん	embassy	大使館は駅の近くです。
昔	むかし	old times	昔、ここは教会でした。
借りる	かりる	to borrow	図書館で本を借ります。
時代	じだい	age; era	学生時代は楽しかったです。
～代	だい	… fee	先月の電気代は高かったです。
代わりに	かわりに	instead	彼の代わりに、仕事をします。
貸す	かす	to lend	来週、車を貸してください。
地図	ちず	map	日本の地図を見てください。
地理	ちり	geography	大学で地理を教えています。
地下	ちか	underground	研究室は地下にあります。

足が好きですか？

Ⅲ ひらがなを漢字に、漢字をひらがなにかえましょう。
　　（かんじ）　　　　　（かんじ）

1. ＿＿＿＿＿＿で＿＿＿＿＿＿＿を＿＿＿＿＿＿＿。
　　としょかん　　　　小説　　　　　かりました

2. ＿＿＿＿＿は今、アメリカ＿＿＿＿＿＿に行っています。
　　ちょうかん　　　　　　たいしかん

3. ＿＿＿＿のスーパーで＿＿＿＿と＿＿＿＿を買いました。
　　ちか　　　　　　　豚肉　　　　鳥肉

4. ＿＿＿＿＿、＿＿＿＿＿がよく見えません。
　　くらくて　　　　ちず

5. ＿＿＿はよく＿＿＿＿＿に行きました。
　　むかし　　　　えいがかん

6. ＿＿＿＿＿になって、学生＿＿＿＿をよく＿＿＿＿＿＿＿。
　　かいしゃいん　　　　　じだい　　　　おもいだします

7. バス＿＿＿が＿＿＿＿＿ので、百円＿＿＿＿ください。
　　　だい　　　たりない　　　　　　かして

8. 祖母が＿＿＿の＿＿＿＿＿、＿＿＿＿＿＿に来てくれました。
　（そぼ）おや　　かわりに　　　　入学式

9. 日本の＿＿＿をよく＿＿＿＿＿＿＿＿＿が多いそうです。
　　　　ちり　　　しらない　　　大人

10. ＿＿＿＿＿は星がきれいに＿＿＿＿＿＿います。
　　今夜　　　（ほし）ひかって

11. 先生を＿＿＿＿＿にして、＿＿＿を＿＿＿＿＿＿。
　　　真ん中　　　しゃしん　　うつしました

Ⅰ 漢字を練習しましょう。

世	世	世			用	用	用		
界	界	界			民	民	民		
度	度	度			注	注	注		
回	回	回			意	意	意		

Ⅱ 単語の読み方を書いて、文を読みましょう。

単　語	読み方	意　味	例　文
世話		care	犬の世話をします。
世界		the world	世界地図を買いたいです。
～度		… time(s)	一年に一度、国に帰ります。
今度		near future; next time	今度の日曜日、何をしますか。
～度		… degree(s)	北海道の気温は五度でした。
～回		… time(s)	その店で一回食事しました。
何回		how many times	週に何回運動しますか。
回る		to turn	地球は回っています。
用／用事		errand; business	明日は用があるので行けません。
市民		citizen	市民は市長を支持しています。
注文する		to order	ピザを注文しました。
意味		meaning	この漢字の意味は何ですか。
注意する		to watch out; to warn	重いので注意してください。
意見		opinion	意見があったら言ってください。
用意する		to prepare	ペンと紙を用意してください。

Ⅲ ひらがなを漢字に、漢字をひらがなにかえましょう。

1. ＿＿＿＿＿＿の＿＿〜〜〜〜〜〜〜＿にはパソコンが＿＿＿＿＿＿いるので
　　　こんど　　　　　　研究　　　　　　　　　　　　にだい

　＿＿＿＿＿＿してください。
　　　よういい

2. すてきなスカートですね。そこで＿＿＿＿＿＿、＿＿＿＿＿＿みてください。
　　　　　　　　　　　　　　　　　　　いちど　　　　まわって

3. 〜〜〜〜〜〜や＿＿＿＿＿の＿＿＿＿＿＿をしました。
　　　牛　　　　ぶた　　　　せわ

4. 〜〜〜〜〜〜は＿＿＿＿＿＿があるので、パーティーに＿＿＿＿＿＿＿＿。
　　　夕方　　　　ようじ　　　　　　　　　　　　　でられません

5. ＿＿＿＿＿＿＿は＿＿＿＿＿＿の＿＿＿＿＿＿を聞きました。
　　　しちょう　　　　しみん　　　　いけん

6. ＿＿＿＿＿＿の〜〜〜〜〜を勉強しようと＿＿＿＿＿＿＿います。
　　　せかい　　　　地理　　　　　　　　かんがえて

7. Ａ：ボタンを＿＿＿＿＿＿＿ ＿＿＿＿＿＿＿＿いいですか。
　　　　　　なんかい　　　　おしたら

　　Ｂ：＿＿＿＿＿＿です。
　　　　　いっかい

8. ＿＿＿＿＿＿を＿＿＿＿＿＿、オーブンを180＿＿＿＿にセットしてください。
　　　やさい　　　あらって　　　　　　　　　　ど

9. インターネットで＿＿＿＿＿＿を＿＿＿＿＿＿しました。
　　　　　　　　　したぎ　　　　ちゅうもん

10. 「はし」には、＿＿＿＿＿＿が二つあります。＿＿＿＿＿＿してください。
　　　　　　　いみ　　　　　　　　　　　　ちゅうい

Ⅰ □にこの課の漢字を入れて、言葉を作りましょう。
　　　　　 か かんじ　　　 ことば つく

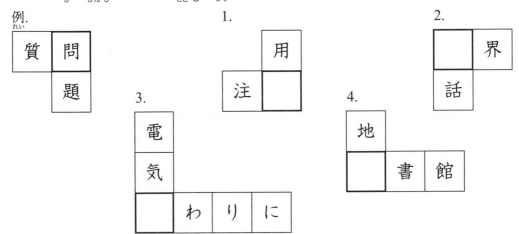

例.
れい

質	問
	題

1.

	用
注	

2.

	界
話	

3.

電
気

| | わ | り | に |

4.

地		
	書	館

Ⅱ 図書館についてのお知らせ

図書館についてのお知らせ

四月に北山市に新しい図書館ができました。図書館には日本文学、世界の文学、旅行や料理の本など、10万冊の本があります。雑誌や新聞も読めます。もし読みたい本が図書館になかったら、市民はいつでも注文ができます。

本は一度に10冊まで、三週間借りられます。他の人が借りている本は予約することもできます。DVDもあって地下のオーディオルームで見られます。オーディオルームは大きい部屋も小さい部屋も用意していますから、一人でもグループでも楽しめます。午前十時から午後七時まで開いていて、毎週木曜日が休みです。来月は三日（水曜日）から一週間閉まっていますから注意してください。

質問に答えましょう。
しつもん こた

1. 図書館にはどんな本がありますか。

2. 読みたい本がなかったら、どうしますか。

3. オーディオルームはどこにありますか。そこで何ができますか。

Ⅰ 漢字を練習しましょう。

頭	頭	頭			別	別	別		
顔	顔	顔			竹	竹	竹		
声	声	声			合	合	合		
特	特	特			答	答	答		

Ⅱ 単語の読み方を書いて、文を読みましょう。

単語	読み方	意味	例文
頭	あたま	head	頭が痛いので、薬を飲みました。
顔	かお	face	顔を洗いました。
声	こえ	voice	大きい声で話してください。
特に	とくに	especially	日本料理で特にすしが好きです。
別れる	わかれる	to separate	先週、別れた夫に会いました。
特別な	とくべつ	special	今日は特別な日です。
別に	べつに	not in particular	明日は別に用事がありません。
別の	べつの	another	今年から別の店で働いています。
竹	たけ	bamboo	これは竹で作ったいすです。
合う	あう	to fit	この服は小さくて私に合いません。
試合	しあい	game; match	明日、野球の試合があります。
間に合う	まにあう	to be in time	電車に間に合いませんでした。
答える	こたえる	to answer	この質問に答えてください。
答え	こたえ	answer	この問題の答えがわかりません。

Ⅲ ひらがなを漢字に、漢字をひらがなにかえましょう。

1. 頭 が痛かったので、 会社 を 休みました 。
   あたま　　　　　　　かいしゃ　　　　　やすみました

2. お酒を 飲む と、いつも 顔 が 赤く なります。
   さけ　　のむ　　　　　　かお　　　あかく

3. 聞こえない ので、大きな 声 で 答えて ください。
   聞こえない　　　　　　　こえ　　こたえて

4. A: 今日 何か 用事 がありますか。
   　　　　何か　　ようじ

   B: 別に ありません。
   　　べつに

5. 林 へ行って、 太い 竹 を 切りました 。
   はやし　　　　ふとい　たけ　きりました

6. 仕事が早く 終わった ので、
   　　　　　　おわった

   試合 に 間に合いました 。
   しあい　　まにあいました

7. 大学に 入った ら、両親と 別れて 住まなくて はいけません。
   　　　はいった　りょうしん　わかれて　住まなくて

8. この 町 には、 特別 な 産業 がありますか。
   　　まち　　　とくべつ　さんぎょう

9. この 上着 は 合わない ので、 別の を見せてください。
   　　うわぎ　あわない　　　　べつの

10. この 問題 は 特に 難しくて、 答え が分かりません。
    　　もんだい　とくに　むずか　こたえ

Ⅰ 漢字を練習しましょう。

正	正	正					集	集	集			
同	同	同					不	不	不			
計	計	計					便	便	便			
京	京	京					以	以	以			

Ⅱ 単語の読み方を書いて、文を読みましょう。

単 語	読み方	意 味	例 文
お正月	おしょうがつ	New Year's holiday	お正月に特別な料理を作ります。
正しい	ただしい	right	この答えは正しくありません。
正式な	せいしき	formal	正式な手紙の書き方を習いました。
正午	しょうご	noon	正午に試合が始まります。
同じ	おなじ	same	私と妹は同じ高校に行っています。
時計	とけい	clock; watch	新しい時計を買いました。
計画	けいかく	plan	春休みの計画を立てました。
東京	とうきょう	Tokyo	夏に東京の大使館へ行きます。
集める	あつめる	to collect	色々な国の切手を集めています。
集まる	あつまる	to gather	家族が集まって食事をしました。
不便な	ふべん	inconvenient	家の近くに店がなくて不便です。
～以上	いじょう	… or more	毎月の電気代は五千円以上です。
～以下	いか	… or less	百万円以下の車を探しています。
～以外	いがい	other than …	私以外、皆宿題を出しました。

Ⅲ ひらがなを漢字に、漢字をひらがなにかえましょう。

1. ___こ と し___ の ___お 正 月___ は ___東 京___ に行きました。
   今年　　　　　　おしょうがつ　　　　とうきょう

2. ___有名な___ ___哥欠手___ が来たので、人が ___集まりました___ 。
   ゆうめいな　　かしゅ　　　　　　　　　　あつまりました

3. ___ちゅがく___ の ___正式___ な ___なまえ___ は中華人民共和国です。
   中国　　　　　　せいしき　　　名前　　ちゅうか じん みんきょう わ こく

4. すし___以外___ に、どんな ___料理___ が好きですか。
   　　　いがい　　　　　　　りょうり

5. ___夏休み___ の ___計画___ を立てなくてはいけません。
   なつやすみ　　けいかく　　　た

6. この___漢字___ は ___正しく___ ありません。
   　　かんじ　　　ただしく

7. ___高校___ の時、___外国___ の ___おかね___ を ___集めて___ いました。
   こうこう　　　　がいこく　　お金　あつめて

8. ___駅___ まで20分___以上___ ___あるく___ ので ___不便___ です。
   えき　　　　　　いじょう　　歩く　　　　　ふべん

9. 私は ___あに___ と ___同じ___ ___時計___ を ___持って___ います。
   　　兄　　　おなじ　とけい　　もって

10. 十七歳___以___ の人は ___運転___ できません。
    さい　いか　　　　うんてん

11. ___きょう___ は ___暑くて___ 、___正午___ の気温は ___さんじゅう___ でした。
    今日　　あつくて　　しょうご　き おん　　三十度

98 第19課(2)

Ⅰ 正しい漢字を選んで（　　）に書きましょう。

1. お酒を飲むといつも（　　　）が赤くなります。　　　【　頭　・　顔　】

2. 友だちに（　　　）います。　　　　　　　　　　　　【　合　・　会　】

3. 日本料理の中で（　　　）にすしが好きです。　　　　【　特　・　持　】

4. この答えは（　　　）しいです。　　　　　　　　　　【　正　・　止　】

5. 漢字を（　　　）って、書きます。　　　　　　　　　【　便　・　使　】

Ⅱ 日本のお正月

　　日本ではお正月は特別な日です。お正月には、家族や親せきが集まって新しい年を祝います。

　　お正月が来る前には、家をきれいにして、お正月の準備をします。そして、年賀状を書きます。年賀状は12月に出しておくと1月1日に届きます。お正月の前の日、12月31日に、そばを食べます。これはそばのように「長く、細く元気にいたい」という意味があります。

　　新しい年になったら、「あけましておめでとうございます」とあいさつをします。そして、みんなでおせち料理という特別な料理やお雑煮という餅の料理を食べます。昔はお正月が来る前に家でおせち料理を作りましたが、今はデパートなどで買うこともできます。そして、神社やお寺にお参りに行きます。着物を着て行く人もいます。子供たちは大人からお金をもらいます。これをお年玉と言います。子供たちはお年玉をとても楽しみにしています。

親せき relatives　　祝う to celebrate　　年賀状 New Year's card　　届く to arrive
あいさつ greeting　　お雑煮 soup with *mochi*　　餅 rice cake
お参り visit to shrines and temples

質問に答えましょう。

1. 日本ではお正月の前に何をしますか。三つ以上書いてください。

2. 日本ではお正月に何をしますか。三つ以上書いてください。

Ⅰ 漢字を練習しましょう。

場	場	場				堂	堂	堂			
戸	戸	戸				都	都	都			
所	所	所				県	県	県			
屋	屋	屋				区	区	区			

Ⅱ 単語の読み方を書いて、文を読みましょう。

単 語	読み方	意 味	例 文
場合	ばあい	case	風が強い場合、中止します。
会場	かいじょう	meeting place	会場に多くの人が集まりました。
工場	こうじょう	factory	この工場で車を生産しています。
売り場	うりば	counter; shop	野菜売り場は地下です。
戸	と	door	戸が開いています。
～所	～ところ	… place	どんな所に住みたいですか。
台所	だいどころ	kitchen	この台所は広くて明るいです。
住所	じゅうしょ	address	紙に住所と氏名を書いてください。
近所	きんじょ	neighborhood	近所に図書館があります。
場所	ばしょ	place	この場所で花見をしましょう。
本屋	ほんや	bookstore	本屋の仕事はおもしろいです。
屋上	おくじょう	rooftop	屋上から遠くの山が見えます。
食堂	しょくどう	cafeteria	大学の食堂は安いです。
東京都	とうきょうと	Metropolis of Tokyo	東京都に住んでいます。

首都	しゅと	capital	東京は日本の首都です。
都合	つごう	convenience	都合のいい日はいつですか。
京都	きょうと	Kyoto	京都には有名なお寺があります。
〜県	〜けん	… Prefecture	長野県には高い山が多いです。
〜区	〜く	… Ward	住所は東京都北区です。

Ⅲ ひらがなを漢字に、漢字をひらがなにかえましょう。

1. ＿＿＿＿（私）は＿＿＿＿（工場）の中の＿＿＿＿（食堂）で＿＿＿＿（働いて）います。
   しゅじん　　こうじょう　　しょくどう　　はたらいて

2. ＿＿＿＿（住所）は、＿＿＿＿（京都）北＿＿＿＿（区）です。
   じゅうしょ　　きょうとし　　く

3. ＿＿＿＿（首都）の＿＿＿＿（東京）には、多くの＿＿＿＿（大使館）があります。
   しゅと　　とうきょう　　たいしかん

4. ＿＿＿＿（ながの県）は＿＿＿＿（空気）がきれいな＿＿＿＿（所）です。
   ながのけん　　くうき　　ところ

5. コンサートの＿＿＿＿（会場）は＿＿＿＿（屋上）です。
   かいじょう　　おくじょう

6. ＿＿＿＿（寒い）ので、＿＿＿＿（台所）の＿＿＿＿（戸）を＿＿＿＿（閉めて）ください。
   さむい　　だいどころ　　と　　しめて

7. ＿＿＿＿（時計）＿＿＿＿（売り）の＿＿＿＿（場所）を＿＿＿＿（教えて）ください。
   とけい　　うりば　　ばしょ　　おしえて

8. ＿＿＿＿（都合）が＿＿＿＿（わるく）なった＿＿＿＿（場合）、＿＿＿＿（知らせます）。
   つごう　　悪く　　ばあい　　しらせます

9. ＿＿＿＿（近所）の＿＿＿＿（本屋）で＿＿＿＿（東京）の＿＿＿＿（地図）を
   きんじょ　　ほんや　　とうきょうと　　ちず
   ＿＿＿＿（買いました）。
   かいました

だい か

① 漢字を練習しましょう。
かんじ　れんしゅう

池	池	池			品	品	品		
発	発	発			旅	旅	旅		
建	建	建			通	通	通		
物	物	物			進	進	進		

② 単語の読み方を書いて、文を読みましょう。
たんご　　　　　　　　　ぶん

単　語	読み方	意　味	例　文
池	いけ	pond	池の近くで写真を撮りました。
電池	でんち	battery	時計の電池がなくなりました。
発音	はつおん	pronunciation	リーさんの発音は正しいです。
出発	しゅっぱつ	departure	午後三時に東京を出発しました。
建てる	たてる	to build	今、家を建てています。
物	もの	thing	大切な物は引き出しに入れます。
建物	たてもの	building	この建物に映画館が入っています。
食べ物	たべもの	food	パーティーの食べ物を用意します。
飲み物	のみもの	drink	飲み物はコーヒーを注文しました。
買い物	かいもの	shopping	仕事の後で買い物をしました。
着物	きもの	kimono	着物を着たことがありません。
動物	どうぶつ	animal	この森にたくさん動物がいます。
品物	しなもの	goods	この店は品物が少ないです。
旅行	りょこう	travel	北海道を旅行しました。

旅館	りょかん	Japanese inn	この旅館はとても古いです。
通る	とおる	to go through; to pass	この道を通って、町に行きます。
通う	かよう	to commute	自転車で学校に通っています。
通り	とおり	street	この通りには本屋がありません。
進む	すすむ	(something) advances	道をまっすぐ進むと駅があります。

Ⅲ ひらがなを漢字に、漢字をひらがなにかえましょう。

1. 池（いけ）の ちかく（近く）に 小さい（ちいさい） 動物（どうぶつ）がいます。

2. あの 建物（たてもの）の 地下（ちか）で、電池（でんち）を 売って（うって）います。

3. 中学校（ちゅうごくご）の 発音（はつおん）は 特に（とくに）難（むずか）しいです。

4. 今朝（きょうらい?）、姉（あね）は 旅行（りょこう）に 出発（しゅっぱつ）しました。

5. 安くて（やすくて）いい 品物（しなもの）がある店で、買い物（かいもの）をします。

6. 毎週（まいしゅう）、着物（きもの）の 学校（がっこう）に 通って（かよって）います。

7. この 通り（とおり）を 進む（すすむ）と、旅館（りょかん）があります。

8. この 場所（ばしょ）に 工場（こうじょう）を 建てる（たてる） 計画（けいかく）があります。

9. この 道（みち）を 通って（とおって）、教会（きょうかい）へ行きます。

10. 食べ物（たべもの）や 飲み物（のみもの）など、いろいろな 物（もの）を 用意（ようい）します。

Ⅰ 下の言葉を漢字で書いて、文を作りましょう。
した ことば かんじ ぶん つく

きょうと　　どうぶつ　　りょかん　　だいどころ　　とうきょう　　きもの

1. ＿＿＿＿＿＿＿は日本の首都です。
とうきょう

2. ＿＿＿＿＿＿＿は日本の昔の首都です。
きょうと

3. ＿＿＿＿＿＿＿は料理する所です。
だいどころ 所

4. ＿＿＿＿＿＿＿はお正月によく着ます。
_着物_

5. ＿＿＿＿＿＿＿は日本式のホテルです。
りょかん

6. ＿＿＿＿＿＿＿は犬や馬や鳥などです。
どうぶつ

Ⅱ 日本への旅行：カナダ人のエイミーさんがインターネットで質問しました。
しつもん

Q はじめまして。日本の文化について勉強しているカナダ人の大学生です。
今度の休みに日本を旅行したいと思っているんですが、どこかおすすめの場
所はありますか。（エイミー）

A 京都はどうですか？　京都には古いお寺や建物がたくさんあって、通りを歩
いていると舞妓さんに会える時もあります。着物をレンタルしたら、一日舞
まいこ　　　　　　　　　　　　　　　　　　　　　　　　　　　　　まい
妓さんになれますよ。それから、京都に行ったらぜひ、北区にあるフレンド
こ　　　　　　　　　　　　　　　　　　　　　　　　　きたく
というカフェで抹茶ケーキを食べてみてください♪　すごくおいしいです。
まっちゃ

A やっぱり日本の首都、東京がいいと思いますよ。六本木や新宿では買い物が
ろっぽんぎ　しんじゅく
楽しめるし、浅草には昔からの文化があります。日本の電化製品やアニメ、
でん か せいひん
マンガが好きだったら、秋葉原がおもしろいと思いますよ。ここには新しい
あき は ばら
日本の文化があります。夜は、東京タワーから見える夜景がきれいです。
や けい

おすすめ　recommendation　　　舞妓　apprentice *geiko*　　　レンタル　rental
　　　　　　　　　　　　　　　　まいこ
抹茶　powdered green tea　　　電化製品　electrical appliances　　　夜景　a night view
まっちゃ　　　　　　　　　　　でん か せいひん　　　　　　　　　　　や けい

質問に答えましょう。
しつもん こた

1. 着物を着てみたい人はどこに行ったらいいですか。
まいこさん 京のおてら

2. カメラやコンピューターを買いたかったら、どこに行ったらいいですか。
あさくさ

3. あなたはどこに行きたいと思いましたか。どうしてですか。
行きたいと思い、私は か夜たいます

Part 3

第21課 − 第32課
(漢字番号 321-512)

Ⅰ 漢字を練習しましょう。

丸	丸	丸				汚	汚	汚			
熱	熱	熱				果	果	果			
冷	冷	冷				卵	卵	卵			
甘	甘	甘				皿	皿	皿			

Ⅱ 単語の読み方を書いて、文を読みましょう。

単　語	読み方	意　味	例　文
丸い	まるい	round	図書館はあの丸い建物だ。
丸	まる	circle	赤いペンで丸を書いた。
熱い	あつい	hot	このお茶は熱くて飲めない。
熱	ねつ	fever	熱があったので、会社を休んだ。
熱心な	ねっしん	enthusiastic	妹は熱心に勉強している。
熱中する	ねっちゅうする	to be absorbed	妻はスポーツに熱中している。
冷たい	つめたい	cold	この川の水は冷たいです。
冷える	ひえる	to become cold	店で冷えたビールを買ってきた。
冷やす	ひやす	to chill	冷蔵庫に飲み物が冷やしてある。
冷ます	さます	to cool	お茶は熱いから、少し冷まそう。
甘い	あまい	sweet	私の父は甘いものが大好きだ。
甘やかす	あまやかす	to spoil	子供を甘やかす親が多い。
汚い	きたない	dirty	手が汚いので、洗った。
汚れる	よごれる	to become dirty	この服は汚れている。
汚す	よごす	to make something dirty	母の着物を汚してしまった。
果物	くだもの	fruit	病気の母に果物を持って行った。
卵	たまご	egg	この料理は卵を二つ使う。
（お）皿	（お）さら	plate; dish	白くて大きい皿を買った。

Ⅲ ひらがなを漢字に、漢字をひらがなにかえましょう。

1. ___正しい___ ___答え___ に ___丸___ を付ける。
   ただしい　　こたえ　　まる

2. そのスープは ___熱かった___ ので、少し ___冷して___ 飲んだ。
   あつかった　　　　　　さまして

3. 子供が悪い ___事___ をしても ___注意___ しないで ___甘やかして___ いる。
   こども　　事　　ちゅうい　　あまやかして

4. ___皿___ を ___洗___ が、まだ ___汚れて___ いる。
   さら　　あらった　　よごれて

5. あの男の人は ___顔___ が ___丸くて___ 、___目___ が大きい。
   顔　　まるくて　　め

6. ___赤___ ちゃんの ___熱___ が高かったから、___病院___ へ行った。
   あか　　ねつ　　びょういん

7. 友達に ___借りた___ ___服___ を ___汚して___ しまった。
   ともだち　かりた　　ふく　　よごして

8. 高校生は ___熱心___ に ___校長___ の ___話___ を聞いていた。
   ねっしん　　校長　　はなし

9. ___教室___ が ___寒かった___ ので、体が ___冷えた___ 。
   きょうしつ　　寒かった　　ひえた

10. ___家___ の前に ___汚い___ 車が ___止まって___ いた。
    いえ　　きたない　　とまって

11. ___朝___ 、果物 ___くだもの___ と ___卵___ を ___食べた___ 。
    あさ　　くだもの　　たまご　　たべた

12. ゲームに ___熱中___ して、___宿題___ を忘れてしまった。
    ねっちゅう　　しゅくだい　　わす

13. ジュースはきのうから ___冷して___ あるから、___冷たい___ 。
    ひやして　　つめたい

14. ___太って___ から、___甘い___ ___物___ を食べないことにした。
    ふとった　　あまい　　もの

① 漢字を練習しましょう。

酒	酒	酒				焼	焼	焼			
塩	塩	塩				消	消	消			
付	付	付				固	固	固			
片	片	片				個	個	個			

② 単語の読み方を書いて、文を読みましょう。

単　語	読み方	意　味	例　文
（お）酒	おさけ	alcohol	日本では二十歳（はたち）から酒が飲める。
酒屋	さかや	liquor store	駅の近くに酒屋がある。
日本酒	にほんしゅ	sake	日本酒は米から作られる。
飲酒運転	いんしゅうんてん	drunk driving	飲酒運転をしてはいけない。
塩	しお	salt	塩を少し足したほうがいい。
付き合う	つきあう	to date	姉は医者と付き合っている。
付ける	つける	to attach	上着に花を付けた。
付く	つく	to stick	この本にはCDが付いている。
日付/日付け	ひづけ	date	手紙には日付を入れる。
片付ける	かたづける	to tidy up	研究室が汚いので片付けた。
片道	かたみち	one way	京都まで片道二時間かかる。
焼く	やく	to burn; to bake	主人が肉を焼いてくれた。
焼ける	やける	to be burned; to be baked	火事で家が焼けた。
消す	けす	to turn off	電気を消して教室を出た。
消える	きえる	something turns off; to disappear	風でキャンドルの火が消えた。

消化する	しょうか する	to digest	食べ物は体の中で消化される。
固い	かたい	hard; firm	父は頭が固くて、話を聞かない。
固まる	かたまる	to harden	それは冷やすと固まる。
〜個	〜こ	counter for small things	りんごを三十個送った。
個人	こじん	individual	それは個人の問題だと思う。

Ⅲ ひらがなを漢字に、漢字をひらがなにかえましょう。

1. <u>飲酒運転</u>　は、<u>酒</u>　を飲んで、<u>運転</u>　することだ。
　　いんしゅうんてん　　　おさけ　　　　　うんてん

2. <u>晩ご飯</u>　に<u>鳥肉</u>　を<u>焼いた</u>　。
　　ばんごはん　　とりにく　　やいた

3. <u>出</u>　前に<u>電気</u>　を<u>消した</u>　。
　　でかける　　　でんき　　　けした

4. <u>上着</u>　にガムが<u>付て</u>　しまった。
　　上着　　　　　ついて

5. <u>台所</u>　を<u>片付</u>　から、<u>買い物</u>　に行こう。
　　台所　　　　かたづけて　　　かいもの

6. <u>塩</u>　が<u>固まって</u>　、<u>使</u>　にくい。
　　しお　　　かたまって　　　つかい

7. <u>卵</u>　が<u>三個</u>　<u>足りない</u>　。
　　たまご　　さんこ　　たりない

8. <u>京都</u>　まで<u>片道</u>　<u>一万三千円</u>　かかった。
　　きょうと　　かたみち　　　一万三千円

9. ここに<u>住所</u>　と<u>氏名</u>　と今日の<u>日付</u>　を書いてください。
　　　　じゅうしょ　　氏名　　　　　　ひづけ

10. 食べ物（たべもの）を消化（しょうか）するのに、三時間以上（いじょう）かかる。

11. 酒屋（さかや）で日本酒（にほんしゅ）を一本（いっぽん）買った。

12. メールに写真（しゃしん）を付けて（つけて）、送った（おくった）。

13. 急に（きゅうに）テレビの音（おと）が消えた（きえた）。

14. 友達（ともだち）のお兄さん（おにいさん）と付き合って（つきあって）いたが、別れて（わかれて）しまった。

15. 近所（きんじょ）で火事（かじ）があって、家が焼けた（やけた）そうだ。

16. サッカーの試合（しあい）では、個人（こじん）プレーが多かった（おおかった）。

17. 夫（おっと）は少し（すこし）頭（あたま）が固い（かたい）。

18. この工場（こうじょう）では正午（しょうご）から昼休み（ひるやすみ）が始まる（はじまる）。

19. 仕事（しごと）が終わらない（おわらない）ので、九時（くじ）のバスに間に合わない（まにあわない）。

20. 弟（おとうと）の部屋は光（ひかり）が入らない（はいらない）ので暗い（くらい）。

21. 出口（でぐち）までは別（べつ）の階段（かいだん）で行くと近い（ちかい）。

① お好み焼きの作り方

【材料（一人分）】

小麦粉（flour）50g　　豚肉　40g

水　50cc　　　　　　青のり（dried seaweed powder）

卵　1個　　　　　　　かつお節（dried, shaved bonito）

塩　少々　　　　　　マヨネーズ

キャベツ　100g　　　お好み焼きソース（甘いソース）

1.　キャベツは小さく切っておく。豚肉も食べやすい大きさに切る。

2.　小麦粉と塩を混ぜておく。

3.　ボウルに水と2を入れて混ぜる。

4.　3の中に切ったキャベツと卵を入れて混ぜる。

5.　熱くしたフライパンに4を丸く広げる。

6.　5の上に豚肉をのせて、しばらくしてから、裏返す。

7.　両面焼けたら、皿にとる。

8.　7にソース、マヨネーズ、かつお節、青のりをかけて食べる。

＊冷たくなったらおいしくないので、熱いうちに食べましょう。

　ビールやお酒にも合いますよ。

＊豚肉の代わりに、いかやえびを入れてもおいしいですよ。

材料　ingredient　　一人分　portion for one person　　少々　a little　　混ぜる　to mix
ボウル　bowl　　広げる　to spread　　裏返す　to turn over　　両面　both sides
かける　to pour; to put on　　いか　squid　　えび　prawn

a～eを、作り方の順番に並べましょう。

Order the following pictures according to the recipe.

（　　　）→（　　　）→（　　　）→（　　　）→（　　　）

 a.

 b.

 c.

 d.

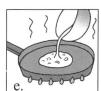 e.

第22課（1）　笑　泣　怒　幸　悲　苦　痛　恥　　337-344

Ⅰ　漢字を練習しましょう。

笑	笑	笑			悲	悲	悲		
泣	泣	泣			苦	苦	苦		
怒	怒	怒			痛	痛	痛		
幸	幸	幸			恥	恥	恥		

Ⅱ　単語の読み方を書いて、文を読みましょう。

単　語	読み方	意　味	例　文
笑う	わらう	to laugh	その映画を見て、何回も笑った。
笑顔	えがお	smile	その女の子は笑顔になった。
泣く	なく	to cry	犬が死んだ時、家族が泣いた。
怒る	おこる	to be angry	昔はよく親に怒られた。
幸せな	しあわせな	happy	赤ちゃんが生まれて、幸せだ。
不幸	ふこう	misfortune	自分が不幸だと思わない。
悲しい	かなしい	sad	友達が帰国するので、悲しい。
悲しむ	かなしむ	to grieve	犬が死んで、家族は悲しんだ。
苦い	にがい	bitter	注文したコーヒーは苦かった。
苦手	にがて	to be weak at	私は化学が苦手です。
苦しい	くるしい	painful	お金がなくて、生活が苦しい。
苦しむ	くるしむ	to suffer	多くの人が病気に苦しんでいる。
痛い	いたい	painful	頭が痛いので、薬を飲んだ。
痛み	いたみ	pain	手の痛みが一週間続いている。
頭痛	ずつう	headache	頭痛がひどくて、会社を休んだ。
苦痛	くつう	pain	長い間立っているのは苦痛だ。
恥ずかしい	はずかしい	to be embarrassed	漢字が読めなくて、恥ずかしい。

Ⅲ ひらがなを漢字に、漢字をひらがなにかえましょう。

1. _____(悲い)_____時は、_____(泣いて)_____もいい。
   かなしい　　　　　　　　ないて

2. 人の_____(不幸)_____を_____(笑って)_____はいけない。
   　　　ふこう　　　　　　わらって

3. _____(新い)_____くつをはいたら、_____(足)_____が_____(痛く)_____なった。
   あたらしい　　　　　　　　　　　　あし　　　　　いたく

4. 子供の_____(笑顔)_____で、_____(幸せな)_____(気持ち)_____になった。
   こども　　えがお　　　　　しあわせな　　　　きもち

5. _____(三十分)_____(走ったら)_____、_____(苦しく)_____なった。
   さんじゅうぷん　　　　はしったら　　　　　くるしく

6. ひどい_____(頭痛)_____がしたので、_____(医者)_____へ行った。
   　　　　ずつう　　　　　　　　　　いしゃ

7. _____(世界)_____には、_____(苦しんで)_____いる人がたくさんいる。
   せかい　　　　　　くるしんで

8. _____(計画)_____が_____(中止)_____になって、皆は_____(怒った)_____。
   けいかく　　　　　中止　　　　　　　みな　　おこった

9. _____(苦い)_____(お茶)_____は好きではない。
   にがい　　　　　お茶

10. 毎日、いやな_____(仕事)_____をするのは_____(苦痛)_____だ。
    　　　　　　しごと　　　　　　　　くつう

11. 火事で_____(図書館)_____が_____(焼けて)_____、町の人は_____(悲しんだ)_____。
    　　　としょかん　　　　やけて　　　　　　　　　かなしんだ

12. _____(心)_____の_____(痛み)_____は、なかなか_____(消えない)_____。
    心　　　　　　いたみ　　　　　　　　　きえない

13. くつが_____(汚れて)_____いて_____(恥ずかしかった)_____。
    よごれて　　　　　　はずかしかった

14. 料理が_____(苦手)_____なので、毎日_____(近く)_____の_____(食堂)_____で食べる。
    にがて　　　　　　　　ちかく　　　しょくどう

Ⅰ 漢字を練習しましょう。

配	配	配			残	残	残		
困	困	困			念	念	念		
辛	辛	辛			感	感	感		
眠	眠	眠			情	情	情		

Ⅱ 単語の読み方を書いて、文を読みましょう。

単　語	読み方	意　味	例　文
心配する	しんぱいする	to worry	試験のことを心配している。
配る	くばる	to distribute	先生は宿題を配った。
困る	こまる	to be in trouble	夜寝られなくて、困っている。
辛い	からい	spicy	料理は辛くて食べられなかった。
眠い/眠たい	ねむたい	sleepy	朝早く起きたので、眠い。
眠る	ねむる	to sleep	家族のことが心配で眠れない。
残る	のこる	to remain	会社に残って仕事を片付けた。
残す	のこす	to leave something	子供はきらいな野菜を残した。
残り	のこり	remainder	残りの宿題は明日しよう。
残念な	ざんねんな	regrettable	旅行に行けなくて、残念だ。
感じる	かんじる	to feel	右の目に痛みを感じた。
感じ	かんじ	feeling; impression	それは暗い感じの音楽だった。
感動する	かんどうする	to be moved; to be touched	その映画を見て、感動した。
感情	かんじょう	emotion	動物にも感情があると思う。
苦情	くじょう	complaint	苦情を言われて困った。
事情	じじょう	circumstances	事情があって、計画を中止した。
友情	ゆうじょう	friendship	友情を大切にしたい。

Ⅲ ひらがなを漢字に、漢字をひらがなにかえましょう。

1. <u>辛い</u> 食べ物が <u>にがて</u> なので、<u>残した</u>。
   からい　　　　　　苦手　　　　　　のこした

2. いろいろな事を <u>心</u> しすぎて、<u>眠れなかった</u>。
   しんぱい　　　　　　ねむれなかった

3. 私は <u>笑ったり</u> 、<u>泣いたり</u> 、よく <u>感情</u> を出す。
   わらったり　　　　　　ないたり　　　　　かんじょう

4. <u>特別</u> な <u>事情</u> があって、<u>残念</u> だが、仕事をやめた。
   とくべつ　　じじょう　　　　　　ざんねん

5. 先生は <u>試験</u> <u>問題</u> を <u>配った</u>。
   しけん　　もんだい　　　くばった

6. ボーナスで <u>北海道</u> に <u>旅行</u> した。
   ほっかいどう　　　　　旅行

   <u>残り</u> のお金で <u>家族</u> と <u>食事</u> をするつもりだ。
   のこり　　　　　かぞく　　しょくじ

7. <u>ふたり</u> の間に <u>強い</u> <u>友情</u> を <u>感じる</u>。
   二人　　　　　　強い　　ゆうじょう　　かんじる

8. <u>はつおん</u> が <u>悪い</u> ので、<u>困って</u> いる。
   発音　　　　　わるい　　　　こまって

9. あの <u>店員</u> はいつも <u>笑顔</u> なので、<u>感じ</u> がいい。
   てんいん　　　　　えがお　　　　かんじ

10. <u>頭痛</u> の <u>薬</u> を飲んだら、<u>眠く</u> なった。
    ずつう　　　くすり　　　　　　ねむく

11. まだ <u>手</u> に <u>痛み</u> が <u>残って</u> いる。
    て　　　いたみ　　のこって

12. <u>夜</u> 、大きい <u>戸</u> で歌っていたら、<u>苦情</u> が来た。
    よる　　　　　こえ　　　　　　くじょう

13. その <u>建物</u> の <u>おくじょう</u> からの景色に <u>感動</u> した。
    たてもの　　屋上　　　　　けしき　　かんどう

第22課(2) <u>115</u>

① ストレス度チェック

あなたのストレス度はどうですか。当てはまるものに○を付けましょう。

1. 朝なかなか起きられない。
2. よく頭が痛くなる。
3. 一人でテレビを見ている時、ほとんど笑わない。
4. 小さい事でよく怒る。
5. ドラマや映画を見て、あまり泣かない。
6. 知らない人と会って話すのは苦手だ。
7. 笑顔がすてきだと言われたことがない。
8. 一人でいるのが好きだ。
9. 自分のベッドじゃないと、眠れない。
10. 最近、きれいな景色を見ても、感動しない。
11. 家を出た時、鍵をかけたかどうか心配になることがある。
12. 苦しい時や困っている時、すぐ親や友達に相談する。
13. 自分は不幸だと思う。
14. 体が重く感じることが多い。
15. あまり感情を出さないほうだと思う。

○が0個～5個の人

ほとんどストレスがありません。楽観的でいつも幸せだと感じています。小さい事をあまり気にしないので、失敗することもありますが、友達も多いです。

○が6個～10個の人

少しストレスがあるようです。今の状態でも問題はありませんが、疲れを感じたら、お風呂に入ったり、音楽を聞いたりして、リラックスするといいでしょう。次の日に疲れを残さないことが大切です。

○が11個～15個の人

かなりストレスがたまっているようです。いろいろな事を苦痛に感じて、いらいらすることが多いかもしれません。疲れがたまってきたら、スポーツや旅行などで気分転換しましょう。

ストレス度　stress level	当てはまる　to apply; to be true	楽観的　optimistic
失敗する　to fail	状態　situation	疲れ　fatigue	リラックスする　to relax
たまる　to accumulate	いらいらする　to feel impatient	気分転換　change of pace

Ⅰ 漢字を練習しましょう。

覚	覚	覚				比	比	比			
忘	忘	忘				受	受	受			
決	決	決				授	授	授			
定	定	定				徒	徒	徒			

Ⅱ 単語の読み方を書いて、文を読みましょう。

単　語	読み方	意　味	例　文
覚える	おぼいる	to memorize	漢字の意味と読み方を覚えた。
忘れる	わすれる	to forget	昔の友達の名前を忘れた。
忘れ物	わすれもの	things left behind	電車で忘れ物をして困っている。
決める	きめる	to decide	夏休みどこへ行くか決めよう。
決まる	きまる	to be decided	新しい住所が決まった。
決して	けっして	never	決して私達の友情を忘れない。
予定	よてい	plan	土曜日の九時に出発の予定だ。
定休日	ていきゅうび	holiday (of a store)	その店は日曜日が定休日だ。
決定	けってい	decision	会議の会場は京都に決定した。
比べる	くらべて	to compare	私の国に比べて、日本は暑い。
受ける	うける	to receive	注文を受けてから、料理を作る。
受付/受け付け	うけつけ	reception	受付で住所と氏名を書いた。
受験	じゅけん	taking an examination	大学受験まで残り三か月だ。
授業	じゅぎょう	class	授業が終わった後、試験がある。
教授	きょうじゅ	professor	教授の研究室はこの建物にある。
授業料	じゅぎょうりょう	tuition	この大学の授業料は高い。
生徒	せと	pupil	生徒は地理の授業を受けている。

Ⅲ　ひらがなを漢字に、漢字をひらがなにかえましょう。

1. <u>冬休み</u>の<u>予定</u>が<u>決まった</u>。
　　ふゆやすみ　　　よてい　　　きまった

2. 私の大学の<u>授業料</u>は、他の大学に<u>比べて</u>かなり高い。
　　　　　　　じゅぎょうりょう　　ほか　　　　くらべて

3. 店は<u>定休日</u>で<u>閉まって</u>いて、<u>残念</u>だ。
　　　ていきゅうび　　閉まって　　　ざんねん

4. ＿＿＿＿は＿＿＿＿に＿＿＿＿＿＿＿＿いる。
　　せいと　　　しょうがっこう　　歩いて　　かよって

5. ＿＿＿＿を＿＿＿＿も、すぐ＿＿＿＿しまう。
　　かんじ　　おぼえて　　　わすれて

6. ＿＿＿＿ので、＿＿＿＿まで＿＿＿＿触ってはいけない。
　　あつい　　　冷える　　けっして　　さわ

7. ＿＿＿＿の大学を＿＿＿＿することに＿＿＿＿。
　　長野県　　　　じゅけん　　　　きめた

8. ＿＿＿＿で＿＿＿＿を書いてから、一時間も＿＿＿＿。
　　うけつけ　　なまえ　　　　　　　まった

9. 山下＿＿＿＿の＿＿＿＿を＿＿＿＿いる。
　　きょうじゅ　じゅぎょう　　うけて

10. ＿＿＿＿へ行った時、＿＿＿＿に＿＿＿＿をした。
　　京都　　　　りょかん　わすれもの

11. 次のアジア大会の＿＿＿＿は＿＿＿＿に＿＿＿＿した。
　つぎ　　たいかい　かいじょう　　東京都　　けってい

12. 先生の＿＿＿＿の後、学生は＿＿＿＿の＿＿＿＿を言った。
　　　しつもん　　　　　じぶん　　いけん

第23課（2）練 復 表 卒 違 役 皆 彼

Ⅰ 漢字を練習しましょう。

練	練	練				違	違	違			
復	復	復				役	役	役			
表	表	表				皆	皆	皆			
卒	卒	卒				彼	彼	彼			

Ⅱ 単語の読み方を書いて、文を読みましょう。

単　語	読み方	意　味	例　文
練習	れんしゅう	practice	道で自転車に乗る練習をした。
復習	ふくしゅう	review	試験の前に復習しよう。
回復	かいふく	recovery	台風の後、天気が回復した。
表	おもて	surface	本の表にサインしてください。
表	ひょう	list; table	この表について説明した。
発表	はっぴょう	presentation	来週、文学の授業で発表する。
表す	あらわす	to express	あの人はすぐ感情を表す。
卒業	そつぎょう	graduation	大学を卒業する前に留学したい。
卒業式	そつぎょうしき	graduation ceremony	卒業式で先生の話に感動した。
卒業生	そつぎょうせい	graduate	彼と私は同じ大学の卒業生だ。
違う	ちがう	to differ	人によって考え方が違う。
間違える	まちがえる	to make a mistake	漢字を間違えて、恥ずかしい。
間違い	まちがい	mistake	間違いに気がつかなかった。
違い	ちがい	difference	文化の違いについて話を聞いた。
役に立つ	やくにたつ	to be useful	社会の役に立ちたい。
市役所	しやくしょ	city hall	市役所へ外国人登録に行った。
皆さん	みなさん	everybody	皆さんの友情は忘れません。
皆	みんな	all	家族は皆、元気にしている。

彼	かれ	he; boyfriend	彼が駅まで車で送ってくれた。
彼ら	かれら	they	彼らは皆、この大学の卒業生だ。
彼女	かのじょ	she; girlfriend	彼女は中国医学を研究している。

Ⅲ ひらがなを漢字に、漢字をひらがなにかえましょう。

1. ___卒業式___の日を___間違えて___しまった。
　　そつぎょうしき　　　　まちがえて

2. ___彼ら___は___皆___、社会の___役に立___と___感じて___いる。
　　かれら　　みな　　　やくにたちたい　　　　かんじて

3. ___頭___が___痛くて___、___熱___も高かったが、少し___回復___した。
　　あたま　　いたくて　　ねつ　　　　　　かいふく

4. ___彼___も___彼女___もこの大学の___卒業___だ。
　　かれ　　かのじょ　　　　そつぎょうせい

5. 封筒の___表___の___住所___が___違って___いた。
　ふうとう　おもて　　じゅうしょ　　ちがって

6. ___作文___に___字___の___間違い___がたくさんあった。
　　さくぶん　　　かく　　まちがい

7. ___皆さん___、6ページの___表___を見てください。
　　みなさん　　　　　ひょう

8. 大学を___そつぎょう___した後、___しやくしょ___で___はたらきはじめた___。

9. あの人はすぐ___おこって___、___かんじょう___を___あらわす___。

10. クラスで___ならった___ことを___ふくしゅう___することが___たいせつ___だ。

11. 明日、___じゅぎょう___で___はっぴょう___するので、家で___れんしゅう___している。

12. ___今___から新しいお茶にしたが、___味___の___違い___が分からない。
　　きょう　　　　　　　あじ　　ちがい

I 悩み相談

相談1

京都の大学で勉強している留学生です。今、好きな男の子がいます。彼は日本人で、同じ授業を受けています。いっしょにグループで発表をして、仲良くなりました。彼はとても親切で、いっしょに授業の復習をしてくれたり、私の日本語の間違いを直してくれたりします。彼ともっと仲良くなりたいと思って、「週末遊びに行かない?」とメールを送ったのですが、彼からの返事は「ごめん。今週は忙しいから、また今度。」でした。日本人ははっきり「NO」を言わないと聞いたことがあります。彼は私と出かけたくないんでしょうか。それとも、私からもう一度誘ってもいいんでしょうか。(M.H.・19歳・女)

回答

もう一度だけ誘ってみたらどうですか。次に誘った時も彼から「また今度」というメールが来たら、あきらめましょう。「また今度」が二度続くのは、「NO」と同じです。

悩み worry	仲良くなる to become friends	それとも or	誘う to invite
回答 answer			

相談2

今、市役所に勤めています。小学生の頃から、人を笑わせるのが好きで、お笑い芸人になるのが夢でした。10年前に大学を卒業した時、その夢を忘れようと決めたのですが、この頃、一度しかない人生だからやってみたいと思うようになりました。去年から大学時代の友人と二人で漫才の練習を始めました。時々、昼休みに市役所の前で漫才をしています。大きい声で笑ってくれる人はまだ少ないですが、皆さん笑顔で見てくれます。仕事を辞めて、芸人になるべきでしょうか。今、付き合っている彼女と来年の春に結婚する予定ですが、まだ彼女には話していません。(未来のスター・32歳・男)

笑わせる to make someone laugh	お笑い芸人 comedian	人生 life
友人 friend	漫才 stand-up comedy by two comedians	笑顔 smiling face
辞める to quit	スター star	

質問に答えましょう。

相談1
そうだん

1. 彼は何をしてくれますか。

2. 彼をもう一度誘ったほうがいいと思いますか。どうしてですか。
　　　　さそ

相談2
そうだん

1. この人の今の夢は小学生の時の夢と違いますか。
　　　　　　　ゆめ　　　　　　　　　　　ゆめ

2. この人は仕事を辞めて、芸人になるべきだと思いますか。どうしてですか。
　　　　　　　　　や　　　　げいにん

3. この人にアドバイスを書きましょう。

Ⅰ 漢字を練習しましょう。

全	全	全				荷	荷	荷			
部	部	部				由	由	由			
必	必	必				届	届	届			
要	要	要				利	利	利			

Ⅱ 単語の読み方を書いて、文を読みましょう。

単 語	読み方	意 味	例 文
安全	あんぜん	safety	日本は安全な国だと思う。
全国	ぜんこく	whole country	この店は全国にある。
全員	ぜんいん	all members	学生は全員卒業できた。
全く	まったく	entirely	彼女の話は彼のと全く違う。
全部	ぜんぶ	all	残さないで、全部食べなさい。
部屋	へや	room	彼女が来る前に部屋を片付けた。
部長	ぶちょう	department head	部長に今日の予定を知らせた。
一部	いちぶ	one part	工場の一部が火事で焼けた。
～部	ぶ	… team; … club	テニス部の皆はいつも笑顔だ。
～学部	がくぶ	department of …	あの人は工学部の教授だ。
大部分	だいぶぶん	most of …	建物の大部分は木で作られた。
必ず	かならず	surely	明日必ず宿題を出してください。
要る	いる	to be needed	その国に行くにはビザが要る。
必要な	ひつような	necessary	必要な物を注文した。
重要な	じゅうような	important	社長と重要な話をした。
荷物	にもつ	baggage	荷物を旅館の部屋に運んだ。
自由	じゆう	freedom	働き始めて、自由な時間がない。
理由	りゆう	reason	宿題を忘れた理由を聞かれた。

届ける	とどける	to deliver	受付に忘れ物を届けた。
届く	とどく	to be delivered	荷物は今日中に届くはずだ。
便利な	べんり	convenient	会場は便利な場所にある。
利用する	りようする	to use	古い着物を利用して洋服を作った。

Ⅲ ひらがなを漢字に、漢字をひらがなにかえましょう。

1. ___紙___ の ___生産___ はこの町の ___重要___ な ___産業___ だ。
　　かみ　　　せいさん　　　　　　じゅうよう　　さんぎょう

2. ___電池___ が ___悪る___ ので、___必ず___ 持って来てください。
　　でんち　　　　いる　　　　　かならず

3. この店は ___全国___ に ___品物___ を ___届けて___ くれるので、___便利___ だ。
　　　　　ぜんこく　　品物　　　　とどけて　　　　　　べんり

4. この大学の ___学部___ を ___受験___ するつもりだ。
　　　　　こうがくぶ　　　　じゅけん

5. テニス ___部___ の ___全員___ が ___集まって___ 話し合った。
　　　　　ぶ　　　　ぜんいん　　　あつまって

6. ___事情___ を聞いて、___運転手___ が辞めた ___理由___ が分かった。
　　じじょう　　　　　うんてんしゅ　　　　　りゆう

7. ___研究室___ にある資料の ___大部分___ は古くて ___役に立たない___。
　　けんきゅうしつ　　しりょう　　だいぶぶん　　　　やくにたたない

8. まだ ___一部___ の人たちが ___利用___ しているから、そのバスは ___必要___ だ。
　　　いちぶ　　　　　　りよう　　　　　　　　　　　　ひつよう

9. 日本は ___安全___ で ___自由___ な国だと ___思う___。
　　　　あんぜん　　じゆう　　　　　おもう

10. ___部屋___ に ___荷物___ が ___全部___ ___届いた___。
　　　へや　　　にもつ　　ぜんぶ　　とどいた

11. ___部長___ は ___全く___ ___悲しまなかった___。
　　ぶちょう　　まったく　　　かなしまなかった

① 漢字を練習しましょう。

払	払	払				活	活	活	
濯	濯	濯				末	末	末	
寝	寝	寝				宅	宅	宅	
踊	踊	踊				祭	祭	祭	

② 単語の読み方を書いて、文を読みましょう。

単 語	読み方	意 味	例 文
払う	はらう	to pay	入学式の前に授業料を払った。
洗濯する	せんたくする	to do laundry	何回洗濯しても汚れがとれない。
洗濯物	せんたくもの	laundry	屋上で洗濯物を干す。
寝る	ねる	to sleep	日曜日は昼まで寝ている。
昼寝	ひるね	nap	家に帰って昼寝する。
踊る	おどる	to dance	皆で歌って踊った。
踊り	おどり	dance	何回も踊りを練習した。
生活	せいかつ	life	もう日本の生活に慣れた。
活動	かつどう	activity	今、クラブ活動に熱中している。
週末	しゅうまつ	weekend	週末の予定が決まっていない。
月末	げつまつ	the end of a month	月末はお金が足りなくなる。
年末	ねんまつ	the end of a year	年末にお正月の料理を作る。
末	すえ/まつ	end of a period	三月の末に卒業式がある。
末っ子	すえっこ	youngest child	私は三人兄弟の末っ子だ。
お宅	おたく	somebody's house (polite)	部長のお宅はどちらですか。
帰宅	きたく	returning home	主人はまだ帰宅していない。
自宅	じたく	one's own house	自宅で料理教室を開いている。
祭り／祭	まつり	festival	週末、祭りを見に行く予定だ。

1. ___雨___で___洗濯物___が干せないので、___困って___いる。
   あめ　　せんたくもの　　　　　　（ほ）　　　　こまって

2. ___月末___に___授業料___を___払う___つもりだ。
   げつまつ　じゅぎょうりょう　はらう

3. ___年末___は___飲酒運転___の事故が多い。
   ねんまつ　　　いんしゅうんてん　　　　（じこ）

4. いつも十時ごろ___帰宅___して、___午前___一時ごろ___寝る___。
   きたく　　　　ごぜん　　　　　　ねる

5. ___週末___、___祭り___に行って、___皆___と___踊った___。
   しゅうまつ　　まつり　　　　みな　　　おどった

6. ___妹___は___末っ子___で、___親___に___甘やかされて___いる。
   いもうと　　すえっこ　　おや　　　甘やかされて

7. 大学___生活___は、___宿題___やクラブ___活動___で毎日忙しい。
   せいかつ　　しゅくだい　　かつどう　　　　（いそが）

8. 八月の___末___に___お宅___に伺ってもよろしいでしょうか。
   すえ　　おたく　　　（うかが）

9. ___今朝___、___部屋___を___片付けて___、___洗濯___した。
   今朝　　へや　　　片付けて　　　せんたく

10. 日曜日の___午後___は、たいてい___自宅___で___昼寝___している。
    ごご　　　　　　じたく　　ひるね

11. ___来週___までに___踊り___と___歌___を___覚えよう___。
    らいしゅう　　おどり　　うた　　おぼえよう

① 一か月に使うお金

右の表はアパートなどに住んでいる学生の一か月の
生活費の平均です。

1. 何に一番お金を使っていますか。

2. あなたの国の大学生と比べてどうですか。

全国大学生活協同組合連合会 学生生活実態調査(2008)より	
一か月に使うお金	
住居費	54,700円
食費	24,500円
交通費	3,500円
本代など	4,000円
電話代	5,000円
その他	32,300円
合計	124,000円

〜費　cost for …　　平均　average
住居　housing　　合計　total

② 山口さんの大学生活

山口美咲さん（20歳）は文学部の2年生だ。山口さんの自宅は東京からバスと電車で3時間ぐらいの所にある。毎日、自宅から大学まで通うのは大変なので、大学の近くにワンルームマンションを借りている。家賃は6万円だ。安くはないが、オートロックなので安全だし、駅から近くて便利なので気に入っている。生活費は全部で10万円ぐらいだ。大部分は親に払ってもらっている。

山口さんは、月曜日から金曜日まで大学へ行く。たいてい9時に授業が始まり、4時半に終わる。ダンスサークルに入っているので週に2回、授業の後3時間ダンスの練習をする。サークル活動がない日はアルバイトで、10時ごろ帰宅する。部屋で晩ご飯を食べて、宿題をして、寝るのは12時を過ぎることが多い。

週末はサークルの仲間と踊りに行ったり、洗濯や掃除をしたりする。来月ダンスの全国大会があるので、今はサークルの仲間全員と「必ず勝とう」と、週末も練習をしている。

大学生活について、山口さんは「今の生活は自由で楽しいです。卒業後の事は少し心配ですが」と話している。

家賃　house rent　　気に入る　to like　　仲間　friends　　大会　competition

質問に答えましょう。

1. 山口さんがマンションを気に入っている理由は何ですか。

2. 山口さんの生活費はいくらですか。だれが払っていますか。

3. 一週間に何時間ぐらいサークルでダンスの練習をしていますか。

4. 今、週末もダンスの練習をしているのはどうしてですか。

Ⅰ 漢字を練習しましょう。

平	平	平			政	政	政		
和	和	和			治	治	治		
戦	戦	戦			経	経	経		
争	争	争			済	済	済		

Ⅱ 単語の読み方を書いて、文を読みましょう。

単 語	読み方	意 味	例 文
平日	へいじつ	weekdays	平日は五時に店が閉まる。
平らな	たいらな	flat	山道の後は平らな道だ。
平和	へいわ	peace	世界の平和について考える。
和食	わしょく	Japanese food	和食は体にいいそうだ。
戦う	たたかう	to fight	テニスの試合で彼と戦った。
戦争	せんそう	war	1945年に戦争が終わった。
争う	あらそう	to fight; to quarrel	兄弟で争うのはよくない。
治る	なおる	to be cured	頭が痛かったが、治った。
治す	なおす	to cure	早く病気を治したい。
政治	せんじ	politics	政治のことを知らない人が多い。
政治家	せいじか	politician	政治家になり、人の役に立ちたい。
経験	けいけん	experience	留学はいい経験だった。
〜経由	〜けいゆ	via ...	パリ経由でドイツへ行く。
経済	けいざい	economy	経済は少しずつよくなっている。
経済学	けいざいがく	economics	大学で経済学を勉強する。
済む	すむ	(something) finishes	洗濯が済んだら、買い物に行く。
済ませる	すませる	to finish (something)	宿題を済ませたら、遊びに行く。

Ⅲ ひらがなを漢字に、漢字をひらがなにかえましょう。

1. _____が_____、_____になった。
   せんそう　　　　おわって　　　　へいわ

2. _____になって、病気で_____人を_____。
   いしゃ　　　　　　　　　くるしむ　　　　　なおしたい

3. _____ _____に _____を_____。
   たいらな　　　みち　　　　　自動車　　　　　　止めた

4. 次の_____では強いチームと_____が、_____勝つもりだ。
   つぎ　　しあい　　　　　　　　たたかう　　　　かならず　　か

5. あの二人は_____が_____ので、いつも_____いる。
   　　　　　　かんがえかた　　　ちがう　　　　　　　あらそって

6. 大学で_____を勉強しているが、将来は_____になりたい。
   けいざいがく　　　　　　　　しょうらい　せいじか

7. _____が_____ら、_____をしようと思っている。
   病気　　　　　なおった　　　りょこう

8. _____は外で食事を_____、10時ごろ_____する。
   へいじつ　　　　　　　　すませて　　　　　　　きたく

9. ロシア_____で、_____へ行き、おもしろい_____をした。
   けいゆ　　　　　中東　　　　　　　　　　　けいけん

10. この_____の店は_____で、_____も食べに来る。
    わしょく　　　　　ゆうめい　　　りゅうがくせい

11. この宿題が_____ _____、_____に行く。
    ぜんぶ　　　　　すんだら　　　　　おどり

12. _____から_____と_____の_____がある。
    昼　　　　　せいじ　　　けいざい　　　　授業

Ⅰ 漢字を練習しましょう。

法	法	法				係	係	係			
律	律	律				義	義	義			
際	際	際				議	議	議			
関	関	関				党	党	党			

Ⅱ 単語の読み方を書いて、文を読みましょう。

単　語	読み方	意　味	例　文
文法	ぶんぽう	grammar	英語で文法の説明をした。
方法	ほうほう	method	別の方法を考えたほうがいい。
法律	ほうりつ	law	新しい法律が作られた。
国際	こくさい	international	国際問題について話した。
国際化	こくさいか	internationalization	日本でも国際化が進んでいる。
～際	～さい	when …	お困りの際は、お電話ください。
関心	かんしん	interest; concern	私は政治にあまり関心がない。
関東	かんとう	Kanto area	彼女は関東の大学を卒業した。
関西	かんさい	Kansai area	父は関西で生まれた。
関係	かんけい	relation	あの人とは何の関係もない。
国際関係	こくさいかんけい	international relationship	大学で国際関係を勉強した。
係	かかり	person in charge	係の人に聞いてください。
主義	しゅぎ	principle; -ism	私は車を持たない主義だ。
民主主義	みんしゅしゅぎ	democracy	日本は民主主義の国だ。
社会主義	しゃかいしゅぎ	socialism	世界には社会主義の国もある。
会議	かいぎ	conference; meeting	明日の午後に重要な会議がある。
国会議員	こっかいぎいん	Member of Congress	彼は国会議員になるつもりだ。

| 不思議な | ふしぎな（handwritten） | mysterious | なぜ荷物が消えたのか不思議だ。 |
| 政党 | せいとう（handwritten） | political party | 新しい政党の名前が発表された。 |

Ⅲ ひらがなを漢字に、漢字をひらがなにかえましょう。

1. ＿＿＿＿＿を＿＿＿＿＿ためのいい＿＿＿＿＿を＿＿＿＿＿。
   ぶんぽう　まちがえない　　　ほうほう　　しりたい

2. 関東（handwritten）の高校を＿＿＿＿＿した後、＿＿＿＿＿の大学に入った。
   かんとう　　　　　そつぎょう　　　　かんさい
   kantoo（handwritten）　sotsugyoo（handwritten）　kansai（handwritten）

3. 学校で＿＿＿＿＿の＿＿＿＿＿をする＿＿＿＿＿になった。
   どうぶつ　　せわ　　　　かかり

4. ＿＿＿＿＿を食べない＿＿＿＿＿で、主に＿＿＿＿＿と＿＿＿＿＿を食べる。
   にく　　　　しゅぎ　　おも　さかな　　豆

5. 東京で＿＿＿＿＿＿＿＿＿＿が＿＿＿＿＿に、彼と会った。
   こくさい　かいぎ　　開かれた　さい

6. ＿＿＿＿＿は＿＿＿＿＿が専門だが、＿＿＿＿＿にも詳しい。
   彼女　　こくさいかんけい　せんもん　ほうりつ　くわ

7. あの＿＿＿＿＿は、どの＿＿＿＿＿にも＿＿＿＿＿いない。
   こっかいぎいん　　せいとう　　入って（ひとつ handwritten）

8. ＿＿＿＿＿はドラマに＿＿＿＿＿しているが、私は＿＿＿＿＿がない。
   妻　　　ねっちゅう　　　かんしん

9. ＿＿＿＿＿は＿＿＿＿＿と＿＿＿＿＿の＿＿＿＿＿について話した。
   教授　　せいじ　　せんそう　かんけい

10. その国は＿＿＿＿＿から＿＿＿＿＿に変わった。
    しゃかいしゅぎ　　みんしゅしゅぎ　　か

11. これからの＿＿＿＿＿は、＿＿＿＿＿が＿＿＿＿＿だ。
    しゃかい　　こくさいか　ひつよう

12. なぜ彼女はいつも＿＿＿＿＿をするのか＿＿＿＿＿だ。
    わすれもの　　　ふしぎ

Ⅰ 広島の千羽鶴
ひろしま　せんばづる

　　広島には広島平和記念公園という公園があります。多くの人が訪れるこの公園
ひろしま　ひろしま　きねんこうえん　　　こうえん　　　　　　　　　　おとず　　　　　　こうえん
には、折り紙で作ったたくさんの千羽鶴があります。外国から来た人の中には、
　　　おがみ　　　　　　　　　　せんばづる
これは何だろうと不思議に思った人もいるかもしれません。

　　1945年8月6日、広島に世界で初めて原爆が落とされ、十万人以上の人が死に
　　　　　　　　　ひろしま　　　　　はじ　　げんばく　お
ました。その後、戦争は終わりましたが、人々はこの経験を忘れないように、平和
記念公園を作りました。この公園の中に、「原爆の子の像」があります。これは、
きねんこうえん　　　　　　　こうえん　　　　　　げんばく　　　ぞう
佐々木禎子という女の子をモデルにした像です。
ささきさだこ　　　　　　　　　　　　ぞう

　　1945年、禎子は2歳の女の子で、原爆が落とされた場所から1.7kmの所に住ん
　　　　　さだこ　さい　　　　　　げんばく　お
でいました。彼女は元気に成長しましたが、小学校六年生の時、白血病になり入院
　　　　　　　　　　　せいちょう　　　　　　　　　　　　　　　はっけつびょう
しました。当時、白血病は治す方法がないと言われていました。しかし禎子は、
　　　　　とうじ　はっけつびょう　　　　　　　　　　　　　　　　　　さだこ
「鶴を千羽折れば、病気が治る」と信じて、痛みに耐えながら、鶴を折り続けまし
つる　せんばお　　　　　　　　　しん　　　　　た　　　　　つる　お　つづ
た。禎子は千羽以上の鶴を残して、12歳でこの世を去りました。その後、彼女の
　さだこ　せんば　　　つる　　　　　　　　　　　　　　　　　　　　　　　　
死を悲しんだ友達が「原爆で死んだ子供たちのために像を作ろ
　　　　　ともだち　げんばく　　こども　　　　　　ぞう
う」という活動を行い、公園の中に像が建てられました。そし
　　　　おこな　こうえん　　ぞう
て、その像の近くに、平和を願う多くの人々によって、千羽鶴が
　　　ぞう　　　　　ねが　　　　　　　　　せんばづる
置かれるようになりました。今では毎年一千万以上の鶴が、広
お　　　　　　　　　　　　　　　　　　　　　　つる　ひろ
島市に届けられます。禎子が死んでから50年以上経った今で
しま　　　　　　　さだこ　　　　　　　　　　た
も、戦争はなくなっていません。国と国が争わない世界になる
ことを願って、あなたも鶴を折ってみませんか。
　　　ねが　　　　　　つる　お

千羽鶴 せんばづる	one thousand *origami* cranes	広島平和記念公園 ひろしま　きねんこうえん	Hiroshima Peace Memorial Park
訪れる おとず	to visit	折り紙 おがみ *origami*	原爆 げんばく atomic bomb　像 statue
成長する せいちょう	to grow up	白血病 はっけつびょう leukemia	当時 とうじ in those days　鶴 crane つる
～羽 わ/ば	counter for birds	耐える た to endure	折る お to fold　この世 this world よ
去る さ	to leave	経つ (time) passes た	

正しいものには○、正しくないものには×を書きましょう。

1. （○）平和記念公園には、千羽鶴がたくさんある。
　　　　きねんこうえん　　せんばづる
2. （×）人々は原爆の経験を早く忘れたほうがいいと思っている。
　　　　　　げんばく
3. （×）禎子が死んだ後、「原爆の子の像」が建てられた。
　　　　さだこ　　　　　げんばく　　ぞう　た
4. （○）平和記念公園の千羽鶴は全部、禎子が作った。
　　　　きねんこうえん　せんばづる　　　　さだこ

Ⅰ 漢字を練習しましょう。

遊	遊	遊				涼	涼	涼	
泳	泳	泳				静	静	静	
疲	疲	疲				公	公	公	
暖	暖	暖				園	園	園	

Ⅱ 単語の読み方を書いて、文を読みましょう。

単　語	読み方	意　味	例　文
遊ぶ	あそぶ	to play	週末、兄が遊びに来た。
遊び	あそび	play	生徒は遊びに熱中していた。
泳ぐ	およぐ	to swim	彼は泳ぐのが上手だ。
水泳	すいえい	swimming	水泳の試合を見に行った。
疲れる	つかれる	to get tired	会議が長くて疲れた。
疲れ	つかれ	fatigue	疲れを感じた時は早く寝る。
暖かい	あたたかい	warm	暖かくなって、花が咲き始めた。
暖める	あたためる	to warm	寒いので、部屋を暖めた。
涼しい	すずしい	cool	秋になると涼しくなる。
静かな	しずかな	quiet	夜、この旅館はとても静かだ。
静まる	しずまる	to become quiet	彼が話し始めて、会場は静まった。
冷静な	れいせいな	calm	彼はいつも冷静だ。
公平	こうへい	impartiality	先生は学生に公平であるべきだ。
公園	こうえん	park	毎朝、近くの公園で運動する。
動物園	どうぶつえん	zoo	卒業後、動物園で働きたい。
遊園地	ゆうえんち	amusement park	週末、息子と遊園地で遊んだ。

ひらがなを漢字に、漢字をひらがなにかえましょう。

1. <u>はるやすみ</u> に子供と <u>遊園地</u> へ <u>遊</u> に行くつもりだ。
春休み　　　　 こども　　ゆうえんち　　　あそび

2. <u>海</u> の水が <u>冷たくて</u> 、 <u>泳ぐ</u> ことができなかった。
うみ　　　　　つめたくて　　　およぐ

3. <u>動物園</u> で <u>にもの</u> を取られた時、彼は <u>冷静</u> だった。
どうぶつえん　　荷物　　　　と　　　　　れいせい

4. 今日の <u>水泳</u> の <u>練習</u> は <u>疲れた</u> 。
すいえい　　れんしゅう　　つかれた

5. <u>法律</u> は国民 <u>全員</u> に <u>公平</u> であるべきだ。
ほうりつ　　　　ぜんいん　　こうへい

6. <u>たいふう</u> が過ぎて、 <u>かぜ</u> が少し <u>静まった</u> 。
台風　　　　　す　　風　　　　　しずまった

7. <u>ごぜんちゅう</u> は <u>涼しかった</u> が、午後は <u>暖かく</u> なってきた。
午前中　　　　　すずしかった　　　　あたたかく

8. <u>平日</u> の <u>ひるま</u> の <u>公園</u> は <u>静かだ</u> 。
へいじつ　　昼間　　　こうえん　　しずかだ

9. <u>彼</u> が <u>来る</u> 前に、 <u>部屋</u> を <u>暖めて</u> おこう。
かれ　　くる　　　　　へや　　　あたためて

10. <u>せんしゅう</u> の旅行の <u>疲れ</u> がまだ <u>残って</u> いる。
先週　　　　　　つかれ　　　　のこって

11. <u>近所</u> の老人に <u>昔</u> の <u>遊び</u> を <u>教えて</u> もらった。
きんじょ　ろうじん　むかし　　あそび　　おしえて

Ⅰ 漢字を練習しましょう。

込	込	込				葉	葉	葉			
連	連	連				景	景	景			
窓	窓	窓				記	記	記			
側	側	側				形	形	形			

Ⅱ 単語の読み方を書いて、文を読みましょう。

単　語	読み方	意　味	例　文
込む	こむ	to get crowded	この時間の電車は込んでいる。
人込み	ひとごみ	crowd	人込みの中を歩くのは疲れる。
連れて行く	つれていく	to take someone	弟を遊園地に連れて行った。
窓	まど	window	暑いので窓を開けてください。
窓口	まどぐち	window/counter in a public office	窓口でお金を払った。
～側	がは	… side	人は右側を歩き、車は左側を走る。
葉	は	leaf	秋になると葉が赤くなる。
言葉	ことば	word; language	彼のやさしい言葉は忘れない。
葉書	はがき	postcard	北海道から母に葉書を送った。
景色	けしき	scenery	山の上からの景色に感動した。
景気	けいき	business conditions	景気が回復してきた。
不景気	ふけいき	recession	不景気で仕事が全くない。
日記	にっき	diary	毎日日記をつけている。
暗記する	あんきする	to learn by heart	暗記するのは苦手だ。
記事	きじ	newspaper article	この新聞の記事はおもしろい。
記者	きしゃ	journalist	彼女はフランスの新聞記者だ。
記入する	きにゅうする	to fill in	この紙に住所を記入してください。

形	かたち	shape	この石はおもしろい形だ。
人形	にんぎょう	doll	着物を着ている人形を買った。

Ⅲ ひらがなを漢字に、漢字をひらがなにかえましょう。

1. _____ に _____ に行ったら、とても _____ 。
   げつまつ　ゆうえんち　　　　　　　　　こんでいた

2. _____ ので _____ の _____ も _____ 。
   あつい　　みぎがわ　　まど　　あけた

3. _____ に _____ もらった _____ がある。
   どうぶつえん　つれていって　　　おもいで

4. この _____ によると、_____ から _____ がよくなるそうだ。
   きじ　　　　　　来年　　　　けいき

5. _____ で _____ と今日の _____ を _____ してください。
   まどぐち　なまえ　　　ひづけ　　きにゅう

6. _____ には、_____ の _____ が変わり、すばらしい _____ だ。
   あき　　　は　　色(か)　　　　　　けしき

7. _____ をもらったので、お礼の _____ を _____ 。
   にんぎょう　　　　　　れい　はがき　　出した

8. _____ で、_____ の _____ は _____ なった。
   ふけいき　　しみん　せいかつ　　くるしく

9. あの _____ は _____ の _____ に詳しい。
   きしゃ　　しゃかいしゅぎ　けいざい　　くわ

10. _____ _____ を _____ して _____ する。
    ならった　ことば　　ふくしゅう　　あんき

11. _____ たちは、先週の _____ のことを _____ に書いた。
    せいと　　　　　祭り　　　　にっき

12. _____ の中で、_____ _____ のイヤリングを拾った。
    ひとごみ　　　丸い　かたち　　　　　　ひろ

① 山の上の動物園

その動物園は山の上にあった。そこから見える景色は最高で、特に秋は木の葉が赤や黄色になり、とてもきれいだった。でも、その動物園はとても小さく、子供たちが大好きなライオンやパンダはいなかった。その代わりに、羊ややぎ、うさぎや鳥などがいた。めずらしい動物はペンギンだけだった。最近、町に大きな遊園地ができて、動物園に来る人は少なくなってしまった。

動物園を見て、もっとたくさんの人に来てほしいと思った。

その日は朝からだれも客が来なかった。よし、動物たちを外に出して遊ばせよう。園長は「客がいないのに、動物たちがおりに入れられてかわいそうだ。」と考えた。園長は羊ややぎたちを動物園の中にある公園に連れて行き、子供たちが遊ぶプールにペンギンを放して、泳がせた。動物たちは広い所に出られて、幸せそうだった。

そこに子供と父親がやってきた。

「お父さん！ぼくも動物たちと一緒に遊んでいい？」子供は一日中、動物たちと遊び、帰る時には「また来るからね。」とペンギンに話していた。子供の父親はある新聞社の記者だった。家に帰ると子供は疲れて寝てしまったが、父親はすぐ、動物と遊べるこの動物園のことを記事にした。プールで遊ぶペンギンの写真も載せた。その日から、動物園は少しずつ変わった。どんどん人が来たがった。すぐにその動物園は人気の場所になり、子供たちは何度も動物園を訪れた。園長は動物と遊ぶ子供たちを見て、うれしそうに言った。「みんな、たくさん友達ができてよかったな。」

やぎ	goat	うさぎ	rabbit	園長 えんちょう	director	おり	cage	よし	yes

放す to release　叫ぶ to scream　一日中 all day long　載せる to publish
はな　　　　　　さけ　　　　　いちにちじゅう　　　　　　　の

どんどん rapidly　訪れる to visit
　　　　　　おとず

---

a〜eを、作り方の順番に並べましょう。　Order the a-e according to the story.
　　　　　　じゅんばん　なら

（　　　）→（　　　）→（　　　）→（　　　）→（　　　）

a.　園長がペンギンをプールで泳がせた。
　　えんちょう

b.　記者が動物園の記事を書いた。

c.　町に遊園地が作られた。

d.　動物園に人がたくさん来た。

e.　子供とお父さんが動物園に来た。
　　こども

Ⅰ 漢字を練習しましょう。

吉	吉	吉			供	供	供		
結	結	結			両	両	両		
婚	婚	婚			若	若	若		
共	共	共			老	老	老		

Ⅱ 単語の読み方を書いて、文を読みましょう。

単　語	読み方	意　味	例　文
結ぶ	むすぶ	to tie a knot	母は着物の帯を結ぶのが上手だ。おび
結果	けっか	result	試験の結果は来週発表される。
結婚する	けっこんする	to marry	姉は来年、結婚する予定だ。
共に	ともに	together	卒業するまで共にがんばろう。
共通	きょうつう	in common	彼女と私は共通の友達が多い。ともだち
公共	こうきょう	public	ここは市民のための公共の場所だ。
子供	こども	child	子供は疲れて寝てしまった。
両親	りょうしん	parents	両親は東京に住んでいる。
両手	りょうて	both hands	荷物が重くて両手でも持てない。
両方	りょうほう	both (sides)	両方の意見を聞いて決めよう。
両側	りょうがわ	both sides	両側にいるのが彼の両親だ。
若い	わかい	young	若い時はよく泣いた。
若者	わかもの	young people	この歌は若者の間で人気がある。にんき
老人	ろうじん	old people	若者は老人に親切にするべきだ。

Ⅲ ひらがなを漢字に、漢字をひらがなにかえましょう。

1. 私が＿＿＿＿＿＿＿＿すると聞いて、＿＿＿＿＿＿＿＿は＿＿＿＿＿＿＿＿になった。
　　　　　けっこん　　　　　　　　　　　　　りょうしん　　　　えがお

2. ＿＿＿＿＿＿＿は ＿＿＿＿＿＿＿の人々の＿＿＿＿＿＿＿＿の願いだ。
　　　へいわ　　　　　　世界　　ひとびと　　　きょうつう　　　ねが

3. その＿＿＿＿＿＿＿はとても元気で、＿＿＿＿＿＿＿教室に＿＿＿＿＿＿＿いる。
　　　　ろうじん　　　　　　　　　　　　すいえい　　　　　　　通って

4. ＿＿＿＿＿＿＿の案を ＿＿＿＿＿＿＿ ＿＿＿＿＿＿＿、これに＿＿＿＿＿＿＿した。
　　りょうほう　　あん　　　　比べた　　　　けっか　　　　　　　　けってい

5. ＿＿＿＿＿＿＿の建物は皆が＿＿＿＿＿＿＿できて、＿＿＿＿＿＿＿であるべきだ。
　　こうきょう　　　　　　　　　　りよう　　　　　　　あんぜん

6. ＿＿＿＿＿＿＿で、＿＿＿＿＿＿＿がロープを＿＿＿＿＿＿＿で＿＿＿＿＿＿＿いた。
　　こうえん　　　　　こども　　　　　　　　むすんで　　　　あそんで

7. ＿＿＿＿＿＿＿＿＿＿＿の＿＿＿＿＿＿＿に立っている＿＿＿＿＿＿＿は
　　　　国会議員　　　　　　　りょうがわ　　　　　　　わかもの

　＿＿＿＿＿＿＿ ＿＿＿＿＿＿＿だ。
　　しんぶん　　　きしゃ

8. 私たちは＿＿＿＿＿＿＿頃から＿＿＿＿＿＿＿にNGOの＿＿＿＿＿＿＿をしてきた。
　　　　　わかい　　ころ　　　　とも　　　　　　　かつどう

9. ＿＿＿＿＿＿＿に＿＿＿＿＿＿＿を持っているので、ボタンが＿＿＿＿＿＿＿＿。
　　りょうて　　　　にもつ　　　　　　　　　　　　　　　おせない

10. ＿＿＿＿＿＿＿＿＿の頃から＿＿＿＿＿＿＿するのは＿＿＿＿＿＿＿だった。
　　　しょうがくせい　ころ　　　　　あんき　　　　　　　にがて

11. ＿＿＿＿＿＿＿に＿＿＿＿＿＿＿＿＿が＿＿＿＿＿＿＿＿＿。
　　　町　　　　　えいがかん　　　　　たてられた

Ⅰ 漢字を練習しましょう。

息	息	息			祖	祖	祖		
娘	娘	娘			育	育	育		
奥	奥	奥			性	性	性		
将	将	将			招	招	招		

Ⅱ 単語の読み方を書いて、文を読みましょう。

単 語	読み方	意 味	例 文
息	いき	breath	寒い日は息が白くなる。
息子	むすこ	son	息子は大使館で働いている。
娘	むすめ	daughter	娘は工学部の学生だ。
奥	おく	inmost; back	引き出しの奥に写真を見つけた。
奥さん	おくさん	someone's wife	森さんの奥さんは大学の教授だ。
将来	しょうらい	future	将来、新聞記者になりたい。
祖父	そふ	grandfather	祖父は昔、高校の校長だった。
祖母	そぼ	grandmother	祖母は毎日洗濯してくれる。
祖先	そせん	ancestor	日本人の祖先の研究をしている。
祖国	そこく	motherland	五年後に祖国に戻るつもりだ。
教育	きょういく	education	祖父と祖母は教育に熱心だ。
育てる	そだてる	to raise	彼女は働きながら子供を育てた。
育つ	そだつ	to grow	日本で生まれて中国で育った。
体育	たいいく	physical education	今日の体育の授業は水泳だ。
男性	だんせい	male	日本の国会議員は男性が多い。
女性	じょせい	female	窓の近くにいる女性が林さんだ。
性別	せいべつ	gender; sex	紙に名前と性別を記入した。

招待する	しょうたいする	to invite	卒業式に彼の家族を招待した。
招く	まねく	to invite	社長を家に招いて、食事した。

Ⅲ ひらがなを漢字に、漢字をひらがなにかえましょう。

1. ＿＿＿＿＿は＿＿＿＿＿、＿＿＿＿の部屋で＿＿＿＿＿＿している。
   そふ　　　　つかれて　　　おく　　　　　昼寝

2. 妹は＿＿＿＿＿＿いる＿＿＿＿を＿＿＿＿に＿＿＿＿＿。
   付き合って　　　　だんせい　　　自宅　　　まねいた

3. ＿＿＿＿＿は＿＿＿＿＿＿に＿＿＿＿を＿＿＿＿。
   そぼ　　　毎年　　　おしょうがつ　きもの　　きる

4. ＿＿＿＿と＿＿＿＿は、＿＿＿＿＿＿に＿＿＿＿いる。
   むすめ　　むすこ　　　　関西　　　　すんで

5. ＿＿＿＿＿が好きなので、＿＿＿＿＿は＿＿＿＿の教師になりたい。
   うんどう　　　　　　しょうらい　たいいく　　きょうし

6. ＿＿＿＿＿、＿＿＿＿＿が＿＿＿＿に＿＿＿＿してくださった。
   しゅうまつ　　部長　　　お宅　　しょうたい

7. 彼の＿＿＿＿＿はベランダで＿＿＿＿や＿＿＿を＿＿＿＿＿いる。
   おくさん　　　　　やさい　　はな　　そだてて

8. その＿＿＿＿＿は二十年＿＿＿＿＿も＿＿＿＿＿に帰っていない。
   じょせい　　　　いじょう　　そこく

9. ＿＿＿＿に＿＿＿＿なく、皆＿＿＿＿を＿＿＿＿権利がある。
   せいべつ　かんけい　　　きょういく　　受ける　けんり

10. 人は＿＿＿＿＿ことや＿＿＿＿＿ことを＿＿＿＿しながら＿＿＿＿。
    たのしい　　　かなしい　　　けいけん　　　そだつ

11. ＿＿＿＿を＿＿＿＿、20メートル＿＿＿＿＿＿。
    いき　　　止めて　　　　　およいだ

12. ＿＿＿＿が＿＿＿＿＿＿＿＿に＿＿＿＿がある。
    そせん　　生きた　　じだい　　かんしん

Ⅰ 日本人女性の結婚観

昔、女性は結婚したら、家にいて子供を育てることが当然だと考えられていました。しかし、男性と同様に教育を受け、働く女性が増えた今、結婚に対する考えは様々です。

今の女性の結婚観について、未婚女性千人を対象に行った調査があります。その調査によると、女性が「結婚をしなくては」と焦り始めるのは三十歳を過ぎた頃、そして「もう無理だ」と思い始めるのは四十歳になってからだそうです。「将来子供が欲しいか」という質問には、25%が「欲しくない」と答えました。その理由で一番多かったのが「子供を育てる自信がない」で、次は「今の社会に不安がある」、その次は「仕事と子育ての両立ができない」でした。最後に「結婚相手に求めることは何か」という質問に対しては、一番多かった答えは「性格」、次は「価値観が合うこと」でした。また、「経済力」よりも、「家事や子育てを手伝ってくれること」や「自分が仕事をすることに理解があること」のほうが大切だと思う女性が多いという結果でした。

今の若い女性は、将来の子育てに不安を感じながらも、男性と共に家事や子育てができる結婚生活を望んでいるようです。

参考資料：「未婚女性1000人に聞いた結婚観」
http://www.macromill.com/r_data/20060803marry/

結婚観 view of marriage　当然 natural　同様に similarly
〜に対する regard to …　様々な various　未婚 unmarried　対象 object
行う to conduct　調査 survey　焦る to be anxious　自信 confidence
不安 uneasy　子育て child rearing　両立 managing both　求める to seek
性格 personality　価値観 concept of values　経済力 ability of making money
家事 household chores　理解 understanding　望む to hope

正しいものには○、正しくないものには×を書きましょう。

1. (　　) 昔、女性は母になるべきだと思われていた。
2. (　　) 未婚女性は三十歳を過ぎると結婚をあきらめてしまう。
3. (　　) 25%の女性は子供が欲しくないと思っている。
4. (　　) 子供が欲しくない一番の理由は、自分の経済力だ。
5. (　　) 相手の性格よりも経済力の方が大切だと考える女性が多い。

第28課（1）取 最 初 番 歳 枚 冊 億

Ⅰ 漢字を練習しましょう。

取	取	取			歳	歳	歳		
最	最	最			枚	枚	枚		
初	初	初			冊	冊	冊		
番	番	番			億	億	億		

Ⅱ 単語の読み方を書いて、文を読みましょう。

単 語	読み方	意 味	例 文
取る	とる	to take	化学の授業を取っている。
受け取る	うけとる	to receive	窓口でチケットを受け取った。
取り出す	とりだす	to take out	引き出しから、薬を取り出した。
取り消す	とりけす	to cancel	旅館の予約を取り消した。
最後	さいご	last	話の最後に二人は幸せになった。
最近	さいきん	recently	最近、悪いニュースばかり聞く。
最高	さいこう	the best	留学は最高の経験だった。
最低	さいてい	the lowest	試験の結果は最低だった。
最新	さいしん	the latest	ネットで最新のニュースを見る。
最も	もっとも	most	富士山は日本で最も高い山だ。
最終電車	さいしゅうでんしゃ	last train of the day	最終電車に間に合わなかった。
最初	さいしょ	first	最初から説明してください。
初めは	はじめは	at first	初めは経済に関心がなかった。
初めて	はじめて	for the first time	初めて北海道を旅行した。
一番	いちばん	number one	料理の中で和食が一番好きだ。
～番目	ばんめ	...th in order	私は三番目に発表する予定だ。
～歳	～さい	... years old	父は二十五歳で結婚した。
二十歳	はたち	20 years old	日本では二十歳からお酒が飲める。

~枚	～まい	counter for flat objects	祖母は着物を十枚持っている。
~冊	～さつ	counter for books	経済学の本を一冊買った。
~億	おく	… hundred million	日本の人口は一億人以上だ。

III ひらがなを漢字に、漢字をひらがなにかえましょう。

1. 仕事を＿＿＿＿＿＿＿、＿＿＿＿＿＿＿＿＿で＿＿＿＿＿＿した。
   すませて　　　　さいしゅうでんしゃ　　　帰宅

2. ＿＿＿＿＿＿は日本語が＿＿＿＿＿分からなくて＿＿＿＿＿だった。
   さいしょ　　　　　まったく　　　　　　ふべん

3. ＿＿＿＿＿から＿＿＿＿＿のプレゼントを＿＿＿＿＿＿＿＿。
   りょうしん　　　さいこう　　　　　　　　うけとった

4. ＿＿＿＿＿は＿＿＿＿＿にだれも＿＿＿＿＿しないつもりだった。
   はじめ　　　そつぎょうしき　　　しょうたい

5. ＿＿＿＿＿が＿＿＿＿＿なったので、＿＿＿＿＿を＿＿＿＿＿＿。
   つごう　　　わるく　　　　　　予定　　　とりけした

6. ＿＿＿＿＿＿＿＿に関する本を＿＿＿＿＿　＿＿＿＿＿＿。
   こくさいかんけい　　かん　　　　いっさつ　　　とりだした

7. ＿＿＿＿＿受けた＿＿＿＿＿は、今までで＿＿＿＿＿だった。
   さいきん　　　　しけん　　　　　　　　さいてい

8. ロシアは＿＿＿＿＿で＿＿＿＿＿大きく、カナダは＿＿＿＿＿だ。
   せかい　　　もっとも　　　　　　　にばんめ

9. ＿＿＿＿＿の時、＿＿＿＿＿＿＿＿＿＿＿＿を飲んだ。
   はたち　　　　はじめて　　　日本酒

10. ＿＿＿＿＿にその＿＿＿＿＿に会ったのは、二十五＿＿＿＿の時だった。
    さいご　　　わかもの　　　　　　　　　さい

11. ＿＿＿＿＿の機械を買うために、＿＿＿＿＿＿＿　＿＿＿＿＿だ。
    さいしん　　き かい　　　　　　　いちおくえん　　　ひつよう

12. ＿＿＿＿＿好きなカードを＿＿＿＿＿　＿＿＿＿＿ください。
    いちばん　　　　　　いちまい　　　とって

Ⅰ 漢字を練習しましょう。

点	点	点			倍	倍	倍		
階	階	階			次	次	次		
段	段	段			々	々	々		
号	号	号			他	他	他		

Ⅱ 単語の読み方を書いて、文を読みましょう。

単　語	読み方	意　味	例　文
点	てん	point; dot	政治の試験で百点を取った。
弱点	じゃくてん	weakness	自分の弱点を知るべきだ。
～階	～かい	the …th floor	この建物の九階に住んでいる。
階段	かいだん	stairs	お手洗いは階段の後ろにある。
～段	～だん	… step(s)	このお寺の階段は百段ある。
一段と	いちだんと	still more	秋になり、一段と涼しくなった。
段階	だんかい	stage	プロジェクトは最後の段階だ。
手段	しゅだん	means	どんな手段を使っても勝ちたい。
番号	ばんごう	number	部屋の番号を教えてください。
記号	きごう	symbol; mark	〒は郵便局の記号だ。
～号車	～ごうしゃ	Car No. …	二号車は自由席だ。
～倍	～ばい	~ times …er	社長の家は私の家より三倍広い。
次	つぎ	next	次の国際会議は京都だ。
目次	もくじ	table of contents	目次を見て、本を買う。
次々	つぎつぎ	one after another	今年の夏は台風が次々に来た。
人々	ひとびと	people	村の人々は親切だった。
色々な	いろいろな	various	色々な人のお世話になった。

時々	ときどき	sometimes	時々、夫は公園で子供と遊ぶ。
少々	しょうしょう	a little	少々お待ちください。
先々週	せんせんしゅう	the week before last	先々週、祖父母に会いに行った。
別々に	べつべつに	separately	父と母は別々に住んでいる。
その他	そのた	others	学生、その他多くの人が来た。
他の	ほかの	another; other	何か他の質問がありますか。
他人	たにん	stranger	家族の問題は他人には関係ない。

Ⅲ ひらがなを漢字に、漢字をひらがなにかえましょう。

1. __他い__ への __階段__ を __一段__ ずつ上がった。
   にかい　　　かいだん　　いちだん

2. __でんきだい__ は __先々週__ __払った__ ので、__次__ は来月だ。
   電気代　　　せんせんしゅう　はらった　　　つぎ　らいげつ

3. __他人__ の __弱点__ ばかり見ないで、いい __点__ も見るべきだ。
   たにん　　じゃくてん　　　　　　　　てん

4. __じけん__ の __結果__ は、今の __段階__ ではまだ分からない。
   受験　　　けっか　　　　　　だんかい

5. __窓口__ で __番号__ を呼びますので __少々__ お待ちください。
   まどぐち　ばんごう　　　　　　　しょうしょう

6. __中国__ やインド、その __他__ __色々__ な国の __人々__ が来た。
   ちゅうごく　　　　　　　　た　　いろいろ　　　ひとびと

7. __げつまつ__ には __一段__ と __暖かく__ なるだろう。
   月末　　　　　いちだん　　あたたかく

8. __子供__ が __一号車__ の __一番__ 前で、__けしき__ を見ている。
   こども　　いちごうしゃ　　いちばん　　　景色

9. __ちず__ のこの __記号__ は __市役所__ を __あらわして__ いる。
   地図　　　　きごう　　しゃくしょ　　　　表して

10. バスや __でんしゃ__ などの交通 __手段__ で、__皆__ __別々__ に来た。
    電車　　　　こうつう　しゅだん　　みな　べつべつ

11. 時々　目次　を見てから、かう　本を　決める。
　　ときどき　もくじ　　　買う　本　　きめる

12. 女性　は　男性　の四　倍　家事をするそうだ。
　　じょせい　だんせい　　ばい　かじ

13. 次　と　新らしい　映画　が　作られて　いる。
　　つぎつぎ　新しい　　えいが　つくられて

14. ばん　は　えんで　いるので、他　の時間に来てください。
　　晩　　こんで　　　　ほか

15. 景気　は　少し　ずつ　回復　するだろう。
　　けいき　すこし　　かいふく

16. 英語　いがい　の　言葉　は話せない。
　　えいご　以外　　ことば

17. 丸くて、中が　赤くて、夏　に　冷やして　食べる
　　まるくて　　赤くて　なつ　冷やして

　　果物　は何？　こたえ　はスイカ。
　　くだもの　　　答え

18. 教科書を暗記　するだけでなく、文法　を理解　することも
　　きょうかしょ　あんき　　ぶんぽう　りかい

　　重要　だ。
　　じゅうよう

19. あの研究者　は　国際　経済学　が専門　だ。
　　けんきゅうしゃ　こくさい　けいざいがく　せんもん

20. 雨の日に、親切　な　本屋　の　てんいん　さんが
　　しんせつ　ほんや　店員

　　傘を　貸して　くれた。
　　かさ　かして

21. 仕事も　えび　も　りょうほう　大切　だ。
　　あそび　　両方　たいせつ

Ⅰ コミック販売サイト
はんばい

コミックマニア オンラインコミック購入サイト
こうにゅう

全国どこでも￥1,500以上送料無料!!
そうりょうむりょう

ただ今、「コナン」3点購入でポスタープレゼント！
こうにゅう

インターネット最大のコミックショッピングモール「コミックマニア」にようこそ！
さいだい
最近話題のコミックはもちろん、昔懐かしい手塚治虫の中古コミックなど、色々な
わだい　　　　　　　　　　　　　　　なつ　　　　　てづかおさむ　ちゅうこ
コミックが手に入るショッピングサイトです。レア物も多く、あなたが今まで探し
はい
続けていた一冊もきっと見つかります。また予約サービスで話題の新刊を一番にゲ
わだい　しんかん
ットできます。

――初めての方は最初にこちらでメンバー登録してください。――
かた　　　　　　　　　　　　　　　　　　とうろく

メンバー登録 （なお、登録は18歳以上の方に限ります）
とうろく　　　　　　　　　　とうろく　　　　　　かた　かぎ

よくある質問　　　　商品検索　　　　注文方法
しょうひんけんさく　　　ちゅうもんほうほう

©青山剛昌／小学館

今週のピックアップ　〜「名探偵コナン」〜
めいたんてい
テレビ・映画にもなった大人気コミック

名探偵として有名な高校生・工藤新一は、ある組織に毒薬
めいたんてい　　　　　　　　くどうしんいち　　　　そしき　どくやく
を飲まされ、子供になってしまう。新一は、「小学生・江
しんいち
戸川コナン」となり、次々と事件を解決する。
とがわ　　　　　　　　じけん　かいけつ

よくある質問　Q：返品はできますか。
へんぴん
　　　　　　　A：商品を受け取り後、一週間以内なら返品ができます。
しょうひん　　　　　　　　　　　　へんぴん
　　　　　　　　　一週間を過ぎたものは返品できません。
す　　　　へんぴん

　　　　　　　Q：注文をキャンセルできますか。

　　　　　　　A：商品の発送前なら取り消すことができます。
しょうひん　はっそうまえ
　　　　　　　　　発送後は、取り消すことができません。
はっそうご

＊その他のご質問はこちらのカスタマーサービスcomicmania@com.jpへ。

質問に答えましょう。

1. 初めてこのサイトを使う時、まず何をしなくてはいけませんか。
   <u>account をつくります</u>

2. このサイトでどんなコミックを買うことができますか。
   <u>まんが</u>

3. どんな場合、送料（そうりょう）が無料（むりょう）になりますか。
   <u>over 1500 yen</u>

4. 注文したコミックが３週間前に届きました。このコミックを返品（へんぴん）することができますか。
   <u>No ちがいます</u>

5. どんな場合、注文を取り消すことができますか。
   <u>前 shipping</u>

購入（こうにゅう） purchase　　送料（そうりょう） shipping charge　　無料（むりょう） free of charge　　〜点 item(s)

最大（さいだい） the biggest　　話題（わだい） topic of conversation　　懐かしい（なつかしい） nostalgic　　中古（ちゅうこ） used

手に入る（はいる） to get　　レア物 rare items　　新刊（しんかん） new publication　　登録する（とうろく） to register

〜に限る（かぎ） to limit to ...　　商品（しょうひん） merchandise　　検索（けんさく） search

名探偵（めいたんてい） famous detective　　組織（そしき） organization　　毒薬（どくやく） poison　　事件（じけん） incident

解決する（かいけつ） to solve　　返品（へんぴん） returning goods　　発送（はっそう） sending out

Ⅰ 漢字を練習しましょう。

Ⅱ 単語の読み方を書いて、文を読みましょう。

単　語	読み方	意　味	例　文
勝つ	かつ	to win	明日の試合に勝ちたい。
負ける	まける	to lose (a game, etc.)	子供の時、よくけんかに負けた。
勝負	しょうぶ	victory or defeat	この勝負に負けたくない。
賛成する	さんせいする	to agree	あなたの意見に賛成する。
成長	せいちょう	growth	子供の成長は早い。
成人	せいじん	adult	日本では二十歳は成人だ。
絶対に	ぜったいに	definitely	絶対に戦争はしたくない。
反対する	はんたいする	to oppose	父に彼との結婚を反対された。
～対～	～たい～	… versus …	今日の試合は日本対中国だ。
続ける	つづける	to continue (something)	卒業後も研究を続けたい。
続く	つづく	(something) continues	最近、雨の日が続いている。
続き	つづき	continuance	この映画の続きを早く見たい。
手続き	れんぞく	procedure	ここで入学の手続きができる。
連続	じしょ	continuity	毎朝、連続ドラマを見ている。
辞書	つづき	dictionary	電子辞書は便利だ。
辞める	やめる	to resign	兄は会社を辞めて、留学した。

Ⅲ ひらがなを漢字に、漢字をひらがなにかえましょう。

1. 日本<u>対</u>（たい）<u>韓国</u>（かんこく）の<u>しあい</u>（試合）は<u>四時間</u>（よじかん）<u>続いた</u>（つづいた）。

2. <u>すいえい</u>（水泳）の<u>全国</u>（ぜんこく）<u>大会</u>（たいかい）は、<u>二年</u>（にねん）<u>連続</u>（れんぞく）で<u>東京都</u>（とうきょうと）の<u>こうこう</u>（高校）が<u>勝った</u>（かった）。

3. <u>会社</u>（かいしゃ）を<u>辞めて</u>（やめて）、<u>自分</u>（じぶん）の<u>みせ</u>（店）を<u>開きたい</u>（ひらきたい）。

4. <u>息子</u>（むすこ）は多くの<u>経験</u>（けいけん）をして<u>成長</u>（せいちょう）した。

5. <u>受け付け</u>（うけつけ）で<u>にゅういん</u>（入院）の<u>手続き</u>（てつづき）をした。

6. どちらが<u>強い</u>（つよい）か<u>勝負</u>（しょうぶ）したが、<u>負けた</u>（まけた）。

7. <u>おや</u>（親）は<u>留学</u>（りゅうがく）に<u>反対</u>（はんたい）したが、<u>絶対に</u>（ぜったいに）行きたい。

8. <u>漢字</u>（かんじ）の<u>辞書</u>（じしょ）を<u>三冊</u>（さんさつ）も<u>持って</u>（もって）いる。

9. <u>用事</u>（ようじ）があるので、<u>宿題</u>（しゅくだい）の<u>続き</u>（つづき）は<u>後で</u>（あとで）する。

10. <u>なんさい</u>（何歳）から<u>成人</u>（せいじん）になるかは、国によって<u>違う</u>（ちがう）。

11. どんな<u>理由</u>（りゆう）でも、<u>戦争</u>（せんそう）を<u>続ける</u>（つづける）ことはよくない。

12. <u>会議</u>（かいぎ）の<u>けってい</u>（決定）には<u>賛成</u>（さんせい）だ。

13. 家族の中で、<u>そふ</u>（祖父）が<u>一番</u>（いちばん）<u>教育</u>（きょういく）に<u>熱心</u>（ねっしん）だ。

Ⅰ 漢字を練習しましょう。

投	投	投			守	守	守		
選	選	選			過	過	過		
約	約	約			夢	夢	夢		
束	束	束			的	的	的		

Ⅱ 単語の読み方を書いて、文を読みましょう。

単 語	読み方	意 味	例 文
投げる	なげる	to throw	息子とボールを投げて遊んだ。
選ぶ	えらぶ	to choose	彼女は市長に選ばれた。
選手	せんしゅ	player	彼は有名なサッカーの選手だ。
予約	よやく	reservation	海の近くの旅館を予約した。
約〜	やく〜	about …	デモに約千人が集まった。
約束	やくそく	promise	午後、人と会う約束がある。
留守	るす	absence from home	両親が留守の間に、祖父が来た。
留守番電話	るすばんでんわ	answering machine	留守番電話に伝言を入れた。
守る	まもる	to protect	必ず約束を守ってください。
過去	かこ	past	過去の苦しかったことを忘れたい。
過ぎる	すぎる	to pass	電車は京都を過ぎた。
〜時過ぎ	〜じすぎ	a few minutes past … o'clock	五時過ぎに荷物が届く予定だ。
過ごす	すごす	to spend (time)	週末は家族と過ごした。
夢	ゆめ	dream	夢は政治家になることだ。
夢中	むちゅう	absorbed	今、踊りに夢中になっている。
目的	もくてき	purpose	歴史を研究する目的で日本に来た。
民主的	みんしゅてき	democratic	この国は民主的な国になった。
社会的	しゃかいてき	social	「いじめ」は社会的問題だ。
国際的	こくさいてき	international	その問題は国際的な関心を集めた。

Ⅲ ひらがなを漢字に、漢字をひらがなにかえましょう。

1. ＿＿＿＿＿＿＿＿＿＿をセットしてから＿＿＿＿＿＿＿＿＿＿。
   るすばんでんわ　　　　　　　　　　　　　　　　出かけた

2. ＿＿＿＿＿＿＿は＿＿＿＿＿＿＿＿に＿＿＿＿＿＿人のことも考えるべきだ。
   せいじか　　　　　しゃかいてき　　　　　よわい

3. 今日の試合で＿＿＿＿＿＿に＿＿＿＿＿＿　＿＿＿＿＿＿は田中だ。
   　　　　　　　さいしょ　　　　なげる　　　　せんしゅ

4. ＿＿＿＿＿＿は＿＿＿＿＿＿＿＿で＿＿＿＿＿＿で遊んでいた。
   こども　　　　　　　遊園地　　　　　むちゅう

5. ＿＿＿百人の＿＿＿＿＿＿＿＿が＿＿＿＿＿＿に＿＿＿＿＿＿＿。
   やく　　　　こっかいぎいん　　　みんしゅてき　　　えらばれた

6. ＿＿＿＿＿＿＿は＿＿＿＿を持って＿＿＿＿＿＿＿ほうがいい。
   なつやすみ　　　もくてき　　　　　すごした

7. ＿＿＿＿＿＿＿に＿＿＿＿＿の店を＿＿＿＿＿した。
   しちじすぎ　　　わしょく　　　　　よやく

8. ＿＿＿＿＿の＿＿＿＿の＿＿＿＿を調べた。
   しんぶん　　　かこ　　　記事　　　しら

9. ＿＿＿＿＿、＿＿＿＿＿＿＿な＿＿＿＿＿をするのが＿＿＿＿だ。
   しょうらい　　こくさいてき　　　しごと　　　　　ゆめ

10. ＿＿＿＿＿＿も＿＿＿＿＿を破るなんて＿＿＿＿＿だ。
    何回　　　　やくそく　やぶ　　　　　さいてい

11. ＿＿＿＿＿を＿＿＿＿＿から、＿＿＿＿＿をつけるようになった。
    二十歳　　　　すぎて　　　　　にっき

12. 彼らは＿＿＿＿＿を＿＿＿＿＿ために毎日＿＿＿＿＿＿＿いる。
    へいわ　　　まもる　　　　　たたかって

13. ＿＿＿＿＿は＿＿＿＿＿に行って＿＿＿＿＿だった。
    かぞく　　　かいもの　　　　　るす

① 谷亮子
たにりょうこ

オリンピックに出場することはスポーツ選手の夢である。
しゅつじょう
そのオリンピックに連続五回出場した日本の柔道選手がいる。
しゅつじょう   じゅうどう
彼女の名前は谷亮子。身長146cmの小さい体で、五回のオリン
たにりょうこ   しんちょう
ピックに出場し、五つのメダルを取った。
しゅつじょう

谷選手は小学二年生で柔道を始めた。始めた時、「体が小
たに   じゅうどう
さいから人の三倍練習しなさい。」と先生に言われ、それを守って練習した。五か
月後、初めての試合で優勝したが、この時、大きい男の子を次々と投げ飛ばして、
ゆうしょう   と
そのうち二人は病院に運ばれたという話である。

1990年に国際大会で優勝し、1992年、十六歳でバルセロナオリンピック代表に選
たいかい ゆうしょう   だいひょう
ばれた。この時は決勝で勝てず、銀メダルを取ったが、彼女に笑顔はなかった。
けっしょう
次のアトランタオリンピックでも決勝で負け、銀メダルの結果となった。2000年
けっしょう
のシドニーオリンピックでは、「最高で金、最低でも金」と言って絶対に金メダル
を取ることを皆に約束し、ついに金メダルを取った。2003年に結婚して、田村亮
た むらりょう
子から谷亮子に名前が変わったが、柔道を続けた。2004年のアテネオリンピックの
こ たにりょうこ   か   じゅうどう
時は「田村で金、谷でも金」という言葉と共に戦い、二つ目の金メダルを取った。
た むら   たに

2005年に子供を産んで、しばらく柔道を休んでいたが、2008年の北京オリンピ
う   じゅうどう   べ きん
ックで復帰。「ママでも金」を目指したが、残念ながら、銅メダルに終わった。金
ふっき   めざ   どう
メダルは取れなかったが、子育てをしながら一対一の厳しい勝負の世界で成長を
こそだ   きび
続ける彼女の姿は、多くの日本人に感動を与えた。
すがた   あた

オリンピック　the Olympics　　出場する　to be in a competition　　身長　height
しゅつじょう   しんちょう
優勝する　to win in a competition　　投げ飛ばす　to throw out　　大会　competition
ゆうしょう   と   たいかい
代表　representative　　産む　to give birth　　北京　Beijing　　復帰　comeback
だいひょう   う   べ きん   ふっき
目指す　to aim　　姿　aspect　　与える　to give
めざ   すがた   あた

下の年表(chronology)を完成させましょう。
ねんぴょう   かんせい

小学（　　　　　）：柔道を始めた　　　　　　2003年：＿＿＿＿＿＿＿＿＿＿＿
じゅうどう

1992年：＿＿＿＿＿＿＿＿＿＿＿　　　　　　2004年：＿＿＿＿＿＿＿＿＿＿＿

1996年：＿＿＿＿＿＿＿＿＿＿＿　　　　　　2005年：＿＿＿＿＿＿＿＿＿＿＿

2000年：＿＿＿＿＿＿＿＿＿＿＿　　　　　　2008年：＿＿＿＿＿＿＿＿＿＿＿

Ⅰ 漢字を練習しましょう。

飛	飛	飛			速	速	速		
機	機	機			遅	遅	遅		
失	失	失			駐	駐	駐		
鉄	鉄	鉄			泊	泊	泊		

Ⅱ 単語の読み方を書いて、文を読みましょう。

単　語	読み方	意　味	例　文
飛ぶ	とぶ	(something) flies	鳥が空を飛んでいる。
飛び出す	とびだす	to jump out	犬が車の前に飛び出した。
飛ばす	とばす	to fly (something)	風船に手紙を付けて、飛ばした。
飛行機	ひこうき	airplane	飛行機は九時過ぎに着く。
機会	きかい	opportunity	仕事で外国に行く機会があった。
洗濯機	せんたくき	washing machine	新しい洗濯機を買った。
失う	うしなう	to lose	彼女は戦争で息子を失った。
失業	しつぎょう	unemployment	兄は失業して一年になる。
地下鉄	ちかてつ	subway	地下鉄は安くて便利だ。
鉄	てつ	iron	この工場では鉄を生産している。
鉄道	てつどう	railroad	村に鉄道が通った。
速い	はやい	fast	この電車は速くて静かだ。
早速	さっそく	at once	服が届いたので、早速着てみた。
遅い	おそい	late; slow	夜遅いので、店は閉まっている。 私の子供は走るのが遅い。
遅れる	おくれる	to be late	道を間違えて、試験に遅れた。
駐車する	ちゅうしゃする	to park	店の近くに車を駐車した。
駐車場	ちゅうしゃじょう	parking area	駐車場は公園の前にある。

二泊三日	にはくみっか	two-night stay	二泊三日の旅行に行った。
～泊する	～はくする	to stay … night(s)	京都の旅館に一泊した。
泊まる	とまる	to stay overnight	週末、祖父の家に泊まった。
泊める	とめる	to let someone stay overnight	先週、友達を家に泊めた。 せんしゅう　ともだち

Ⅲ ひらがなを漢字に、漢字をひらがなにかえましょう。

1. この町は＿＿＿＿＿や＿＿＿＿＿が発達していて、＿＿＿＿＿だ。
　　　　　　てつどう　　　　ちかてつ　　はったつ　　　　　べんり

2. 九月の＿＿＿に＿＿＿＿＿の〰〰〰に行くことに＿＿＿＿＿。
　　　　　すえ　　にはくみっか　　旅行　　　　　きめた

3. ＿＿＿＿＿する＿＿＿＿＿がなくて、＿＿＿＿＿に＿＿＿＿＿。
　　ちゅうしゃ　　ばしょ　　　　　じゅぎょう　　おくれた

4. 〰〰〰＿＿＿＿＿に＿＿＿＿＿子供が＿＿＿＿＿。
　　急に　　じてんしゃ　　のった　　　　とびだした

5. ＿＿＿＿＿は＿＿＿＿＿へ帰る＿＿＿＿＿を＿＿＿＿＿。
　　そぼ　　そこく　　　　きかい　　うしなった

6. ＿＿＿＿＿＿＿＿＿＿ので、＿＿＿＿＿＿は＿＿＿＿＿いた。
　　よる　　おそかった　　　　ちゅうしゃじょう　　しまって

7. ＿＿＿＿＿で＿＿＿＿＿を〰〰〰、＿＿＿＿＿。
　　かみ　　ひこうき　　作って　　　とばした

8. ＿＿＿＿＿で＿＿＿＿＿している人が＿＿＿＿＿と増えた。
　　ふけいき　　しつぎょう　　　　いちだん　　ふ

9. 青森で＿＿＿＿＿してから、秋田の＿＿＿＿＿に＿＿＿＿＿。
　あおもり　いっぱく　　　あきた　　りょかん　　とまった

10. ＿＿＿＿＿を＿＿＿＿＿＿＿＿＿＿を見た。
　　そら　　とぶ　　ゆめ

11. ＿＿＿＿＿ ～～～～～～～ からの＿＿＿＿＿を家に＿＿＿＿＿＿。
　　　ときどき　　　　外国　　　　　　　がくせい　　　　　　とめる

12. ～～～～～ は世界で＿＿＿＿＿足が＿＿＿＿＿ ＿＿＿＿＿だ。
　　　彼　　　　　　　もっとも　　　　はやい　　　せんしゅ

13. ＿＿＿＿＿した＿＿＿＿＿が＿＿＿＿＿ ＿＿＿＿＿。
　　ちゅうもん　　　せんたくき　　　さっそく　　　とどいた

14. ＿＿＿＿＿が＿＿＿＿＿、＿＿＿＿＿。
　　　てつ　　　　ひえて　　　　かたまった

15. ～～～～～が＿＿＿＿＿いるので ～～～～～を立てないください。
　　　子犬　　　　　ねむって　　　　　　音　　　た

16. ソウル～～～～～～～～で行くと＿＿＿＿＿12時間かかる。
　　　　　経由　　　　　　　かたみち

17. ＿＿＿＿＿ ～～～～～～～の中にも＿＿＿＿＿の人と
　　おなじ　　　　政党　　　　　　　はんたい

＿＿＿＿＿の人がいた。
　さんせい

18. ～～～～～～～には＿＿＿＿＿の友人だけを＿＿＿＿＿ことにした。
　　結婚式　　　　　きょうつう　ゆうじん　　　　まねく

19. ～～～～～～～の＿＿＿＿＿さん、
　　卒業生　　　　　みな

これから＿＿＿＿＿ ～～～～～が＿＿＿＿＿います。
　　　あかるい　　　未来　　　　まって

第30課（2）　船 座 席 島 陸 港 橋 交

Ⅰ 漢字を練習しましょう。

船	船	船			
座	座	座			
席	席	席			
島	島	島			

陸	陸	陸			
港	港	港			
橋	橋	橋			
交	交	交			

Ⅱ 単語の読み方を書いて、文を読みましょう。

単 語	読み方	意 味	例 文
船		ship	船に乗ると気分が悪くなる。
船便		surface mail	荷物は船便で送るつもりだ。
風船		balloon	お祭りで風船を売っていた。
座る		to sit	電車は込んでいたが、座れた。
口座		bank account	銀行で口座を開いた。
席		seat	窓側の席に座った。
出席		attendance	会議には全員出席した。
空席		empty seat	この飛行機は空席が全くない。
島		island	沖縄は日本の南にある島だ。
半島		peninsula	伊豆半島を旅行した。
大陸		continent	この大陸には色々な動物がいる。
陸		land	船から遠くに陸が見えた。
空港		airport	新しい空港を建てる計画がある。
港		port	港に船が着いた。
橋		bridge	この橋からの景色は最高だ。
交番		police box	交番で道を聞いた。

Ⅲ ひらがなを漢字に、漢字をひらがなにかえましょう。

1. _____がないので、_____でその_____へ行った。
　　　 はし　　　　　　　　 ふね　　　　　　　　 しま

2. _____があったので、学生は_____ _____した。
　　 はっぴょう　　　　　　　　　　　　 ぜんいん　　 しゅっせき

3. _____は_____に_____に_____。
　　 ろうじん　　　　 しずか　　　　 せき　　　　 すわった

4. _____で次の_____の_____を待った。
　　 くうこう　　　　　　 ひこうき　　　　 くうせき

5. _____に_____ _____を見られないように_____した。
　　 たにん　　　　 こうざ　　　 ばんごう　　　　　　　　　　　　 ちゅうい

6. _____で_____と、〜〜〜〜〜〜は1か月半で_____。
　　 ふなびん　　　 おくる　　　　　　　 荷物　　　　　　　　　 つく

7. おもちゃ_____の_____で_____を_____いる。
　　　　　　 うりば　　　 まえ　　　 ふうせん　　　 くばって

8. _____を〜〜〜〜〜〜〜して、_____を_____。
　　 くるま　　　　　　 運転　　　　　　 はんとう　　　 まわった

9. _____を_____してから、〜〜〜〜〜〜〜〜〜後、_____が見えた。
　　 みなと　　 しゅっぱつ　　　　　　　　 一週間　　　ご　　 りく

10. 〜〜〜〜〜〜が分からなくて、_____で〜〜〜を〜〜〜〜。
　　　 会場　　　　　　　　　　　　 こうばん　　 道　　 聞いた

11. _____を〜〜〜〜〜〜〜〜で旅行して、
　　 たいりく　　　　　　 鉄道

_____な_____に_____。
　　 いろいろ　　 ひとびと　　　 あった

12. 病気を_____ために_____の_____が_____。
　　　　　 なおす　　　　　　 さいしん　　　 ほうほう　　　 つかわれる

① 沖縄旅行
おきなわ

名古屋発 毎週火曜日出発 5万8千円〜
なごやはつ

人気ホテルに泊まる 二泊三日 **沖縄の旅**
にんき   おき なわ たび

青い空と青い海。暖かい南の島で、美しい景色を
うつく
楽しみ、沖縄の歴史、文化に触れてみませんか。
おきなわ れきし   ふ

一日目
いちにちめ

飛行機で那覇へ → 那覇空港着 → 水族館・公園
なは   なは くうこうちゃく   すいぞくかん
→ ビール工場 → 市場で買い物 → 那覇泊（ロイヤルガーデンホテル）
なははく

二日目
ふつかめ

飛行機で宮古島へ → 半島をドライブ → 橋を渡って池間島へ
みやこじま   わた いけまじま
→ 港から船でクルーズ → 宮古島泊（オーシャンビューホテル）
みやこじまはく

三日目
みっかめ

飛行機で那覇へ → 出発までフリータイム（オプショナルツアーあり）
なは
→ 夜、名古屋着
なごやちゃく

注意） 飛行機が遅れた場合は予定が変わることがあります。
か

食事：朝食二回、昼食二回、夕食二回
ちょうしょく   ちゅうしょく ゆうしょく
（夕食は和食と洋食をご用意。お好きな料理をお選びいただけます）
ゆうしょく   ようしょく

◆オプショナルツアー

A. 動物園とみいばるビーチ（ガラスボートに乗り、色々なサンゴや魚をご覧
いただけます）

B. 首里城と琉球村（沖縄の歴史に触れ、伝統文化をお楽しみください）
しゅりじょう りゅうきゅうむら おきなわ れきし ふ   でんとう

●ご出発の一か月前までにご予約された方への特典
とくてん
・空港までお車をご利用の場合は、駐車場の料金が割引になります。
りょうきん わりびき
・お帰りのお荷物は、空港からご自宅まで無料でお届けします。
むりょう

質問に答えましょう。

1. 那覇で何泊しますか。
   なは

2. 沖縄の文化を知りたい人は、どちらのオプショナルツアーに行きますか。
   おきなわ

3. 夕食は、和食ですか、洋食ですか。
   ゆうしょく　　　　　　　ようしょく

4. いつまでに予約すると、空港の駐車場の料金が安くなりますか。
   りょうきん

～発　leaving …　　旅　trip　　触れる　to touch　　～着　arriving …
はつ　　　　　　　　たび　　　　ふ　　　　　　　　　ちゃく

水族館　aquarium　　～泊　staying at …　　朝食　breakfast　　昼食　lunch
すいぞくかん　　　　　　はく　　　　　　　　ちょうしょく　　　　　ちゅうしょく

夕食　dinner　　洋食　western dish　　サンゴ　coral　　首里城　Shuri Castle
ゆうしょく　　　　ようしょく　　　　　　　　　　　　　　しゅ　り　じょう

伝統　tradition　　特典　benefit　　料金　fee　　割引　discount　　無料　free of charge
でんとう　　　　　とくてん　　　　りょうきん　　わりびき　　　　　　むりょう

Ⅰ 漢字を練習しましょう。

申	申	申				調	調	調			
神	神	神				査	査	査			
様	様	様				相	相	相			
信	信	信				談	談	談			

Ⅱ 単語の読み方を書いて、文を読みましょう。

単　語	読み方	意　味	例　文
申す	もうす	to tell; My name is …	山田と申します。
申し上げる	もうしあげる	I humbly tell you	社長にお礼を申し上げた。
申し込む	もうしこむ	to apply	一泊二日の旅行に申し込んだ。
神社	じんじゃ	shrine	京都にはお寺や神社が多い。
神経	しんけい	nerve	あの選手は運動神経がいい。
神/神様	かみさま	god	困った時は神様にお願いする。
～様	～さま	Mr./Mrs. …	田中様は三時にご出発です。
様々な	さまざまな	various	留学して、様々な経験をした。
様子	ようす	condition	子供が遊ぶ様子を見ていた。
同様に	どうように	similarly	うちの犬は家族同様に大切だ。
信号	しんごう	traffic light	信号が赤になったら止まろう。
信じる	しんじる	to believe	彼が約束を守ると信じている。
自信	じしん	confidence	自分に自信を持つべきだ。
信用	しんよう	trust	彼の言うことは信用できる。
調べる	しらべる	to investigate	知らない言葉を辞書で調べた。
強調する	きょうちょうする	to emphasize	その点を強調して彼に伝えた。
調子	ちょうし	condition	コンピューターの調子が悪い。
調査	ちょうさ	investigation	調査の結果を表にまとめた。

相手	あいて	partner	結婚の相手は同じ会社の人だ。
首相	しゅしょう	prime minister	首相は今海外にいる。
相談する	そうだんする	to consult	困った時は姉に相談する。

Ⅲ ひらがなを漢字に、漢字をひらがなにかえましょう。

1. ＿＿＿＿＿＿の田中と＿＿＿＿＿＿。
   しゃくしょ　　　　　もうします

2. ＿＿＿＿＿は＿＿＿＿＿な＿＿＿＿＿を＿＿＿＿＿。
   しゅしょう　　こくさいてき　　しんよう　　　失った

3. ＿＿＿＿＿と＿＿＿＿が落ちる＿＿＿＿＿を＿＿＿＿から見ていた。
   次々　　葉　　　　　ようす　　　まど

4. 試合の時、私と＿＿＿＿＿に、＿＿＿＿＿も＿＿＿＿＿が良くなかった。
   どうよう　　　あいて　　ちょうし

5. ＿＿＿＿＿を＿＿＿＿と＿＿＿＿＿に＿＿＿＿＿がある。
   しんごう　　過ぎる　　みぎがわ　　じんじゃ

6. ＿＿＿＿＿をしてデータを＿＿＿＿＿、＿＿＿＿＿を＿＿＿＿＿した。
   ちょうさ　　　　あつめ　　けっか　　　発表

7. 木や＿＿＿や水の中に＿＿＿＿＿がいると＿＿＿＿＿＿いた。
   石　　　　かみさま　　　しんじられて

8. ＿＿＿＿＿に＿＿＿＿＿＿事があります。
   たなかさま　　もうしあげたい

9. ＿＿＿＿＿は、＿＿＿＿＿ことは＿＿＿＿＿ではないと＿＿＿＿＿した。
   りょうしん　　かつ　　じゅうよう　　　きょうちょう

10. ＿＿＿＿＿と＿＿＿＿＿して、その奨学金に＿＿＿＿＿＿ことにした。
    きょうじゅ　そうだん　　しょうがくきん　　もうしこむ

11. ＿＿＿＿＿の＿＿＿＿＿な＿＿＿＿＿について＿＿＿＿＿。
    からだ　　さまざま　　しんけい　　　しらべた

12. ＿＿＿＿＿時は、自分に＿＿＿＿＿が持てなかったが、今は＿＿＿＿＿。
    わかい　　　　じしん　　　　　ちがう

Ⅰ 漢字を練習しましょう。

案	案	案			星	星	星		
内	内	内			雪	雪	雪		
君	君	君			降	降	降		
達	達	達			直	直	直		

Ⅱ 単語の読み方を書いて、文を読みましょう。

単　語	読み方	意　味	例　文
案		plan	会議の結果、彼の案が選ばれた。
案外		unexpectedly	試験は案外よくできていた。
答案用紙		answer sheet	先生は学生に答案用紙を配った。
案内する		to guide	係の人が工場を案内してくれた。
～以内		within …	三日以内に作文を出してください。
家内		my wife	家内は今出かけている。
国内		domestic	国内をのんびり旅行したい。
～君		Mr. …	駅の前で山本君に会った。
君		you	君の本を貸してくれないか。
友達		friend	結婚式に大学の友達を招待した。
私達		we	私達には将来の夢がある。
速達		express mail	父から速達で手紙が届いた。
上達する		to improve	彼の日本語はずいぶん上達した。
配達		delivery	新聞配達のバイトをしている。
達する		to reach	失業者は百万人に達した。
星		star	空には星が光っている。
雪		snow	雪のため電車が止まった。

降りる		to get off	次の駅で電車を降りよう。
降る		(rain/snow) falls	雨が降って、祭が中止になった。
～以降		after …	三時以降なら自宅にいる。
直す		to correct; to fix	辞書を見て、間違いを直した。
直る		to be fixed	洗濯機が直ってよかった。
正直な		honest	彼は頭が固いが、正直な人だ。
見直す		to take another look	試験の答えをもう一度見直した。

Ⅲ ひらがなを漢字に、漢字をひらがなにかえましょう。

1. _____を_____、_____の_____で_____。
　　ちかてつ　　　おりて　　　えき　　　　北口　　　　　まった

2. _____が家に_____ので、_____の日、町を_____した。
　　ともだち　　　　とまった　　　　つぎ　　　　　あんない

3. _____の日本語は、_____ _____にずいぶん_____したね。
　　きみ　　　　　みじかい　　あいだ　　　　　じょうたつ

4. _____は明日_____なら_____できる。
　　品物　　　　　いこう　　　はいたつ

5. 車が_____ので、_____、_____まで海を見に行った。
　　なおった　　　　　早速　　　みなと

6. _____が_____ _____が_____。
　　ゆき　　　ふって　　　　急行　　　おくれた

7. _____でも_____ _____がきれいに見える。
　　とうきょう　あんがい　　ほし

8. その_____に_____した人は、_____した人より多かった。
　　あん　さんせい　　　　　はんたい

9. 一週間_____に_____と言われて、_____で送った。
　　いない　　　　届かない　　　　　そくたつ

10. 山本＿＿＿＿は壊れた～～～～～～～～～～を＿＿＿＿＿＿くれた。
　　　　くん　　こわ　　　　　　洗濯機　　　　　　　なおして

11. ＿＿＿＿＿＿＿＿＿を出す前にもう～～～～～～　＿＿＿＿＿＿＿＿＿。
　　　とうあんようし　　　　　　　　　一度　　　みなおした

12. ＿＿＿＿＿＿してから、＿＿＿＿＿には何でも＿＿＿＿＿に話している。
　　　けっこん　　　　　　　かない　　　　　　しょうじき

13. ＿＿＿＿＿＿の～～～～～～～～を、＿＿＿＿＿＿＿忘れない。
　　　わたしたち　　　　友情　　　　　　けっして

14. その商品の＿＿＿＿＿＿での売り上げが～～～～～～～～に＿＿＿＿＿。
　　　しょうひん　こくない　　　う　あ　　　　五億円　　　たっした

15. ＿＿＿＿＿＿＿、＿＿＿＿＿の＿＿＿＿＿＿は～～～～～～ですか。
　　　たなかさま　　　　よやく　　　てつづき　　　お済み

16. ＿＿＿＿＿＿＿　＿＿＿＿＿＿に～～～～を～～～～なさい。
　　　ただしい　　　　こたえ　　　丸　　付け

17. テニス～～～～を＿＿＿＿＿＿＿で、＿＿＿＿＿＿＿いる。
　　　　部　　　やめない　　　　　つづけて

18. その～～～～をまっすぐ＿＿＿＿＿＿と～～～～がある。
　　　通り　　　　　　　すすむ　　　池

19. ～～～～～～～～には＿＿＿＿＿お茶がよく＿＿＿＿＿。
　　甘い物　　　　　にがい　　　　　あう

Ⅰ 日本人と宗教

　ある新聞の調査によると「あなたは何かの宗教を信じていますか」という質問に日本人の約七割が「信じていない」と答えたそうだ。これは「日本人は宗教を信じない国民だ」ということを意味しているのだろうか。

　日本人の宗教と言えば、神道と仏教が代表的だ。神道は日本で生まれた宗教で、木や山などの自然の中に神がいるという考えから始まったものだ。そのため、日本全国に様々な神様を祭った神社がある。仏教は六世紀に日本に伝えられた後、全国に広がり、多くのお寺が建てられている。

　日本人の生活を見てみると、神道と仏教に関係した行事が多くある。子供が生まれた時には神社にお参りに行くし、人が死んだ時はお坊さんを呼んで葬式を行う。結婚式を神社やお寺でする人もいる。お正月には一年の幸せを願って、何千万人の人が神社やお寺に行く。また、全国各地で行われるお祭りの多くも神社やお寺と関係している。

　神道と仏教だけでない。日本のキリスト教徒は国民の約1～2％だと言われているが、クリスマスは大きなイベントになっている。寒くなり始めるころから街はクリスマスのイルミネーションで飾られ、友達や家族とパーティーをしたり、恋人とロマンチックな時間を過ごしたりする。また、キリスト教徒ではないのに、教会で結婚式をする人も少なくない。一人の人が、生まれた時は神社にお参りし、教会で結婚し、葬式はお寺で行うことも案外珍しいことではない。

　このように見ると、日本人にとって宗教は生活の中の様々な行事や習慣となっている。「ある宗教を信じている」という意識がなくても、宗教は生活の一部になっていると言えるのではないだろうか。

宗教　religion	七割　70%	国民　citizen	～と言えば　speaking of ...
仏教　Buddhism	代表的　representative	自然　nature	祭る　to worship
世紀　century	広がる　to spread	行事　event	お参りする　to go praying
お坊さん　Buddhist monk	葬式　funeral	各地　various regions	
キリスト教徒　Christian	街　town	恋人　boyfriend/girlfriend	
意識　consciousness			

A. 本文を読んで、【 　　　】の中の当てはまるものすべてに○を付けてください。

1.【 神道・仏教・キリスト教 】は日本で生まれた。

2.【 神道・仏教・キリスト教 】では、自然の中に神様がいると信じられている。

3.【 神道・仏教・キリスト教 】は六世紀ごろ日本に伝えられた。

4. 子供が生まれた時、【 神社・お寺・教会 】に行く人が多い。

5. 多くの人はお正月に【 神社・お寺・教会 】に行って、幸せを願う。

6.【 神道・仏教・キリスト教 】を信じている人は日本人の約1〜2%だと言われ
ている。

B. あなたの国では、宗教に関係するどんな行事がありますか。

Ⅰ 漢字を練習しましょう。

危	危	危			戻	戻	戻			
険	険	険			吸	吸	吸			
拾	拾	拾			放	放	放			
捨	捨	捨			変	変	変			

Ⅱ 単語の読み方を書いて、文を読みましょう。

単　語	読み方	意　味	例　文
危ない		dangerous	暗い道を一人で歩くのは危ない。
危険		danger	雪の中を運転するのは危険だ。
拾う		to pick up	道で千円拾った。
捨てる		to throw away	ごみをここに捨ててはいけない。
戻る		to return to (a place)	昼ご飯の後、図書館に戻った。
戻す		to return (something)	本を前にあった場所に戻した。
払い戻す		to refund	ホテル代を払い戻してもらった。
たばこを吸う		to smoke	たばこを吸うのは体に悪い。
吸う		to breathe in	大きく息を吸ってください。
放す		to release	小鳥を空に放した。
放送		broadcast	その番組は六時からの放送だ。 ばんぐみ
変な		weird	前の部屋から変な音が聞こえた。
変わる		(something) changes	信号が赤から青に変わった。
変える		to change (something)	計画を変えて、車で行った。
大変		very; hard	山本さんには、大変お世話になった。 毎日忙しくて大変だ。 いそが

Ⅲ ひらがなを漢字に、漢字をひらがなにかえましょう。

1. ＿＿＿＿＿＿の時、煙を＿＿＿＿＿＿＿＿と、＿＿＿＿＿＿＿＿だ。
   火事　　けむり　　すう　　　　きけん

2. お金を＿＿＿＿＿＿＿＿ので、＿＿＿＿＿＿に＿＿＿＿＿＿＿。
   ひろった　　　　こうばん　　とどけた

3. 日本での＿＿＿＿＿＿＿＿は、＿＿＿＿＿＿はとても＿＿＿＿＿＿だった。
   せいかつ　　　　はじめ　　　　たいへん

4. ＿＿＿＿＿の＿＿＿＿＿＿がテレビで＿＿＿＿＿＿された。
   祭り　　　ようす　　　　ほうそう

5. ＿＿＿＿＿ ＿＿＿＿がしたので、＿＿＿＿＿＿した料理を＿＿＿＿＿。
   へんな　　あじ　　　　　　注文　　　　のこした

6. チケットの＿＿＿＿＿＿＿＿を＿＿＿＿＿＿＿＿＿＿ので、
   枚数　　　　　まちがえた

   ＿＿＿＿＿＿＿で＿＿＿＿＿＿＿＿＿＿もらった。
   窓口　　　　　はらいもどして

7. ＿＿＿＿＿＿は＿＿＿＿＿を＿＿＿＿＿＿＿＿　＿＿＿＿＿で行った。
   わたしたち　　よてい　　かえて　　　　　船

8. この＿＿＿＿＿＿の中でたばこは＿＿＿＿＿＿＿＿。
   じんじゃ　　　　　　すえない

9. ＿＿＿＿＿＿で犬を＿＿＿＿＿のは＿＿＿＿＿＿＿のでやめてください。
   こうえん　　　　はなす　　　あぶない

10. ＿＿＿＿＿＿に＿＿＿＿＿＿と、誰かが私の＿＿＿＿＿に＿＿＿＿＿いた。
    へや　　　もどる　　　だれ　　　　せき　　　座って

11. サイズが＿＿＿＿＿＿ので＿＿＿＿＿服は＿＿＿＿＿＿ ＿＿＿＿＿＿。
    かわった　　　　古い　　　ぜんぶ　　すてた

12. 元の＿＿＿＿＿＿に＿＿＿＿＿＿のを＿＿＿＿＿＿＿＿＿でください。
    もと　ところ　　もどす　　　　わすれない

Ⅰ 漢字を練習しましょう。

歯	歯	歯				当	当	当			
髪	髪	髪				伝	伝	伝			
絵	絵	絵				細	細	細			
横	横	横				無	無	無			

Ⅱ 単語の読み方を書いて、文を読みましょう。

単　語	読み方	意　味	例　文
歯		tooth	一日に三回歯を磨く。
歯医者		dentist	明日、歯医者の予約がある。
虫歯		decayed tooth	虫歯が痛い。
髪		hair	髪を短く切った。
絵		picture	その絵を見て感動した。
絵本		picture book	子供達に絵本を読んであげた。
横		side; beside	横にいるのは彼のお兄さんだ。
横切る		to cross	その道を横切るのは危険だ。
本当に		really	山本君は本当に正直な人だ。
当たる		to be hit	ボールが頭に当たった。
伝える		to convey	電話があったと部長に伝えた。
手伝う		to help	姉が服を選ぶのを手伝った。
伝言		message	先生からの伝言を彼に伝えた。
細い		thin	このパンツは細すぎて入らない。
細かい		detailed	細かい事は後で決めよう。
細長い		long and narrow	イタリアは細長い形だ。
無理な		impossible	明日までに調査するのは無理だ。
無料		free of charge	五歳以下の子供は無料だ。
無い		there is no ...	この部屋には時計が無い。

1. 田中さんが＿＿＿＿＿＿＿＿と彼に＿＿＿＿＿＿＿＿。
    もどった　　　　　　　　つたえた

2. ＿＿＿＿＿が＿＿＿＿＿＿＿日の朝は、＿＿＿＿＿のようにきれいだ。
    ゆき　　　　ふった　　　　　　　　え

3. 一日に＿＿＿＿＿＿＿＿＿＿を磨くので、＿＿＿＿＿＿が＿＿＿＿＿。
    　　　三回　　　　は　み が　　　　　むしば　　　　ない

4. 子供は＿＿＿＿＿が＿＿＿＿＿好きで、いつも＿＿＿＿＿前に読んでいる。
    　　　えほん　　ほんとうに　　　　　　ねる

5. あの＿＿＿＿が長くて＿＿＿＿＿＿が山本君の＿＿＿＿＿＿だ。
    　　かみ　　　　ほそい　　　女性　　　　　　　おくさん

6. ＿＿＿＿＿が＿＿＿＿＿＿なので、私はいつも＿＿＿＿＿＿で診てもらう。
    娘　　　　はいしゃ　　　　　　むりょう　　　　み

7. 彼から「＿＿＿＿＿＿の＿＿＿＿にある店にいる」と、＿＿＿＿＿＿＿があった。
    　　　ちゅうしゃじょう　よこ　　　　　　　　でんごん

8. ボールが＿＿＿＿＿、＿＿＿＿＿＿が壊れたので、＿＿＿＿＿＿もらった。
    　　　あたり　　　　自転車　　こわ　　　　なおして

9. ＿＿＿＿まで行き、＿＿＿＿＿＿の＿＿＿＿＿を＿＿＿＿＿＿つもりだ。
    島　　　　　　　彼ら　　　ちょうさ　　てつだう

10. 銀行で、＿＿＿＿＿について＿＿＿＿＿＿＿＿＿＿＿＿＿をしてもらった。
    　　　口座　　　　　こまかい　　せつめい

11. ＿＿＿＿＿＿影が、前を＿＿＿＿＿＿＿ので驚いたが、＿＿＿＿＿だった。
    ほそながい　かげ　　　よこぎった　　おどろ　　　　犬

12. この＿＿＿＿＿を＿＿＿＿＿のは＿＿＿＿＿に＿＿＿＿＿だ。
    　　やくそく　　まもる　　　絶対　　　むり

Ⅰ ボランティア募集

山田市からのお知らせ　ボランティア募集

山田市では、ボランティア活動に参加してくださる方を募集します。仕事をお持ちの方も休日など空いている時間に参加できます。無理せず、できることから、ボランティア活動を始めてみませんか。

●クリーン運動

山田川は、山田市出身の絵本作家、小森明子さんの作品の舞台として有名になった所です。昔はきれいな水が流れ、魚が住み、子供たちがよく遊んでいました。しかし、今、川は全く変わってしまいました。水は汚れ、ごみも多く捨てられていて、子供たちにとって危険な場所になっています。先日も川の様子がテレビで放送され、市民の方から何とかしてほしいという意見が多く寄せられました。昔のきれいな川を取り戻すため、日曜日の朝に川のごみを拾い、清掃を手伝ってくださる方を募集します。

○問い合わせ
環境課（☎三五一―九〇〇〇）

【日時】毎週日曜日・九時～十一時

●通訳ボランティア

山田市に住んでいる外国人の方は年々増えていますが、日本語ができず大変困っている人がいます。そのような方たちをサポートするために、英語、中国語、ポルトガル語などの通訳ボランティアを募集します。病院や歯医者に付き添い、横に座ってお医者さんの話を伝えたり、お子さんの学校の先生からの伝言を翻訳したりする活動です。

○問い合わせ
国際課（☎三五一―七〇〇〇）

募集 recruitment	参加する to participate	作品 artistic piece	舞台 stage
流れる to flow	～にとって for …	先日 the other day	
何とかする to do something about it	寄せる to send	取り戻す to restore	
清掃 cleaning	日時 time and date	問い合わせ inquiry	
環境課 environment division	通訳 interpretation	年々 year by year	
付き添う to accompany			

質問に答えましょう。

1. 山田川はどうして有名ですか。
   <small>やまだがわ</small>

2. 昔に比べて山田川はどう変わりましたか。
   <small>やまだがわ</small>

3. クリーン運動では何をしますか。

4. 通訳ボランティアは、病院や歯医者で何をしますか。
   <small>つうやく</small>

5. 通訳ボランティアについて質問がある人は、どこに聞きますか。
   <small>つうやく</small>

追加練習
ついか

1. _____が_____に_____ので車を_____。
   しんごう　　あか　　　　かわった　　　　　　　　　　　　　とめた

2. _____は_____で_____できる人だ。
   やまもとくん　　しょうじき　　しんよう

3. _____に_____ _____を_____してください。
   とうあんようし　　がくせい　　ばんごう　　　きにゅう

4. _____が道を_____として_____。
   こども　　　　　　よこぎろう　　　　　　とびだした

5. _____が_____、_____に行った。
   むしば　　　いたくて　　　　はいしゃ

6. _____の_____のスピーチに_____した。
   しゅしょう　　さいご　　　　　　　　かんどう

7. _____を_____、お金を_____もらった。
   よやく　　　とりけして　　　　　　はらいもどして

8. _____に_____からの_____が入っていた。
   るすばんでんわ　　　かない　　　　　　でんごん

9. _____、_____なったので、夜はエアコンを_____。
   さいきん　　すずしく　　　　　　　　　　　　　　　　けす

10. _____が_____、_____の_____の
    ひこうき　　　　　おくれて　　　くうこう　　よこ

    ホテルに_____した。
    　　　　いっぱく

11. _____で_____を_____で_____いた。
    どうぶつえん　　ふうせん　　むりょう　　　くばって

12. _____の_____に古い_____が入っていた。
    ひきだし　　　　おく　　　にんぎょう

13. その＿＿＿＿＿＿はまだ＿＿＿＿＿＿ので、＿＿＿＿＿＿＿＿＿＿ください。
　　　　　　じしょ　　　　　　　いる　　　　　　　　すてないで

14. ＿＿＿＿＿＿＿で送られてきた＿＿＿＿＿＿を＿＿＿＿＿＿＿＿＿＿。
　　　ふなびん　　　　　　　　　　にもつ　　　　うけとった

15. ＿＿＿＿＿＿＿になって、この国を＿＿＿＿＿＿で＿＿＿＿＿＿な国にしたい。
　　　せいじか　　　　　　　　　　　　じゆう　　　みんしゅてき

16. その〜〜〜〜〜〜〜は＿＿＿＿＿に＿＿＿＿＿＿、＿＿＿＿＿＿した。
　　　　　兄弟　　　　　べつべつ　　そだてられ　　せいちょう

17. ＿＿＿＿＿＿の人生を＿＿＿＿＿＿に＿＿＿＿＿＿＿＿＿＿。
　　　のこり　　じんせい　　しあわせ　　　すごしたい

18. 十日＿＿＿＿＿＿に＿＿＿＿＿＿を自転車で一周するのは＿＿＿＿＿＿だ。
　　　　　いない　　　　はんとう　　　　　　いっしゅう　　　　　　むり

19. スキーは＿＿＿＿＿＿＿＿だったので＿＿＿＿＿＿がなかったが、
　　　　　　はじめて　　　　　　　　じしん

＿＿＿＿＿＿＿やさしかった。
　　あんがい

20. 毎週＿＿＿＿＿＿されている日本の＿＿＿＿＿＿ドラマを見ていたので、
　　　　ほうそう　　　　　　　　　　れんぞく

日本語が＿＿＿＿＿＿＿した。
　　　　じょうたつ

21. あの人は＿＿＿＿＿＿のために＿＿＿＿＿＿を＿＿＿＿＿＿＿＿＿＿。
　　　　もくてき　　　　　　しゅだん　　　　えらばない

22. ＿＿＿＿＿＿、＿＿＿＿＿＿が来るので、町を＿＿＿＿＿＿するつもりだ。
　　　こんど　　　ともだち　　　　　　　　　あんない

23. 皆の前で＿＿＿＿＿＿から落ちて、＿＿＿＿＿＿に＿＿＿＿＿＿＿＿＿＿。
　　　　かいだん　　お　　　　　　　ほんとう　　はずかしかった